P9-DNX-255

ALSO BY MICHAEL J. TOUGIAS

A Storm Too Soon

The Finest Hours
(coauthored with Casey Sherman)

Overboard!

Fatal Forecast

Ten Hours Until Dawn

Until I Have No Country

There's a Porcupine in My Outhouse

The Cringe Chronicles

Derek's Gift

King Philip's War
(coauthored with Eric Schultz)

ALSO BY DOUGLAS A. CAMPBELL

The Sea's Bitter Harvest

Eight Survived

RESCUE OF THE *BOUNTY*

DISASTER AND SURVIVAL IN SUPERSTORM SANDY

MICHAEL J. TOUGIAS
AND
DOUGLAS A. CAMPBELL

SCRIBNER
New York London Toronto Sydney New Delhi

SCRIBNER
A Division of Simon & Schuster, Inc.
1230 Avenue of the Americas
New York, NY 10020

First Scribner hardcover edition April 2014

SCRIBNER and design are registered trademarks of The Gale Group, Inc., used under license by Simon & Schuster, Inc., the publisher of this work.

For information about special discounts for bulk purchases, please contact Simon & Schuster Special Sales at 1-866-506-1949 or business@simonandschuster.com.

The Simon & Schuster Speakers Bureau can bring authors to your live event. For more information or to book an event contact the Simon & Schuster Speakers Bureau at 1-866-248-3049 or visit our website at www.simonspeakers.com.

Jacket design by Ervin Serrano
Jacket photograph © Tim Kuklewski/Lightroom Photos/USGC/Alamy

Manufactured in the United States of America

1 3 5 7 9 10 8 6 4 2

Library of Congress Control Number: 2013042684

ISBN 978-1-4767-4663-0
ISBN 978-1-4767-4665-4 (ebook)

Permission granted by the Cassie Brown Estate for the excerpt printed in this publication from Cassie Brown's *Standing into Danger.*

Photograph credits: 1 courtesy of Scott McQuire; 2–3 courtesy of Jim McNealy; 4–5 courtesy of Susan Tamulevich; 6 courtesy of Adam Prokosh; 7 courtesy of Andy Beck; 8–9 courtesy of Marc Castells; 10–11 courtesy of Tim Kuklewski; 12 courtesy of Dan Todd; 13–18 courtesy of the U.S. Coast Guard.

To all the librarians who have helped my writing and speaking careers. Our public libraries are national treasures.

MICHAEL TOUGIAS

To those who loved Robin Walbridge and Claudene Christian and who now grieve.

DOUG CAMPBELL

Contents

Part I

Part II

PART III

RESCUE OF THE *BOUNTY*

PART ONE

CHAPTER ONE

THE SPEECH

The autumn afternoon was perfect, untroubled on the New London, Connecticut, waterfront. The rippled river water sparkled; the blue sky was washed clean as fresh laundry. The late-October sun came low behind the woman's right shoulder, casting sharp, long shadows before her. For twenty years Beth Robinson had been part of the engrossing world of tall ships and she still thought, *This is why we go to sea, days like this.* She walked onto the City Pier, where, ahead of her, a crew of sailors hustled to their assignments on deck below the three towering masts of the historic square-rigger *Bounty*. Robinson, a relief skipper on a nearby schooner, knew the ship, a 180-foot, fifty-year-old wooden ship—an expanded replica of the original 1784 ship HMS *Bounty*. She made a casual inspection, passing the soaring sixty-foot bowsprit, thrust upward toward shore, before reaching the freshly painted black hull. She knew *Bounty*'s captain, too, Robin Walbridge, and thought her friend of two decades had his boat looking pretty good.

Robinson had come to see Walbridge for just a passing hello.

"Hi, Captain," she called out.

Walbridge gave a similar greeting—nothing elaborate. He, like Captain Robinson, was native New England stock, a taciturn man who saw eloquence in one's work and ideals, not in words or attire.

Walbridge mentioned that *Bounty* was preparing to leave port, but the exchange was brief as the captain was focused on a serious problem and had urgent business to attend to.

During the day, several of Walbridge's fifteen subordinates had received text messages or phone calls from family and friends who knew the ship was set to embark on its annual southward voyage, heading for a winter dock. The callers were concerned about a hurricane, brewing in the Bahamas and heading north, named Sandy.

A twenty-five-year-old crewman, Joshua Scornavacchi, had received a text message from his mother in Pennsylvania. She was worried about the storm. "I'll be fine," he replied, adding that *Bounty* had been through rough weather before.

Another twenty-five-year-old got a worried text message from her mother on Cape Cod. The young woman, a maritime academy graduate, was not concerned, though, nor were most of the other crew members, many of them considered "green" sailors as far as experience aboard *Bounty* was concerned.

However, among the more experienced crew, there were worries. The chief mate, John Svendsen, forty-one, now in his third season aboard *Bounty*, had spoken earlier with his junior officers. The third mate, Dan Cleveland, on board *Bounty* five years, and the bosun, Laura Groves, on board three years, had doubts about sailing offshore toward a hurricane. The second mate, Matt Sanders, was moderately concerned. The conversation convinced Svendsen that he needed to talk with Walbridge and present the captain with options.

Svendsen knew that the New London City Pier, which projects out from the west bank of the Thames River, would be exposed to heavy weather by way of Long Island Sound, which lay two miles south via a straight path of open water. *Bounty* was moored to the exposed south side of the dock, where the fetch to the Sound invites trouble. Svendsen knew that if *Bounty* remained where she was and Sandy arrived, the storm's winds and surge could race up that fairway, presenting the possibility of serious damage to the ship.

Svendsen, who had become aware of the hurricane two days earlier, thought there were better choices than heading offshore. *Bounty* could simply sail farther up the Thames to where the US Coast Guard Academy's tall ship *Eagle* had docked. *Bounty* could sail east, to where the city of New Bedford, Massachusetts, had a hurricane barrier—a stone wall across its deep harbor. *Bounty* could also sail farther north, to Boston. Svendsen even thought sailing toward Bermuda, 650 miles to the southeast, might be an option.

• • •

From the moment the crew awoke on Thursday, October 25, 2012, *Bounty* had been crammed with activity. The crew was preoccupied with more important considerations than their coming departure. Company was expected—special visitors. *Bounty*'s owner, a wealthy Long Island businessman, had invited the crew of the navy's newest submarine, the *Mississippi*, for a daysail aboard *Bounty* on Long Island Sound.

Soon after daybreak, the crew was busy preparing. One team washed the decks. Two hoses were neatly stowed on deck: one to reach forward to the bow, and the other to extend to the stern. On the ship's third and lowest deck, down a set of stairs and then a ladder, two diesel engines powered electric generators whose most important function was to run the electric bilge pumps that kept the ship afloat. Without pumps, like any other leaky wooden boat, *Bounty* would eventually sink.

Below the floorboards of the third deck, which housed crew quarters and fuel and water tanks, pipes and hoses extended from the two pumps to the bilge space. The hoses sucked up water in the bilge space and discharged it amidships back into the sea. But the process could also be reversed and seawater could be sucked up into the deck-washing hoses. As the team used this seawater that bright autumn morning, one team member noticed something different, troubling. Instead of a powerful stream, the washdown hoses gave him barely enough spray to wet the deck boards. Normally, the pressure in the hoses would be too high if some of the water wasn't diverted overboard. Yet this morning, even using the full capacity of the pump, the crewman could not fully charge the hose. He mentioned the problem to his two teammates, who seemed unconcerned, and then reported his observation to the ship's engineer. In the end, the pump problem was ignored.

The sun was high when the crew from the *Mississippi* arrived at the City Pier. *Bounty*'s owner, Robert Hansen, and her captain, Robin Walbridge, greeted them. Then *Bounty*'s crew cast off the dock lines and, engines running, pointed her lancelike, uptilted bowsprit south on the Thames.

Bounty's crew led the visiting submarine sailors as they climbed aloft in the 111-foot-high rope rigging, teaching them how to set the sails in a light breeze. For a while, the canvas billowed white and full until the wind died. *Bounty* circled the Ledge Lighthouse, a redbrick, two-story cube just off the mouth of the Thames, drifted in place for a while, and about midafternoon motored back to the City Pier.

Walbridge made a point to catch one of his guests—New London dockmaster Barbara Neff—before she went ashore. He told her that although *Bounty* had originally been scheduled to spend another night in the city, he had decided to leave that evening due to the oncoming hurricane. He explained that sailing around the hurricane could give *Bounty* a good boost of following winds after the storm passed.

Neff was mildly disappointed. When she got ashore, she and some others planned to set up a Halloween corn maze on the waterfront—she thought that *Bounty*'s tall masts in the background would add a nice touch. However, having been acquainted with Walbridge for over fifteen years, she knew him to be low-key and intelligent, never cocky or pompous, and she felt his explanation for the change of plans both understandable and reassuring. She trusted his judgment.

As Walbridge talked with Neff, his crew accepted an invitation to visit the *Mississippi*. Walbridge joined them, but was among the first to return to *Bounty*, sometime before five o'clock.

Now Chief Mate Svendsen saw his chance. Asking Walbridge to join him on the dock and away from the rest of the crew, he told the skipper about the apprehension among the junior officers.

"There are people concerned about the hurricane," Svendsen told his boss. "I want to discuss options, including staying here."

Walbridge listened to his chief mate, as he always did, then offered his own thoughts. "A ship is safer at sea than in port," he told Svendsen, and said he would hold a meeting with the crew and explain his plan.

At about five o'clock everyone returned from the visit on the *Mississippi*. Often a recluse aboard *Bounty*, Walbridge nevertheless conducted an all-hands meeting every day, so this muster was far from unusual. Walbridge used these musters as teaching opportunities, for in part he saw his purpose aboard *Bounty* as an educator. He had come from a family of teachers as far back as his grandparents and some of his great-grandparents.

This muster would be different, though. Walbridge, celebrating his sixty-third birthday that afternoon—a low-key event he marked by splurging on a bottle of ginger ale—climbed atop a small deckhouse called the Nav Shack (below its roof were the ship's navigational equipment and chart table) and in his quiet way began talking.

In retrospect, this moment seemed preordained. Even as a boy, Walbridge thought through his options in silence, arriving at a decision well before those around him realized there were choices to be made. Similarly on this afternoon, he had decided, selected a path—his path—and he did not seek suggestions. Certainly there were alternative routes for *Bounty* in the days to come. Yet, like the chess player he'd been for fifty-five years, the captain considered all those moves and dismissed them.

"There is a hurricane headed this way," he told his fifteen shipmates with the falling sun at his back. "It's called Frankenstorm. There will be sixty-knot winds and rough seas. The boat's safer being out at sea than being buckled up at a dock somewhere." Then he laughed a little and, as if in jest, added, "You guys will probably be safer if you take a train inland." The levity ended there.

"I know that some of you have received phone calls and text messages from worried friends and family. If anyone wants to go ashore, now is the time. I won't think any less of you. Come back to *Bounty* when the weather clears up."

No one budged, nor did anyone speak.

"My plan is to sail south by east, to take some time and see what the storm is going to do." He told them about hurricanes *Bounty* had encountered under his command. The ship had made it through then, and she would do so now.

Still, no one spoke. Chief Mate Svendsen, who had given his captain his best advice, did not now share his thoughts. He had accepted the Walbridge plan as prudent.

Nor did the second mate, third mate, or the bosun voice their doubts.

Some of the crew members were nervous as they looked up at Walbridge. Some were excited for a new adventure after a summer of tranquil voyages. The moment for objections passed, and everyone—even the new cook, who had first boarded *Bounty* the night before—went to work, preparing to set sail.

The sun slipped behind the railroad terminal just inshore from the City Pier. Dockmaster Neff and her crew were creating the Halloween maze when one of them looked up and saw *Bounty* was leaving. They all stood for a moment and enjoyed the spectacle: the dignified progress of a stately vessel of ancient proportions departing into the gathering dusk, heading south toward a monster storm.

CHAPTER TWO

THE STORM

Bounty has departed New London CT . . . Next Port of Call . . .
St. Petersburg, Florida.
Bounty will be sailing due East out to sea before heading
South to avoid the brunt of Hurricane Sandy.

—Entry on HMS *Bounty* Facebook page, 6:06 p.m., October 25, 2012

Adam Prokosh had been aboard *Bounty* for almost eight months. On the evening of October 25, he watched as the ship passed the red-brick Ledge Lighthouse and entered Long Island Sound, following the dusk as it dissolved into darkness. Prokosh, twenty-seven, of Seattle, had spent several years on a number of tall ships and schooners before he arrived at *Bounty*'s dock in San Juan, Puerto Rico, as an able-bodied seaman, or AB, the lowest coast guard rating, but a step above an ordinary deckhand. He had been impressed with much of what he found aboard the old ship, which was at times referred to as a "movie prop."

While there was truth to the description—*Bounty* had been built in 1960 in Lunenburg, Nova Scotia, for use in the movie *Mutiny on the Bounty*, starring Marlon Brando, and had more recently played a role in two *Pirates of the Caribbean* movies—the ship's architect had created a rugged vessel that could actually sail. Whether sailing for MGM studios to Tahiti or doubling as the base of operations for the film crew and actors, *Bounty* was more than just a movie set. The ship was an expanded version of the HMS *Bounty*, with a 120-foot waterline as opposed to the original 86 feet that had been commanded by William

Bligh. Inside were diesel-powered generators, air-conditioning, and other amenities necessary for moviemaking in the tropics.

Some of the film-crew equipment, such as cameras and lighting, had been scuttled by the time Prokosh boarded *Bounty*. But he had heard stories about the ship's adventures under Robin Walbridge and believed her to be fundamentally seaworthy. He was further impressed by how organized and informed the crew were. Prokosh felt that communications aboard *Bounty* were the best he had ever encountered aboard any vessel. He felt far more excitement than fear about sailing during Hurricane Sandy. Out on Long Island Sound, Prokosh felt his spirits soaring.

"Sailing is a sport and a team sport," he would say. "This is the big game. End of the season. This is what we train for. I've been on boats before that don't emphasize seamanship. So those boats have a very set routine of Boston Harbor cruises. They will come back to the same dock after three hours. So, the little things about seamanship don't get emphasized." *Bounty*, having sailed all over the world in every weather and with crew members whose experience ranged from nonexistent to several licensed captains, had a special emphasis on seamanship training that he'd never experienced elsewhere.

The past season had been spent on tranquil seas. Prokosh could remember only two instances of sudden squalls that required the crew to douse sails on the double. There had been no sustained storms like what he had experienced on other boats. In his opinion, there was nothing quite like foul, exciting weather to drive home why you practiced good seamanship.

With these thoughts in mind Prokosh had gone into a New London bar earlier in the day. A patron who recognized him as a member of *Bounty*'s crew approached him. Prokosh knew few details about the approaching hurricane, although the crew who had heard from worried family members had been chattering about it.

"You guys will be crazy leaving the dock," the bar patron told Prokosh.

"Are you kidding me?" he replied. "This is going to be great weather!"

At 11:00 a.m., Monday, October 22, commercial weather router Chris Parker predicted that the eighteenth tropical depression of the season would turn into Tropical Storm Sandy. In an email to his boating clients, Parker suggested that by Wednesday night Sandy could cross Cuba as a Category 1 hurricane. Yet Parker's email did not get to Robin Walbridge aboard *Bounty*. The tall ship was not one of Parker's subscribed customers. Parker's forecast a day later carried other sobering suggestions: "We're used to thinking of Hurricanes as geographically-small systems. Tornadoes cause 200+ mph winds along a swath less than 1 mile across. Most Hurricanes' strongest winds occur along a swath less than 30–40 miles across. The difference with Sandy is, as she transforms into a non-Tropical LO, her wind-field will expand geographically . . . AND she is expected to continue strengthening."

The predicted level of low pressure in Sandy "would normally support a [Category 4] Hurricane. In Sandy's case (as a non-Tropical LO), [that pressure] will probably support only 70–80 [-knot] winds . . . but those winds could blanket an area more than 500 miles across."

A large blanket, indeed, covering most of the Atlantic Ocean between the US East Coast and Bermuda.

"So, whatever your plans are in the next week-or-so, you MUST have a PLAN for what you'll do if Sandy brings 70–80k Hurricane Force winds (and maybe VERY LARGE surge of water) to your area."

At 4:42 p.m. on Thursday, about an hour before *Bounty* left City Pier, Parker emailed his clients with his latest insights: "Obviously, Sandy is the BIG STORY!" Landfall, he predicted, would be somewhere along the Delaware-Maryland-Virginia coast, possibly New Jersey sometime on Tuesday, October 30.

Parker had a number of clients who, like *Bounty*, were making southbound voyages at the time. Many of them were "snowbirds"—live-aboard sailors who headed for warmer harbors when autumn arrived—and they sought refuge. One of them had pulled into a marina in Atlantic City, where he was protected behind the tower of a casino.

Other weather experts had come to a similar conclusion about the storm. Weather router Herb Hilgenberg, who provides sailors with free weather reports from his home base in Burlington, Ontario, had among his regular listeners the crew of the Maine-based schooner *Harvey Gamage*. Captain Christopher Flansburg had sailed the schooner south to Fernandina Beach, Florida, on a voyage to the Dominican Republic and was two days into the next leg when he learned from Hilgenberg that Sandy was forming. He turned the schooner around and docked in Jacksonville, Florida, for the next ten days.

By Thursday, October 25, when *Bounty* left City Pier in New London, Hilgenberg's reports had steered three sailboats to anchor in Bermuda, where they remained for the duration of the hurricane.

Like Hilgenberg, Parker had no clients at sea that Thursday.

The open ocean came into view around midnight. As *Bounty* approached the flashing white light on a tower at the end of Montauk Point, Long Island, the B-Watch came on duty—Second Mate Matt Sanders, deckhands John Jones and Jessica Hewitt, and able-bodied seaman Adam Prokosh. They found the seas calm and the skies clear. For an hour at a time, each watch stander steered *Bounty* by its big wooden steering wheel, called the helm, located aft of the rear mast (or mizzen) and used in Hollywood movies as far back as the 1935 film *Mutiny on the Bounty* starring Clark Gable. They also stood watch for an hour on the foredeck, where they were responsible for spotting traffic or obstacles, spent another hour doing boat checks in the engine room with bilge-pumping duties, and were on standby for an hour, in case their labor was needed.

In the six hours since leaving the dock, all of *Bounty*'s crew members had been on duty. Walbridge had told the new thirty-four-year-old cook, Jessica Black, to hold off on the evening meal. So she put the chili on simmer in the galley, which was located at the forward end of the middle, or tween, deck, and pitched in with the others. Everyone was "sea stowing," securing everything on deck and belowdecks to prevent items from dislodging in the violent rocking of the ship during foul weather.

Tables on deck had to be tied down, and sails needed lashing. Prokosh organized the work on the top, or "weather," deck knowing that if a piece of sail even as small as a handkerchief caught the wind in heavy weather, the entire sail would yank free and havoc would ensue. Walbridge had trained the crew to have the storm sails—smaller than sails used in moderate weather—ready in the case of rising winds. Prokosh oversaw that work, too.

When all was done and dark had settled over *Bounty*, the crew went down to the tween deck and then forward to the galley, where the steaming chili awaited them. Perhaps the hard work had primed their appetites, but all aboard felt Jessica's cooking had exceeded their expectations.

During the meal the A-Watch was on duty—their hours were always from eight until twelve, day or night. Chief Mate John Svendsen, the watch captain, did not have much tenure aboard *Bounty*. Walbridge had hired him in February 2010 as an able-bodied seaman. While he would say he had spent most of his life on the water, Svendsen's primary maritime employment before *Bounty* was as a dive instructor and dive-boat operator in Hawaii. He had sailed for a year aboard a modest tall ship, the *Californian*, a ninety-three-foot topsail schooner based in San Diego, and aboard another vessel operated by an environmental organization.

Svendsen was recognizable aboard *Bounty* by his shoulder-length, smoothly groomed, brown hair and his square build. At forty-one, the Minnesota native was articulate and measured. He was aware that aboard a tall ship there was much to learn, and he had once even searched for mentors in the maritime industry. But aboard *Bounty*, he was second-in-command. Only Robin Walbridge stood above him, and there was talk that when Walbridge retired in three years, Svendsen would replace him.

The able-bodied seaman on the A-Watch was an unpaid volunteer, Douglas Faunt, from Oakland, California. Though *Bounty* carried paid crew who received about $100 a week and some officers who received a bit more than that, at sixty-six Faunt was retired and not only didn't need the money, but also enjoyed being able to sail at will and not on command.

Faunt had made a fortune selling a business and was now spending his money as he pleased. He rode motorcycles, traveled the world, and, being something of an electronics whiz, participated in ham-radio contests that took him to far-flung locales. But on *Bounty* Faunt found something—someone—who made the experience stand out above all other adventures: Robin Walbridge. Faunt loved him and saw Walbridge as a logical thinker, a consummate teacher, and someone that others should emulate.

Also on the A-Watch were deckhands Mark Warner, thirty-three, of Milton, Massachusetts, and Claudene Christian, forty-two, originally from Alaska and a former Miss Teenage Alaska. Of the two, Christian was known as the outgoing one with a "bubbly" personality.

Christian claimed to be a distant relative of Fletcher Christian, the master's mate aboard the original *Bounty* who, in Tahiti in April 1789, led a mutiny and seized control of the ship from Captain William Bligh. Christian didn't need to mention her notorious ancestor to attract attention, however. A petite blonde who had been a cheerleader at the University of Southern California, she once got the idea for a business—fashion dolls with cheerleader outfits from specific colleges and universities. In a sour ending to the Cheerleader Doll Co., Christian was sued by Mattel, maker of Barbie dolls. Before she reached *Bounty*'s decks, she had returned to live with her parents in Oklahoma. She shared with her college friend Michelle Wilton that she didn't want to be there, was bored, and wanted a new start in life. Single and over forty, she felt that her life had hit a dead end. Then in May, with no significant tall ship experience, she joined *Bounty*'s crew as a volunteer and loved life aboard. For the first time in a long, long time, she told Wilton, she felt at peace and happy.

Among the four A-Watch crew members, Faunt had the most tall ship experience, having for several years sailed off and on aboard *Bounty* and other square-rigged ships. By any measure, the watch was the oldest on board, with an average age of over forty-five years.

Prokosh was pleased to be sailing toward a hurricane with the four members of the A-Watch and the other eleven crew members who stayed aboard *Bounty* for her voyage to *Bounty*'s 2012–2013 winter dock in Galveston, Texas. Yes, with only sixteen aboard, *Bounty* had her smallest crew since leaving San Juan in April. *But these sixteen,* Prokosh thought, *they are the right ones. They have stuck with* Bounty *the whole season, they know the boat well, and they really will give it their best.*

CHAPTER THREE

A VOYAGE WITH PURPOSE

MY REVISED FORECAST: Landfall in S New Jersey, between Cape May and Atlantic City . . . during the night [Monday, October 29], and before Dawn [Tuesday, October 30] morning.

I caution either [of two computer models] could easily be correct.

Further, regardless where Sandy makes landfall, the entire region may see a long-duration (1–2 day) wind event, with nearly-uniform winds of 60–80 knots sustained (gusting 80–100k)—anywhere within 300 miles of Sandy's landfall in all directions (600-mile-wide swath of destructive winds and potential Storm Surge).

—Chris Parker, October 26, 2012, 6:36 a.m.

Chris Parker's forecast did not reach *Bounty*'s Nav Shack. HMS Bounty Organization LLC had not chosen to buy Parker's service, at a fee ranging up to $195 a year.

At the time of Parker's report, *Bounty* was sailing with both diesel engines hammering at full throttle, on a course of about 165 degrees from true north, about forty miles south of Montauk Point. She carried instruments for gathering weather information, including a single-sideband radio, on which she received faxed weather reports; a satellite telephone, from which she could call home base in Setauket, Long Island; a radar to view approaching weather; and Winlink 2000, a ham-radio-based email service.

That Walbridge and Hansen had not engaged a professional weather router to guide their ship's voyage—not even the free service provided by Herb Hilgenberg—may have spoken more to Walbridge's noble attitude and lifelong habit of self-reliance than to penury. But as with any wooden-tall-ship operator, Walbridge fought an ongoing battle for funds and was always selecting which of the ship's many pressing needs would absorb the limited cash on hand. It was a difficult and lonely role. Richard Bailey, skipper of the tall ship *Rose* in the 1990s when Walbridge was his mate, recalls his own feeling of being not "just the hired captain, but the chief visionary of the project, always trying to increase revenue just so you have more money to spend. I think you become very alert to financial opportunities but also to financial losses or failures." Needing to make the economics work creates pressures.

Walbridge had left *Rose* in 1995 to take the helm of *Bounty* and had been her skipper ever since. But he and Bailey had stayed in touch. Walbridge, a year older than his former boss, told Bailey about his fund-raising schemes and dreams, among them a plan to make frequent stops in Copenhagen, Denmark, where *Bounty* had drawn huge crowds. If you could do that often enough, you could make hundreds of thousands of dollars a year. Bailey got the impression that *Bounty* was surviving on a rather low budget.

Some of Walbridge's big dreams worked out. Thanks to her role in the *Pirates of the Caribbean* films, in 2005 *Bounty* was able to dock in Bayou La Batre, Alabama, where the Steiner Shipyard was building boats for the same films. There, she got completely new rigging, replacing much of her ten miles of rope. The crew did the work but the materials and dock fees had been paid for by Disney, Walbridge told friends.

Not every deal is a blockbuster, though. Some income walked up *Bounty*'s gangplank one person at a time. The ship was licensed by the US Coast Guard as a "dockside attraction" only and was not permitted to engage in the more lucrative business of taking customers sailing. Although at times the HMS Bounty Organization LLC had made stabs at qualifying for a coast guard sail-training license—and at times advertised that it would take paying customers sailing—no such license had ever been earned.

So Walbridge's chore was to find ways to lure people off the dock in any city the ship visited, and a unique opportunity surfaced in January 2012 when *Bounty* was at its 2011–2012 winter dock in San Juan.

An Ohio photographer and event promoter, Gary Kannegiesser, wanted to become a private contractor who would take photographs of visitors in every port where *Bounty* docked. Since the primary source of *Bounty*'s income—other than the money spent on the ship by its owner, Robert Hansen—was the $10 fee visitors paid to board the ship, Kannegiesser's scheme could be a nice addition. Once *Bounty* was inspected by the coast guard at a new dock, guests began walking the deck, climbing down to the tween deck, and imagining where, in Captain Bligh's day, various events would have occurred. If they had known *Bounty*'s recent history, they might silently have visualized Johnny Depp swaggering over the same deck boards now under their feet. They would be primed, Kannegiesser believed, for a photo op.

Kannegiesser suggested that he take pictures of visitors standing at *Bounty*'s impressive wooden helm and sell them copies. He wanted a two-year contract, hoping to cash in during the 2013 season when *Bounty* was scheduled to join other tall ships for a tour of the Great Lakes.

Robert Hansen had flown to San Juan and Kannegiesser met with him and Walbridge aboard *Bounty*. "Bob was a businessman and he thought it [the idea] was cool, but he left the decision-making up to Robin," Kannegiesser said. "Robin felt, 'I really don't know if I want to tie up the crew so they can have pictures taken.' He was lukewarm. Very cordial, but lukewarm at best."

During a break in the visit, Kannegiesser and a colleague who had made the trip with him went to a restaurant. At a nearby table sat an Alabama woman, Connie DeRamus, and her friend. The women were in Puerto Rico on vacation, and they eavesdropped and heard the men talking about *Bounty*. DeRamus's friend began asking questions about *Bounty,* and soon all four were conversing.

DeRamus had one topic she liked to discuss: her twenty-nine-year-old daughter, Ashley, a blond young woman with Down syndrome. For years, DeRamus had thought of building a clothing line around Ashley, garments that would take into account the unique figure of Down syndrome girls and women, whom department-store clothing seldom fit. She told the men about her dreams.

"That's a great idea," Kannegiesser said. "Why don't you do it?"

They continued to talk, and Kannegiesser began envisioning a role for Ashley DeRamus that would connect her with *Bounty*. He had in mind a concession on the dock beside *Bounty* where silicone bracelets promoting Ashley by Design—the name DeRamus had chosen for her daughter's clothing line—could be sold. He imagined a charitable, nonprofit organization under whose auspices the bracelets would be marketed and which would raise funds for the needs of Down syndrome children and adults.

Eventually, Robin Walbridge agreed to Kannegiesser's photography scheme, and Kannegiesser decided to begin slowly. When the season started in April and *Bounty* sailed north from Puerto Rico, the photographer and a crew of five boarded a recreational vehicle, joining *Bounty* at its first stops in St. Augustine and Jacksonville, Florida.

DeRamus's friend Kim lived in Jacksonville. Her home on the St. Johns River had a pool. Kannegiesser and his crew stopped there for a break from travel and discussed how to make the photo operation at the next port—Savannah—more functional.

"Then Kim and I decided to go to Savannah and help out," DeRamus said. "I just brought Ashley's bracelets along because I could, and I set up a picture of her and [an] Ashley by Design [sign]. We just had that sitting on the corner of the photo table. It ended up that a remarkable number of parents stopped by to see what it was all about."

DeRamus recognized then that having her daughter present would help boost donations to the nonprofit.

"The idea evolved [from] actually talking to the captain about Ashley," she said.

DeRamus and her friend stayed with Kannegiesser through the next two ports, Charleston, South Carolina, and Wilmington, North Carolina. DeRamus was busy the next few weeks, and not until the end of May did she and Ashley return to *Bounty,* in Greenport, New York, *Bounty*'s registered home port. By then, Kannegiesser had an agreement from Walbridge that Ashley could set up a small area near the photo booth to sell bracelets and tell her story.

At first, DeRamus says, she didn't know which of the crew members was *Bounty*'s skipper. "Robin was so humble and unassuming that he never announced to anyone that he was the captain," she said. "He was always wearing a *Bounty* T-shirt or sweatshirt, cruising the deck, talking with visitors."

From Greenport on, the recreational vehicle, with Kannegiesser, DeRamus, Ashley, and the five photo employees, arrived at every port where *Bounty* stopped. There was a swing north up the Hudson River and then a voyage south to the Chesapeake Bay and Annapolis, Maryland. Next was a stop in Philadelphia, in the midst of a hundred-degree heat wave that kept visitors away in droves, and then *Bounty* returned to Long Island, where it docked at Port Jefferson, below the bluffs of Setauket, home to the ship's corporate offices as well as her owner, Robert Hansen.

The ship, her crew, and the photo team visited Plymouth, Boston, Gloucester, and Newburyport, Massachusetts, and sailed to Star Island in the Isles of Shoals, six miles offshore from Portsmouth, New Hampshire. Two weeks later, they were in Nova Scotia, where they visited Lunenburg, *Bounty*'s birthplace.

Along the way, DeRamus saw Walbridge developing what she later described as "a kind of rapport" with her daughter. To DeRamus, Walbridge seemed sweet and compassionate.

DeRamus also said she and her daughter developed a friendship with everybody in the crew. "They were just really genuinely nice people, but they were sailors and they weren't into giving tours of the ship and stuff, except for Claudene," DeRamus said.

When Kannegiesser's summer help went home near the end of the season, Claudene Christian was recruited to become part of the photo crew. In port, she donned the Tahitian-print dress provided by DeRamus and helped with Kannegiesser's and DeRamus's operations.

In Plymouth, Massachusetts, Walbridge welcomed Ashley and Connie DeRamus on board as crew members. They sailed to Portsmouth, New Hampshire, and then, watched over by other crew members, Ashley sailed on *Bounty* without her mother for the better part of a week, handling some of the duties of sailing a tall ship, perhaps a first for a person with Down syndrome.

In every port, Ashley was at the dock with her colorful bracelets, taking donations. "We got anywhere from one dollar to twenty dollars for donations, depending on the persons," her mother said. "We had a table set up where we had printers for the photo operation. The people who had the pictures taken at the helm would come back to our table.

We had an extra little extension table at the end of our photo booth. She [Ashley] had a sign explaining what she was doing."

Meanwhile, Kannegiesser's brain was churning out ideas connecting *Bounty* and Ashley. He and Walbridge talked of bringing Down syndrome children aboard for voyages the following summer, 2013, on the Tall Ships America fleet tour of the Great Lakes.

"They [*Bounty*] would either bring a parent [to supervise their child] or one of the crew members would supervise," DeRamus said. "We were all very excited about that, giving Downs kids an opportunity for independence and learning about sailing, the education, self-esteem, responsibility, and the self-discipline. We spent a lot of time, and Gary and Robin especially, discussing the logistics of this next summer and what we were going to do," DeRamus said. Walbridge wanted to make Ashley the liaison for special needs on *Bounty*, DeRamus said.

While she helped Kannegiesser with his photo operation, DeRamus was not his employee. "He took me and Ashley and gave her the opportunity to raise money. We used his photo opportunity to promote [Ashley's] foundation."

When, in September, *Bounty* was hauled out at the Boothbay Harbor (Maine) Shipyard for maintenance and repairs, Ashley and her mother returned to Birmingham, Alabama, where Ashley was a volunteer at the Bell Center, which helps special-needs children. She and her mother made a $6,300 donation to the center from the money they collected at *Bounty*'s side.

But the connection among *Bounty*, Walbridge, and Down syndrome did not end there. Kannegiesser had located the Down Syndrome Network of Tampa Bay. "Gary had approached me [in September]," said Shirley Lawyer, head of the nonprofit group. "I guess he was kind of calling around, trying to find some connection to Down syndrome in the Tampa area."

Lawyer was familiar with *Bounty*, which had spent many winters as a dockside attraction in neighboring St. Petersburg.

In 2012, Walbridge wanted *Bounty* to visit St. Petersburg one more time. He and his wife, Claudia McCann, had a home there. But there was another reason: the St. Petersburg Pier, where, for many years, *Bounty* was a seasonal fixture moored on the pier's south side during the winter, was scheduled for demolition.

"When she [*Bounty*] came to St. Petersburg," Lawyer said, "we would bring as many people as we could get down to the [dock]. We have 450 families on our mailing list." Kannegiesser, the promoter, envisioned Ashley DeRamus leading the crowd in reciting the Pledge of Allegiance. "That was one component of the event," Lawyer says. "And then it was asked if we would have three or four families who would be interested in sailing on the ship. We were going to sail across the Gulf of Mexico to Texas," where *Bounty* was scheduled to spend the winter in Galveston.

Ashley DeRamus was not the first special-needs person Captain Robin Walbridge had ever met. Nor was Gary Kannegiesser the first person to suggest that Walbridge pay attention to and have concern for the handicapped. Walbridge's father, Howard, had worked as a vocational and rehabilitation counselor for the State of Vermont. In that work, he saw the needs of the blind and developed the Vermont State Division for the Blind and Visually Impaired. Often when his children were growing up, Howard would bring them to events for those with special needs.

"Dad was a very compassionate person," said Lucille Walbridge Jansen, Robin's older sister. "In the course of working with challenged people, Dad saw a need for them to socialize and be with others and [to] realize they were not alone. He developed the Indoor Sports Club, which met once a month. There was food involved, refreshments," and the Walbridge children were invited. Mingling with those whom some might view as "different," Lucille Walbridge "felt like a queen when Dad allowed me to come with him." Her little brother, four years younger, enjoyed similar experiences.

Thus Robin Walbridge had several reasons to agree when Kannegiesser proposed the Down syndrome event in St. Petersburg. Publicity for Walbridge's beleaguered ship was but one. He let his crew know about the Florida event and Ashley's involvement. Reflecting on the decision to sail from New London, Connecticut, in the face of an advancing hurricane, crew member Doug Faunt later remarked that had *Bounty* not sailed when it did, "We would have disappointed all the people in St. Pete. The captain wanted to push to make that destination."

CHAPTER FOUR

THE CAPTAIN

> *Sandy passed* [east and north] *of Abacos* [the Bahamas] *this morning, exactly as expected.* [A buoy] *sampled* [east and south] *winds (indicating East side of Sandy) about 5 miles off Elbow Cay, Abacos, at 9am. Throughout Abacos, winds as Sandy approached were sampled* [from the northeast] *@ 45–85 knots sustained . . . and after Sandy passed . . . winds backed* [to the north-northwest] *as expected in 45–75 knots sustained range.*
>
> —Chris Parker, report, Friday, October 26, 3:00 p.m.

At about 8:00 a.m. on Friday, October 26, around the time the east and most violent side of Hurricane Sandy was hammering the Abacos Islands about a hundred miles or more off the Florida coast, the officers of *Bounty* gathered at the stern on the tween deck in what was called the Great Cabin. Eating breakfast while they talked, Walbridge, Chief Mate Svendsen, Second Mate Sanders, Third Mate Dan Cleveland, Bosun Laura Groves, and Engineer Chris Barksdale discussed the weather. The forecasts that they were getting—weather faxes off the single sideband radio and emails from Tracie Simonin, *Bounty*'s land-based office manager—continued to show the same path for Hurricane Sandy.

They talked about work that would be performed that day by *Bounty*'s crew. A yard—the horizontal wooden spar that holds the top of a square sail—would be lowered to the deck to reduce weight aloft. More sea stowing had to be accomplished so that when the seas grew and the ship rocked, no loose items would be flying across the ship's thirty-one-foot beam and threatening the crew.

The officers also talked about the navigation plans. The engines were running hard—uncommon aboard *Bounty*. Usually, when the ship lost sight of land, the captain, for authenticity and as a means of teaching, turned off most mechanical equipment—even navigational tools—and reverted to authentic practices used in the days of sail. But time and distance needed to be made—three hundred miles to the south in the next couple of days—according to Walbridge's plan to place *Bounty* at the same latitude as Cape Hatteras, where, if the hurricane performed as the captain expected, he thought he would be able to sail with favorable winds.

Once the officers' meeting concluded, it was time for the daily Captain's Muster, when all hands gathered around the ship's capstan, a giant winch in front of the third, or mizzen, mast, which hauled lines when the force needed was greater than what the deckhands alone could provide.

Muster was the one time in any normal day when all the crew saw Walbridge, a time when the skipper might tell a joke or two, but when, invariably, he would use the opportunity to teach his young followers—he called them future captains of America—something new about seamanship.

Walbridge was a modern-day Socrates. He taught by asking questions. On this day, the question was "Two hundred years ago, how would sailors know a hurricane was coming?"

"I don't think they would have known at all that a hurricane was coming," replied Joshua Scornavacchi, twenty-five, who had been on board most of the time since San Juan. Walbridge didn't agree or disagree. This was part of his teaching technique. He allowed people to think out the solution to a problem and encouraged them to try their ideas, even when those efforts resulted in mistakes, as long as the mistakes were not dangerous. Then he would urge that person to teach others what he or she had learned. Moreover, crew members, even the greenest, found Walbridge willing to listen to what they had to say. But everyone, regardless of his or her experience, found that the captain was several steps ahead in his thinking. Respect for his deep knowledge was widespread, a dividend of not only the life Walbridge had led but his singular personality. At least superficially, this explains why no one left *Bounty* back in New London. If he or she stayed aboard long enough, as Third Mate Dan Cleveland had, a crew member learned to believe what the captain said. But you had to experience Walbridge's expertise in the context of life aboard *Bounty*. Taken out of that context, Walbridge was capable of being misunderstood, as he had been during an interview one day in the summer of 2012.

On that day, August 9, *Bounty* had pulled up to the municipal dock in the hillside community of Belfast, Maine, with preparations under way to welcome visitors. The past week or so had seen dense fog on Penobscot Bay. In Belfast, one of the northernmost ports on the bay, it was a grim morning, the tips of *Bounty*'s three masts blurred by the sagging belly of the low, gray overcast. *Bounty*, big and dark with a blue band on her topsides, dominated the waterfront, where normally the largest visiting vessels were small cruise ships.

Ned Lightner, host of a local public-access television program, knew that *Bounty* was coming. Her visit was the subject of conversation in the local government. The city harbormaster, Kathy Pickering, had lobbied for the visit. Lightner, whose program, *Somewhere in Waldo County*, would often tackle such subjects as the purchase of a new fire truck, was delighted to have a more exotic topic. He thought some of his homebound listeners might appreciate a video tour. He contacted Walbridge, who agreed to allow filming.

Lightner arrived around seven thirty that morning. Much of the *Bounty* crew was still asleep, and at first Lightner didn't know that the captain was the older fellow up on deck, holding a cup of coffee.

Walbridge, soft-spoken as always, was perfectly affable when he greeted Lightner. They began talking, and the camera rolled with a mast and webs of rigging as a backdrop.

About eleven minutes into the interview, Lightner asked, "Have you ever run into some pretty nasty weather while at sea?"

"Actually, I'm going to answer that with a no," Walbridge replied in his somewhat gravelly voice. "We say there's no such thing as bad weather. There's just different kinds of weather."

Lightner, laughing, changed his question. "Have you run into stormy seas?"

"We chase hurricanes." Walbridge grinned. "You try and get up as close to the eye of it as you can and you stay down in the southeast quadrant, and when it stops, you stop. You don't want to get in front of it. You stay behind it. But you also get a good ride out of a hurricane."

Lightner speculated that Walbridge must have sailed in some pretty towering waves.

"The biggest waves that I personally have ever been in have been about seventy feet. That's a pretty good sea." Walbridge said that particular ride in the wake of a hurricane was no more uncomfortable than "you and I standing right here."

Dan Cleveland understood that his captain's comments were not bravado because in his first year aboard *Bounty*, he had twice seen how Walbridge dealt with hurricanes. And by observation, Cleveland had learned.

Before he boarded *Bounty* in 2008 as a deckhand, Cleveland had no nautical experience. That year, the ship took a Pacific tour. On the way back to the Atlantic Ocean, *Bounty* transited the Panama Canal and entered the Gulf of Mexico, where a Category 1 hurricane was stalled between the Yucatán Peninsula and Cuba, blocking *Bounty*'s progress to the north.

Walbridge ordered *Bounty*'s crew to heave to, a maneuver in which the ship faces into the wind, trimming its sails to back-wind them while steering in the opposite direction. Heaving to parks a vessel, which then will drift slowly with the wind while riding at a relatively comfortable attitude.

The storm was moving north at four knots. The ship made a knot or two. Cleveland saw that the point was to avoid overtaking the storm.

Another crew member for that voyage, Cliff Bredeson, explained that the problem was that while *Bounty* needed to pass through the gap between the peninsula and Cuba, the hurricane was in the way. Under Walbridge's direction, Bredeson said, the crew "poked our nose up into the hurricane as far as we were comfortable so as the hurricane moved north, we could be as close getting to the gap as we could. We were in the southeast quadrant. If things got bad, we could go southerly and get away if it decided to go south or east. That became the joke, that we were hurricane chasers."

The logic, Bredeson said, was that "with a hurricane, we could always know where the winds were coming from. The winds around the hurricane are counterclockwise. You watch the hurricane reports and you know where the center of the hurricane is. If you're in the south and east quadrant, winds are going to be coming out of the west, or, higher up, out of the south."

That predictability made Walbridge's choice a wise decision, according to Bredeson, and the conditions were tolerable, with winds in the forty- to fifty-knot range. *Bounty* was designed as a collier, a ship that hauls coal, and her stout build made her capable of handling such a breeze.

Earlier that season, *Bounty* had been caught in a Pacific hurricane as the ship made its way from Mexico to Costa Rica. Cleveland, then the novice, endured three days of "crappy" weather and fatigue. But he took a lesson from his master: "You try to make sure you're going slower than the hurricane so it's going away from you. If one is in the vicinity, we want to follow it. We actually had a very fine sail."

Those two hurricanes taught the inexperienced Dan Cleveland something about his captain's knowledge and his thoughts about seamanship. But Walbridge often took a more active role as teacher and used his ship as a classroom, just as he had on Friday morning when he asked his crew about weather predictions two hundred years before.

Bounty was not officially a sail-training ship as it lacked the necessary coast guard certification. But in Belfast the previous August, Walbridge had told Ned Lightner, "I consider us kind of an educational ship. We're trying to teach the public about what sailing was like two hundred years ago.

"This [ship] was the tractor-trailer of two hundred years ago. This was the space shuttle of two hundred years ago. People don't understand the heritage. I like to use the analogy of a manual speed transmission. If you buy a car with a manual speed transmission, [the owner's manual won't] tell you to push the clutch down because everybody knows that you have to push the clutch down. So picture two hundred years from now, somebody gets in that car. They're not going to be able to drive it because nobody told them to push the clutch down.

"That's kind of what's happened," Walbridge continued. "We're rediscovering the very basics [of square-rig sailing]. And I think this is important for our youth to understand our basics, to understand where we came from and why we got to where we did."

Walbridge was genetically wired as an educator, not a sailor. Born Robert Walbridge in St. Johnsbury, Vermont, on October 25, 1949, he came into the world as the second child of two teachers. At the time, his father was a teacher in Lyndonville, Vermont. But soon after Robert arrived, Howard Walbridge was hired to work for the state in its vocational rehabilitation office in Montpelier, the state capital.

The Walbridges moved into a hundred-year-old farmhouse on the north edge of town, on a hillside facing east, bathed by the first sunlight of the morning. There were thirty-five acres and a three-hundred-foot-long driveway.

Anna Walbridge, Robert's mother, took a job teaching the first four grades in a two-room schoolhouse on the Winooski River in Middlesex, Vermont, a few miles west and downstream from Montpelier.

But the teaching roots were much deeper than this. Robert had grandparents on both sides of the family who were teachers, and one great-grandfather was a state superintendent of schools.

Learning was an enjoyable and constant part of life in the Walbridge family. Walbridge could remember the day when he was in the sixth grade and the family made a Thanksgiving trip to Quincy, Massachusetts, to visit Anna's parents, the Palmers.

The Walbridges had one of the first Volkswagens in Vermont, but on this trip they drove their powerful French car, a Citroën. The two-lane road crossing the heart of New Hampshire was dark as the car climbed and descended the many hills.

"Dad being my dad was commenting on the cars, talking about cars," Lucille Walbridge Jansen said. "As we started going up a hill, we passed a Volkswagen, and Dad was explaining how the Citroën had a twelve-volt battery and the VW only six volts," and how the power of the two batteries were different and how cars were built to travel at a certain optimal speed. The Citroën passed the Volkswagen going up a hill, and Howard explained that was because the Citroën had so much more power.

"Then going down the hill, these guys passed us," said Lucille. "And Dad commented that they were exceeding the safe speed for that VW to be going. We also observed that they were drinking and they were feeling quite victorious in their behavior. I remember seeing a beer can. They certainly were not hiding the fact.

"In front of us, they rolled that car several times," Lucille recalled. "It landed right side up, perpendicular to the road. The wheels were still spinning and it went off the road, missed a very solid tree. One of the boys was thrown out."

Speaking the whole time in a calm voice, like a teacher in a classroom, Howard observed that an accident like that could cause a fire or an explosion.

"And you shouldn't park in front of [the wreck] because you don't want to obstruct the view" of motorists following you and arriving on the scene.

It was as if the Walbridge kids—Lucille, the oldest; Robert, four years younger; and Delia Mae, about nineteen months younger still—were watching a movie. Their father's voice, calm and confident, kept teaching as he drove past the wreck and parked.

Howard got out and took Lucille with him, approaching the Volkswagen. "You have to know how many people we're looking for," he told her as they reached the boy who had been thrown from the car and, now stunned, staggered around.

"Son, how many people were in that car?" Howard asked the boy. "Three," the boy answered. Howard told him to sit down. He turned to Lucille and instructed her to stay with the boy and keep him in place while he looked for the others.

Once the injured boys had been sent to a hospital, Howard explained to his children that you didn't go by the scene of an accident without helping. At the next pay phone, Howard stopped to call the Palmers and explain that he and the family would be late.

"I didn't understand why we would do that," Lucille recalls. When she asked, Howard patiently explained that you didn't let people worry about you.

Lesson taught—and lesson learned.

In a sense, Robin Walbridge, the ship's captain, couldn't help himself. He was a teacher as well.

CHAPTER FIVE

A HAPPY, HAPPY CREW

This will be a tough voyage for Bounty. Here is Bounty's current position and the weather front (Hurricane Sandy) that is approaching.

Bounty is approx 100 miles off shore. Speed 8.6 knots on a course South by west.

—*Bounty* Facebook page, Friday, October 26, 9:45 a.m.

Sandy is generating deep convection near her center . . . but as soon as it's generated, strong SSW-to-NNE wind-shear strips them away from Sandy's center, and spreads "debris" clouds (which are not significant), some showers, and lesser-intense squalls throughout areas . . . all the way from FL E Coast . . . to Norfolk VA . . . and E-ward to beyond Bermuda.

—Chris Parker, email, Friday, October 26, 5:50 p.m.

Among his fifteen crew members—ten men and five women—aboard *Bounty*, Walbridge enjoyed unquestioning loyalty.

Douglas Faunt, the oldest crew member and three years older than Walbridge, would say that the *Bounty* crew was his family—"closer than my family"—and a group who would risk their lives for one another. Walbridge, Faunt felt, was his mentor and someone whom he held in high regard.

Although there seemed to always be eager applicants for crew positions, not every sailor who stepped aboard *Bounty* shared

Faunt's enthusiasm for the skipper when he or she returned ashore. At least one, Andrew Seguin, felt lucky to have been able to get off the boat alive.

In late November 2010, Seguin, from Osterville, Massachusetts, twenty-three at the time and recently unemployed, got a call telling him that *Bounty* was looking for crew for a voyage to Puerto Rico, leaving Boothbay Harbor, Maine, the next day. Seguin, who held a coast guard captain's license, had studied naval engineering at Stevens Institute of Technology, a prestigious New Jersey university. There he had met Marc Castells, three years older, a computer science major.

Seguin called Castells, who had also lost his job, and told him about *Bounty*.

"You have twenty-four hours if you want to do this."

Seguin said, "The only information I had before getting on the boat was that it was leaving Maine and was ending up in Puerto Rico. We drove through the night to get there and literally pulled into Boothbay Harbor when the sun was coming up." It was November 27, past the end of the hurricane season.

Seguin had sailed a few vessels up and down the East Coast, including the seventy-four-foot, steel-hulled *Liberté*, from Annapolis, Maryland, to Cape Cod. *Liberté* was as close as he had come to sailing a tall ship. Castells had no such experience.

"It was like a giggly feeling," Seguin said. "Wow, I'm going to take that boat from here all the way to Puerto Rico."

In time, Robin Walbridge got up, and he and the crew invited Seguin and Castells to have breakfast. They got to do a bit more exploring before Walbridge held muster at the capstan.

"Then it was 'Here's a list of things we have to do before we leave the dock.'" They spent the rest of the day helping their new shipmates tie everything down that was loose, assuring that the ship's cannon were secured and that the dockside furniture that welcomed guests was stowed.

When the work was done, Seguin was satisfied that *Bounty* was prepared to sail offshore. "We really didn't know what to expect from the boat. There's so many systems on the boat and it's so complicated that it's difficult to say it's seaworthy unless you are a full-time crew," he said. "We ended up leaving Boothbay under motor. Everything seemed perfectly normal. I do know that hours before we left, they were diving over the boat. The seacocks were leaking slightly." Seacocks are valves in the hull of a vessel, below the waterline, that either admit seawater or are used for pumping out bilge water. Before the dock lines were cast off, Seguin said, the seacocks were sealed. "Motoring out the first day it was gorgeous. It was cold. There were dolphins jumping off the bow." As *Bounty* headed south, the friends spent the first couple of days getting used to the routine of the ship. Each morning, Walbridge came to the weather deck and gave a speech.

On the first morning, Walbridge told the crew that he didn't worry about fire on the boat because it was old and wet. He also was unconcerned with sinking. "He said he's had many engineers who said the boat has enough buoyancy in itself that it won't sink," Seguin recalled.

"One thing that he emphasized was that man overboard was the most dangerous thing on the boat. The boat can't sail into the wind," so anyone in the water would quickly be left behind.

"We did overboard drills almost every day," Castells recalled. In the drill, a dinghy was lowered overboard and used to pick up an object thrown into the water in place of an actual man overboard.

Then the weather worsened, and Walbridge told the crew that in these conditions *Bounty* could not even be turned around should someone fall into the water. For those cases of man overboard, a drum at the stern was packed with safety and survival gear, even an Electronic Position Indicating Radio Beacon (EPIRB), the device that, when triggered, contacts a satellite that relays a distress signal to the National Oceanic and Atmospheric Administration (NOAA), which notifies coast guard search-and-rescue units.

All were taught that if they fell overboard, they could find the big drum floating in *Bounty*'s wake.

The first day out of port, with calm seas and no wind, the crew was sent up the rigging to furl and set sails for practice. It was exhilarating.

"After the sun set the first day, everyone was in really high spirits,"

Seguin recalled. "It seemed like it was going to be a good trip. Even day two was not bad, with enough wind to sail the boat, a little sea-state."

But then, making boat checks while standing watch, the friends each noticed that the bilges contained more water than when *Bounty* had left the dock.

"It becomes a blur from then on, the order of stuff going to hell," Seguin said, laughing. "It might have been the night of day two, morning day three, when the wind started to really build up." There were no more man-overboard drills.

For a while, the winds were consistently in the thirty-knot range. Then one morning the winds eased. "The captain said, 'We've gone through the worst of the weather.'"

But the wind returned and the crew started to see sails tearing and blowing out. At one point, Seguin said, he went to Walbridge and questioned the amount of sail area *Bounty* was flying. "I'm a conservative sailor," Seguin said. "It's easier to let more sail area out than to put it away. We had four or five sails up.

"Robin told me, 'I've gone through hurricanes with three of them up.' That's when I was, like, 'Okay, I don't like this situation, but I'm not in control, so I do what I'm told.'"

When the fore course sail, the lower square sail on the foremast, blew out, eight hands were sent aloft. Castells followed Chief Mate John Svendsen—in his first year aboard *Bounty* and his first year aboard a square-rigged ship—up the ratlines. Castells was wearing a head-mounted video camera that memorialized the event. *Bounty* rolled thirty degrees to each side, a huge metronome, driven by gale-force winds that blew up the shredded sections of the torn sail into canvas balloons. Overhead the sky was blue, with patchy white clouds, a beautiful day to look up. When the crew looked down, they saw a surging sea.

And then the topmast broke and folded over its lower half.

Seguin had stayed on deck. At first, he saw the backstays, ropes that hold the masts up and keep them from falling forward, sagging. Then he saw the mast break above where Castells was working.

Then the weather got worse.

"At one point, I was down in the galley and Captain Robin

whispered something," Seguin said. "The cook yelled, 'What? We're sailing directly into a force-nine gale? Don't you think the cook would want to know?'"

Seguin said he asked several times to be shown the weather faxes, but it was two watch shifts before he got to see them, and when he did, he discovered that *Bounty* was headed dead center into the storm.

Meanwhile, *Bounty*'s bilges were filling with water. On watch, Seguin inspected the bilge, expecting to find baffles there to keep the water near the suctions for the bilge pumps. There were none. Every time the boat rolled, the water sloshed up the inside of the hull, away from the suction lines, and the bilge pump lost its prime.

Seguin said he asked the ship's engineer, Caleb, why there were no baffles. He said Caleb replied that a couple of years earlier, when *Bounty* was in dry dock, the baffles that had been there were removed to make repairs, and half of them were rotten, so they were not replaced.

"Once we got into the thick of the storm, I don't know how far we were rolling, but it was huge," Seguin said. "There's stuff all over the floor. At the same time, the timbers of the boat worked endlessly in bone-crunching moaning, creaking [so loudly] that you pretty much have to yell, not over the motors but over the boat."

Seguin recalled a time when he awoke to go on watch and met one of his shipmates whose face was parted in a huge grin.

"Guess what I did last night," the fellow said. "I saved the boat. I put out a fire." The crewman didn't say where the fire was, but later in the day, when he was doing boat checks, Seguin lifted an engine cover. The day before, it had been yellow. Now it was white from fire-extinguisher foam. Seguin learned from Castells, who had been on watch at the helm when the fire was extinguished, that the shipmate who saved the ship never told anyone in authority.

This bothered Seguin, but probably not as much as the story he said the engineer told him. Two wires had been shorting when anyone stepped on a certain floorboard in the crew quarters. The engineer said he didn't know what the wires were for, but his solution was to pull them out.

Upon hearing this, Seguin said, "I was prepared to end up in the life raft."

Seguin noted that Walbridge stayed in his cabin except when he gave his morning talk. He ran the boat by delegation. Seguin was unsettled by the fact that Svendsen, to whom Walbridge entrusted command of the day-to-day handling of his ship, had, as recently as two years earlier, been a dive boat captain. This was not the sort of credential Seguin expected of the person second-in-command of a massive tall ship.

As *Bounty* neared Bermuda, with the bilge pumps overwhelmed, Seguin came up behind Walbridge, who was writing an email to home base. In it Walbridge wrote that things were not going so well and requested that parts be sent overnight to Bermuda.

"This is not what he's telling everyone," Seguin said.

In a last-ditch effort, old bilge pumps were hauled out of a forward hold and dragged back to the engine room. The crew spent two hours hooking one pump to the bilge manifold system. It was time wasted. The pump never worked, Seguin said.

Bounty did dock in Bermuda and Seguin and Castells informed Walbridge they were leaving. The skipper was pleasant when he accepted their resignations. Ashore, the friends paid for lodging and airfare home. They were told on the dock that when people applied for their berths on *Bounty*, they were told that the two friends had left because they were seasick.

CHAPTER SIX

BECOMING ROBIN WALBRIDGE

December 1951. A Volkswagen Bug, one of the first imported, was headed from northern Vermont to a Boston suburb, a family Christmas trip. In the backseat were a six-year-old girl and her brother, two months past his second birthday. The boy was silent. So far in his short life, he hadn't spoken a word. His sister thought he was difficult to fathom. His parents were getting worried about the child's learning ability.

As the Volkswagen slowly negotiated the winding country roads on the way to the grandparents' home, the girl was mulling over a quandary. The family was spending hours—long, boring hours—to travel from Montpelier to Quincy, Massachusetts. If she compared the distance they had to cover to, say, the entire world, it was not that far. How, then, was it possible that in one short night—Christmas Eve—Santa Claus visited the home of every child in the world? She struggled with her puzzle until she couldn't bear it. Then she asked Dad, who was driving. Dad was honest with his children.

"Every little girl's father is her Santa Claus," he said.

Amazed, she turned to her brother. "Did you hear that? Daddy is Santa Claus."

"Yeah, yeah, yeah," the toddler said. "I knew it all the time." And from then on, Robert—not Bob or Bobby—Walbridge, having apparently waited to select what he judged was the right moment, spoke in complete sentences.

Concealed by Robert's two-year silence was a level of analysis most adults don't imagine in two-year-olds. He spoke and the evidence was revealed. Both the analysis and the silence would continue, however, and lead to startling convictions as the boy grew.

His sister Lucille adored Robert and perhaps understood him as well as any adult. She saw, when he was four, that he had already selected a course for his life.

From time to time, a visitor or a relative would hand the boy a coin or two as a gift. Robert would take the change, slip it in his trousers pocket, and thank the person. "That's for my truck," he would tell the gift giver, who would assume that the boy had his eye on some special toy.

Lucille knew otherwise. Robert had decided that when he grew up, he would be a long-haul trucker. He was saving for his first rig. (The idea of that vocation probably didn't pop into his imagination uninvited. Howard Walbridge loved to drive, and he would often say that in another life he would be a long-haul trucker and see the world.)

Three years later, in the old farmhouse whose shelves were stacked with books and world atlases and dictionaries and various games, chessboards began appearing on every flat surface, as if delivered by elves, and on the boards were chessmen positioned as if in the midst of battle. Robert, age seven, had discovered the game and had, by mail, begun competing with other players from around the country. Quiet as always, he made no announcements but, with a passion that would last a lifetime, immersed himself in the game, exercising and strengthening his analytical powers.

In four more years, in the winter of 1960—when hundreds of miles to the northeast the shipbuilding firm of Smith and Rhuland was building the tall ship *Bounty*—Robert Walbridge began haranguing Lucille to turn over an acre of land on which she had been raising corn. She was fifteen now, he ten, and she had been harvesting her corn and selling it to raise money for college. She saw no need for Robert to have that land. There were thirty-four other acres on the Walbridge farm.

Robert didn't say why he wanted that particular land. Like most rural New Englanders, he was taciturn. It's a cultural thing. But with Robert Walbridge, it was different. Unlike other children his age, he kept his own counsel, always.

Howard Walbridge was aware that his daughter was under siege. He may have decided to intervene because he wondered what his son was up to. In a family meeting, he noted that Lucille had been raising the same crop on that acre for some time. Now might be the moment to move her crop to another location so the nutrients were not drawn out of that acre, he suggested. The family listened, and although Lucille may have sighed, she relented.

Robert now had his acre, in front of the house and adjacent to the roadway—Vermont Route 12—that climbed past the driveway. He had thought ahead, had a plan, and that's why he wanted this specific plot.

Montpelier had a public swimming pool, a quarter mile beyond the Walbridge farm. To get to the pool, every kid in town had to walk past Robert's land. No one in the family knew what he planned to plant there. They knew which catalog the seeds came from but didn't know what crop the seeds would become.

As summer progressed, the land turned green with vines supporting yellow blossoms. Small pumpkins followed, and by autumn, all those passing children had selected the pumpkin that would be theirs at Halloween. Robert's profit from his one acre was over $1,000, ten weeks' pay for many grown men in 1961.

The pool up the street was the closest water to the largely landlocked Walbridge family. The grandparents from Quincy had a summer home in Post Mills, Vermont, near Lake Fairlee, where the children had access to a canoe and rowboats. The home was within walking distance of the lake, which at the time had a good beach. Most weekends during the summer, the family drove the forty miles from Montpelier southeast to the lake, where the birthdays of Lucille and her younger sister, Delia, were celebrated.

The three Walbridge children got to see salt water from time to time as well.

Anna Walbridge's parents, the Palmers, lived on Hilda Street in Quincy, about a mile from the beach, and the family visited there often. "It [the beach] was the family's escape from the city," said Lucille.

"Mom would tell us to smell the salt air, feel the slippery seaweed, examine the seashells. We had countless numbers of picnics down there. Dad also liked the sea but not as intensely as my mother. In the whole family, Mom seemed to have the most intense liking for the sea." She also loved a poem by John Masefield:

> *I must go down to the seas again, to the lonely sea and the sky,*
> *And all I ask is a tall ship and a star to steer her by,*
> *And the wheel's kick and the wind's song and the white sail's shaking,*
> *And a grey mist on the sea's face and a grey dawn breaking.*

Like a mantra, someone in the family was always reciting the poem along the thin beach in a bay of the Atlantic Ocean.

On these visits to Quincy, Lucille Walbridge had, in addition to the beach, a favorite excursion. Although nearby Boston was filled with historical sites, Lucille's compass always directed her gaze toward Old Ironsides, the USS *Constitution*, the historic tall ship docked near the heart of the city.

"It held a certain fascination [for me] that Paul Revere's house didn't have," Lucille said.

So that's where the family went, again and again, with Robert in tow.

One memorable summer vacation led not to Quincy but to a campground in Eastport, Maine, near the Canadian border. Robert was about ten, and the family had packed everything in and on the Volkswagen. When Howard struck up a conversation with a fellow, the man invited the whole family to stay in his cabin at the ocean's edge. In fact, the cabin was built out over the water, and nearby, lobster boats floated on their moorings. The Walbridges ate lobster from the sea and slept over the lapping waves of the Atlantic. When they got home, young Robert wanted his own lobster boat.

The request was not granted, and this angered the boy, turning him against his mother. But the boy was going to be a long-haul trucker, anyway. That was his focus. When he entered high school, he concentrated on acquiring the money to fund that vision. He had jobs delivering two local newspapers. He worked at a ski area helping to pack the snow. He had an egg route, selling eggs from the family chickens. He raised three hundred turkeys at a time to sell for Thanksgiving. At night, he had a job at a local Howard Johnson restaurant.

"He had fudged a bit on his age," Lucille said. He was thirteen, not the required sixteen, when he was hired. "He was rapidly promoted to opening and closing" the restaurant, she said. "His theory was [that] wherever you worked, you learned everything you could, every job in the place."

By the time he was fifteen, Robert had a steady business buying, repairing, and selling cars, even though he wasn't old enough to hold a driver's license. At times, the long driveway at the farm would be cluttered with old cars. As a sideline, he sold scrap metal.

The price that the boy was willing to pay was academic. He thought school was a good place to catch up on his sleep. Like the son of a preacher, this son of teachers seemed to snub the family trade. He managed to earn B's, but thought his plan would be advanced more quickly if he quit school altogether. He informed his parents.

Learning was considered fun in the old farmhouse north of Montpelier. What was the boy thinking? His mother was distraught, pleading with Robert to stay in school.

Robert Walbridge relented and completed high school. He had another reason to be angry with his mother. But the hostility did not interfere with the boy's drive to excel. He earned the rank of Eagle in Boy Scouts, an achievement announced in the local newspaper. Among his badges was one for canoeing.

Nor were these years in Montpelier devoid of simple joy for the boy. In winter, he would climb the hill behind their home and ski down before school with his sisters. After supper, Anna Walbridge would read to her children. In the summer, during family picnics, one of the larger rocks on a hillside field served as the table. Everyone would sit and talk around a campfire. Anna quoted different poems, Howard quoted Shakespeare, Grandfather recited Longfellow, Milton, and Shelley, and Grandmother a little bit of everything.

Robert and his sisters helped set the table; washed dishes; dusted; fed the farm animals—they raised their own cows and chickens, as well as vegetables; mowed lawns; weeded their assigned three rows of peas each day during the summer; drove the tractor for haying; assisted in canning the vegetables—anything their parents were doing, the Walbridge children did.

In Boy Scouts, Robert learned to cook. One morning, Lucille started to cook eggs in the farmhouse kitchen. "He put his arm around me and gently shoved me aside and said, 'Let me do that,'" Lucille recalled. "He took four eggs, two in each hand, and then simultaneously cracked all four of them and dumped the shells in the wastebasket in one smooth motion. Eggs went in the frying pan and shells went in the trash. He was thirteen. It was a few days after that that he got the job cooking at Howard Johnson's."

Nor, Walbridge told his sister, did he ever stop cooking. Aboard *Bounty*, he said, he baked eight loaves of bread every other day. He said he taught bread-baking to his crew members.

The Vietnam War was raging when Robert graduated from Montpelier High School. That summer, he took a job as a cook at a prestigious golf resort on Vermont's Lake Morey. He wanted a truck but he wasn't twenty-one yet, and the Lake Morey Inn was a move up from Howard Johnson.

The resort provided its guests with small boats on which to sail the lake, where the pink summer evening clouds reflected majestically on the lake surface. Robert Walbridge borrowed a friend's sailboat and sailed across the lake. He was hooked. The feel of the wind in the sails thrilled the teenager, who as a boy had seen lobster boats and lusted. But for a while, boats and sailing would have to wait.

He applied for conscientious objector status and took a defense-industry job at Pratt & Whitney in East Hartford, Connecticut. During his time at the aircraft company, he was always busy but found time to enroll in art and algebra courses at a community college. His trucking plans were on hold, and he felt that in taking courses, he also was wasting his time. He told his sister that he had earned A's in both courses but that he had learned all that college could teach him.

On October 25, 1970, Walbridge turned twenty-one and was eligible to get a truck driver's license. As soon as that was accomplished, he paid cash for a new semitractor—money from the egg routes and paper routes and car sales and restaurant jobs and even from the coins he'd accepted in his childhood "for my truck"—and hit the road as a long-haul trucker. He had planned for seventeen years for this moment and had made it happen.

It would be another decade or more before Robert Walbridge turned away from the highways and toward the sea. Just before he did that, he made another move he had apparently been contemplating for some time.

Few people outside the Walbridge family called him Robert. They seemed to feel that Bob or Bobby was a better name. This apparently grated on him, and in his midthirties he took action.

In some court the date is recorded when Robert Walbridge officially changed his name to Robin. He was like that, headstrong and determined. These qualities would have grave consequences as *Bounty* headed toward Hurricane Sandy.

CHAPTER SEVEN

JOSHUA'S STORY

Friday, October 26, 2012, was a good day at sea. The winds were moderate and the seas relatively calm as *Bounty*'s bluff bow plowed south across the Atlantic. Long Island had disappeared in her wake overnight. Now, dark blue water was in every direction, with only thin lines of foam atop small waves. The crew knew a change was coming, though. They had their weather fax, among other modern conveniences, to remind them that Sandy was headed north. So those sailors not on watch began tackling the jobs on Bosun Laura Groves's list.

The C-Watch, Joshua Scornavacchi's crew, finished its last tour at eight o'clock, ate breakfast, and now was available to help Groves. Safety ropes called jack lines had to be strung along the top—or weather—deck and on the wide-open sections of the tween deck just below. "Sailor strainer" netting had to be raised along the exposed sides of the weather deck. And Groves wanted to lower the unused royal yard to the deck to bring its weight down.

Jack lines are long lines or straps running along a sailing vessel's deck from bow to stern. In rough seas they give crew members a place to hold on or on which to clip a tether attached to a harness to prevent them from falling and sliding overboard.

The sailor strainer is netting raised along the aft rails to catch crew members before they are washed overboard.

The royal yard is the spar that supports a royal sail, a small, light-air sail flown at the very top of a mast.

Scornavacchi, as nimble as any of the other crew members, was sent aloft first with Drew Salapatek to reef some of the sails, a normal tactic prior to foul weather and rising winds. Reefing is gathering up part of a sail into folds, thus reducing the area of sail exposed to the wind.

With the reefing accomplished, Scornavacchi alone was sent higher, to disconnect and lower the royal yard. Although *Bounty*'s stability letter—an official document stating under what circumstances a vessel is stable in the water—prohibited use of royal sails, she was rigged with the spars, and at times Walbridge ordered that canvas flown.

One hundred feet up the mast, where he could see far beyond the horizon that would be visible to the helmsman on deck, Scornavacchi rode the mast as it rocked gently. Salapatek was below, keeping an eye on him for safety. It was a perfect day for this job, and shortly the yard was lying on the weather deck, where Scornavacchi joined the rest of the crew.

Next the crew strung two jack lines—one on each side—on the weather deck. The lines were loose, giving anyone holding on to them the ability to go near the outer rails. Then Scornavacchi and the crew went below, where they strung two tight lines on the tween deck and another, short line athwartships in the galley to give the cook, Jessica Black, something to hold on to while she prepared meals.

In all the time Scornavacchi had been aboard *Bounty*, the crew seldom had need of jack lines, nor did they need the sailor strainer netting, which they now attached to the vertically slanting ropes that, like guy wires on a telephone pole, rose from the hull to support the main- and mizzenmasts. Scornavacchi had endured the calm summer weather while longing for some action at sea. Now, he was happy preparing for the storm.

Bounty was in San Juan, Puerto Rico, when Scornavacchi met her. He arrived in the early-morning hours in a downpour. Rainwater streamed down the street as he approached the dock. Through the rain, he saw the ship, dark, huge, breathtaking. Everyone on board was asleep, but he made enough noise to awaken a watch stander sleeping near the companionway. He was shown to a display case on the tween deck, and there he bunked until dawn.

A month later, *Bounty* began her season sailing north for St. Augustine, Florida. On that first day out of San Juan, Scornavacchi climbed the rigging with others in the crew to set the four topmast staysails and the main topsail. From high on a mast, he saw dolphins bounding by the ship's sides.

Then a squall struck, and quickly the seas built to eight to twelve feet.

Scornavacchi and two other young men, following orders to furl the jib, went out on the jibboom, a spar holding down the bottom of a triangular sail above *Bounty*'s sixty-foot bowsprit.

"Whenever you're furling a sail, you're going to be standing just on a footrope and that's it," Scornavacchi said. "It's pretty cool. Man, you do things that you think you would never do."

Sailing in his first storm, Scornavacchi worked with the snapping sailcloth, the wind blowing so hard he couldn't hear his shipmates. One of the other crew members, Johnny, was yelling, but his words were carried away in the howl. The rain stung and the ship's bow plunged and spray rose in great, soaking fans.

The furlers climbed back down to the deck, where, without breaking stride, Scornavacchi vomited off the leeward rail. Then he went up the mainmast to set the main topsail. The ship moved side to side and fore and aft and up and down, and the yard that he was approaching moved side to side. He hadn't quite reached the yard when a humpback whale breached immediately beside the ship. Then another, big as a small bus, broke the surface, and soon whales were jumping out of the water everywhere.

The crew set the sail but, gawking at whales, they were not quick. Scornavacchi watched in awe, all the while worrying that the next wave of nausea would rain the remaining contents of his stomach down on the crew members below. He finished his work aloft, then vomited once he returned to the deck. He took a turn at the helm, then had to hand off the job to race once again to the leeward rail. And still the whales and dolphins leaped as if they, indoctrinated into *Bounty*'s routine, knew—as did Scornavacchi—that you didn't stop working for anything.

That night had its own reward for the young sailor. As the boat broke through the water, it agitated floating phosphorescence, and as if a switch had been thrown, the sea swirling along the hull turned green, and the dolphins, still swimming beside *Bounty*, glowed.

Life seemed perfect. These were the best days. But unknown to Scornavacchi, he had contracted a virulent infection through some cuts and scrapes. After a week at sea, boils began appearing on his skin, eleven of them when the ship was two days from St. Augustine. By then, he was unable to walk.

As soon as *Bounty* docked, he was given a heavy dose of antibiotics and sent home to Pennsylvania to recover. More shots and pills and nasal antibiotics and antibiotic soap took care of the staph infection. But it took weeks, while everyone Scornavacchi knew attempted to keep him from returning to sea.

The Center for Infectious Diseases had to clear him, but so did his mother and family and friends and his girlfriend. "They were just really worried," he recalled. "I felt like I was just starting on that [nautical] journey. I wanted to finish it. My girlfriend left me pretty soon after that, and then I just continued on the ship."

Already, Scornovacchi had discovered something compelling aboard *Bounty*. In that, he was not alone. Many of his shipmates were tugged aboard in the same way. For Scornavacchi, unique ingredients in the stew of his first twenty-five years may have steered him toward *Bounty* and Robin Walbridge.

In his early memories there is the divorce. He was five when his father and mother separated. He stayed with his mother, learned to resent his father.

Two years later, when Scornavacchi was in first grade, he had what he now describes as his "midlife crisis." It began in a moment when he stopped and looked around him, at everything, and thought, *If I died right now, I wouldn't have accomplished anything in my life.*

He felt old. He looked down at a small patch of grass—he was standing in his own yard—and stared at it. He saw what he now says were fourteen different species of plants and many types of insects.

"A patch of grass the size of a dinner plate. It made me realize it wasn't just grass. I didn't even know what was in my own yard. And if you put that in perspective with Earth, I know nothing about what is around me. I just started exploring everything," Scornavacchi recalled.

Even as a young adult, he would have difficulty being content. He would always need to do more, see more. There would always be something to explore, even in a barren room. But the feeling began back then, in grade school.

In the first grade, he looked ahead and saw twelve more years of school. He started abhorring routines. They were monotonous, inhibited his ability to live. He became depressed.

The feeling lasted until he was fifteen. Then he realized that he was wasting time. Obsessing about his inability to constantly experience the world around him, he was also doing little.

He decided to stop thinking and start living. He was in high school now and joined every group he could find: the orchestra, the concert band, the jazz band, the choir, the wrestling team, hockey, tae kwon do, the Christian Club. He became president of the outdoor club and the dance club. He joined the ski and snowboarding club.

Having switched into overdrive, he found that though he was well-rounded, he was mediocre at everything and an expert in nothing.

"If I was to climb Mount Everest at that point in time, I would have done more than I had ever done in my life, but looking out over that expanse, I would see that there was more to do out there than I knew before," he said now. He was overwhelmed.

For a while in high school, Scornavacchi suffered from narcolepsy. He fell asleep randomly and as a result began missing school. He was medicated and the sleep disorder vanished.

He earned his Eagle rank in Boy Scouts and had the grades to enroll in Penn State University after high school. There, in rural central Pennsylvania, he found a passion for the outdoors.

He camped, backpacked, did rock climbing and scuba diving. In the summer, he worked as a white-water rafting and kayaking guide in nearby Jim Thorpe, Pennsylvania.

Scornavacchi lived to hike in the snow. In this and other activities, he found that he was alone. Others were content to remain indoors in front of a television. When he worked, his fellow employees would, at the end of the day, go to a bar. He wanted to go hiking and backpacking. He went alone.

Ten inches of snow covered the forest one February day when, alone, he headed into the woods. Reaching a campsite, he set up his tent and spent the night. The following morning, he was headed out of the woods with a sixty-pound pack on his back when his knee snapped, tearing his meniscus. His leg was stuck in one spot.

"I couldn't put much weight on it," he said. "I used the two ski poles I had brought with me and then dragged myself out of the woods. It started raining and it got dark and a lot of times I had to crawl. Every time I took a step, I would thank God I was able to take one more step."

He made it out of the woods. Undeterred, he would go back for more. Perhaps he was testing himself. He wanted the whole experience and believed if he held back, he would only get part of it.

He felt the same way when the infection interrupted his voyage on *Bounty*. And so, when the boils healed and the infection was gone, Scornavacchi got back aboard the tall ship.

CHAPTER EIGHT

A VIGILANT WATCH

Joshua Scornavacchi was but one of sixteen aboard *Bounty* when, twenty-four hours into her voyage and nearing sunset, she was making seven knots across the Atlantic Ocean, about 110 miles south of Montauk Point, Long Island, and due east of Atlantic City, New Jersey. C-Watch—with watch captain Dan Cleveland, Anna Sprague, Drew Salapatek, and Scornavacchi—was on duty on the weather deck, and at the forward end of the tween deck, the evening meal was being prepared in the galley.

The seas had been between three and four feet, the wind ranging from ten to fifteen knots, but by now, everything aboard *Bounty* was lashed in place and prepared for the coming storm. The big diesel engines thrummed two decks below the helm. Those on watch rotated through all four positions during their four-hour duty. Up front, the person standing forward watch had a clear view ahead of the gathering darkness. Another watch stander spent an hour in the bowels of the ship, checking the bilges and monitoring the engines. The fourth person was on standby, and this evening that duty called for little effort.

Dan Cleveland, twenty-five, the watch captain, had served aboard *Bounty* longer than anyone else except Robin Walbridge. He boarded her in 2008 with little sailing experience—a few daysails on schooners—and became a deckhand with no authority except to take orders. He found his skipper quiet, not much of a yeller. Walbridge never got excited, even when problems arose, never showed nerves or fear. In Cleveland's view, the captain was a problem solver, always two steps ahead of anyone else.

Cleveland stood his watch, observed, and learned. At the beginning of the 2009 season, he was promoted to able-bodied seaman—AB—of the watch, and halfway through that summer, when *Bounty* needed a bosun, he applied for the job and got it.

The bosun was in charge of the deck in all-hands situations—sail handling, docking, or leaving the dock. Cleveland was twenty-one years old and had major authority on a storied tall ship. In the winter of 2011, Cleveland earned a hundred-ton coast guard license, which qualified him to be captain of a substantial vessel. On *Bounty*, he was promoted to third mate.

Anna Sprague, twenty, had been on the sailing team at Auburn University when *Bounty* arrived in her hometown of Savannah, Georgia, for the Tall Ship Festival in the first week in May 2012. Her mother, Mary Ellen Sprague, a Savannah alderwoman, was working on the event and had an extra ticket that she gave to Anna.

Sprague had been sailing her whole life. The family had small boats—Sunfish and Lasers—that they sailed in the Savannah River. One time when she was much younger, her father, Larry, took her sister and Anna out on the river and threw them overboard so they would be comfortable off a boat in the water. The family chartered catamarans in the Caribbean islands from time to time as well.

Anna Sprague, then, was no novice in sailing and salt water, and that gave her the confidence when she visited *Bounty*, moored dramatically along Savannah's picturesque waterfront promenade in the center of the fleet, to ask how the ship selected crew.

The answer: we're looking for three new crew members. On Saturday, she was interviewed by John Svendsen, the chief mate, and on Monday, when the festival was over and the dock lines were dropped, Anna Sprague sailed down the river, the youngest member of *Bounty*'s crew.

Drew Salapatek, twenty-nine, boarded *Bounty* at about the same time as Sprague, but it was for his second season. He'd been a deckhand in 2011 and had sailed across the Atlantic and back. When he boarded that first time, he had no maritime licenses, but in the fall of 2012, while *Bounty* was hauled out for repairs, he went to Ft. Lauderdale, Florida, and earned both an AB certificate and a hundred-ton license. When the Chicago native returned, he was the AB on the C-Watch.

While Salapatek was aboard *Bounty* crossing the Atlantic, his father, Jim, sitting in his television repair shop in Chicago, was curious. "It just grew interesting, and as I went more and more digging into it, I found *Bounty*'s Facebook page," the father recalled. "I was just a regular person who liked the page. I kept posting, asking some questions. There were a lot of parents who were concerned. Their children were sailing on the ship. When [my son] got to England, I found pictures from people who had toured the *Bounty* [and were posting] on their Flickr pages."

In time, Jim Salapatek would become the Internet voice of *Bounty*, making all its Facebook postings, and he would visit the ship. He was so connected to the vessel that when the ship left New London, he got a quick text message from a crew member.

The tight-knit *Bounty* community was even closer when standing watch together. C-Watch was a good team. Cleveland, Sprague, Salapatek, and Scornavacchi shared one thing above all: their mentor and the source of virtually all of their tall ship knowledge was Robin Walbridge.

Only twelve crew members were standing watch on the voyage toward Hurricane Sandy. This was almost a minimum crew. Had a handful decided not to sail, the watch standers would have been spread thin.

Three members of the crew—in addition to the captain—were exempt from standing watch.

Laura Groves, twenty-eight, of Apalachee Bay, Florida, the bosun, was in charge of deck work and thus was spared the rigors of the four-hours-on, eight-hours-off watch system. She had plenty of her own work to keep her occupied.

Groves was raised in a sailing family, had a bachelor's degree in environmental studies, and had worked as a science instructor on a research ship. She joined *Bounty* in 2010. In the off-season, she'd earned a hundred-ton coast guard intercoastal license and an AB rating. She had had no experience on wooden vessels before she joined *Bounty*, but when the bosun job opened in February 2012, she applied for it and Walbridge gave her the duties.

The bosun's job, as Groves saw it, was to create work lists to meet the ship's needs, prioritize those lists, then to delegate jobs to crew members and oversee their work, whether it be on deck under sail or onshore when the ship was hauled out for maintenance and repairs.

Bounty was the only tall ship on which Groves had worked. But she'd formed an opinion of the captain. Walbridge was knowledgeable, caring, analytical, thoughtful, and a good teacher.

Unlike Groves, the ship's engineer, Chris Barksdale, had minimal sailing experience when he came aboard *Bounty*. As a ship's officer, he was exempt from standing watch, a role through which others learned the ropes of the ship.

Barksdale's role was to keep the machinery running, and *Bounty* had lots of machines: two large John Deere diesel engines for propulsion, two smaller John Deere diesels to turn two electric generators, and various pumps to keep the bilges dry.

Chief Mate John Svendsen had met Barksdale on a vessel operated by the Nature Conservancy and invited him to join *Bounty* in September 2012, in Boothbay Harbor when the previous engineer left. Barksdale characterized his experience as thirty years in "horticulture," operating and maintaining loaders and backhoes. On the Nature Conservancy vessel, his job was maintaining the drinking-water system.

Aboard *Bounty*, if he had not known it before, Barksdale learned he was prone to seasickness when out on the high ocean.

Like Svendsen, Barksdale said he could not remember a time in his life, even at an early age, when he was not on the water. As a teen, he worked at a marina. He was a small-craft operator, but his work was primarily shore-side support.

Bounty was hauled out of the water when Barksdale arrived in Maine. He found a copy of his job description posted in the engine room on the bottom deck, down a stairway and then a ladder from the weather deck. It said the engineer was responsible for operation and maintenance of the engines, electrical systems, plumbing and water systems. Even after the ship left the dock in New London, Barksdale wasn't certain the bilge pumping system came under his authority.

The cook, Jessica Black, had never been aboard a tall ship before the night of October 24, when her train pulled into the New London train station. She disembarked, and there *Bounty* was, just a few steps away on the City Pier.

Black, thirty-four, was a graduate of the New England Culinary Institute in Burlington, Vermont, and after working in catering, she had applied her kitchen skills for the most recent two years in the galleys of motor yachts sailing out of Florida. The smallest of these multimillion-dollar vessels was 75 feet long, the largest 150 feet. These vessels spent much of the time steaming to the Bahamas and the islands of the Caribbean.

Black was looking for a job and had posted her résumé in a shop in Ft. Lauderdale. She got a call from John Svendsen on October 16, eight days before she arrived on board. On the motor yachts, she had been required to do a bit of deckhand work. On *Bounty*, she stood watch over two electric ranges and a microwave in the galley near the bow of the boat. Never was she required to stand with a regular watch. As soon as she was on *Bounty*'s deck, though, she felt compelled to be a loyal crew member. When, the afternoon after she arrived, Robin Walbridge gave everyone permission to leave in the face of Hurricane Sandy, Black stayed. In part, she didn't want to leave the boat without a cook. As it turned out, whether *Bounty* had a cook would be the least of its problems.

CHAPTER NINE

KEEPING *BOUNTY* AFLOAT

The seas were eight to twelve feet and the wind was touching twenty-five knots, the force needed to propel a bulky ship such as *Bounty*, when the B-Watch came on deck at midnight as the day became Saturday, October 27. The sailing was precisely what the members of the watch had hoped for. All that was needed was to steer the course that Robin Walbridge had dictated, about 165 degrees true—dead south on the compass mounted on the binnacle before the helm. They could man that helm. They could steer that course.

Indeed, B-Watch had, among the three assigned watch teams, the most wide-ranging experience. Watch Captain Matt Sanders was a 2001 graduate of Maine Maritime Academy. After he got his degree, he served in the tug-and-barge industry, using his training to advance. Then he took positions on schooners in the Maine windjammer fleet as a deckhand. He had joined *Bounty* in San Juan, about the time Scornavacchi did but with vastly greater knowledge of ships and sailing. He found *Bounty* to be run "professionally." Everyone knew his job. Sanders's job was navigator. He prepared the voyage plan for each trip, kept the charts updated, and, of course, ran the B-Watch.

Captain Robin Walbridge was, Sanders thought, someone he could learn from, even after an academy education and more than a decade at sea.

Sanders, thirty-three, from West Palm Beach, Florida, was joined on watch by another Maine Maritime graduate, Jessica Hewitt, twenty-five, from Harwich, a town on Cape Cod. Sanders was eleven years past college when *Bounty* left New London, Hewitt three years. During college, she had worked on the Maine schooner *Margaret Todd* and the next summer on the schooner *Bowdoin* as a trainee. After graduation, she worked as third mate on the schooner *Harvey Gamage*. She got her hundred-ton coast guard license and moved up to second mate.

Prior to joining *Bounty*, Hewitt was the captain of a ferry running out of Portsmouth, New Hampshire, taking luggage and supplies between that port and Star Island in the Isles of Shoals archipelago, six miles offshore along the Maine–New Hampshire border. The island served as a summer retreat, and she drove the ferry as long as the season lasted, then joined *Bounty* in early September.

Aboard *Bounty*, Hewitt—although she held an AB rating—was a deckhand. The AB on her watch was Adam Prokosh. He had served on several tall ships, including the *Lady Washington*, the *Sultana*, the *Amistad*, the *Spirit of Massachusetts,* and the *Harvey Gamage*, all in the past five years, many of them inspected vessels with higher ratings than that of *Bounty*.

Prokosh, who talked in machine-gun bursts, had heard in the tall-ship community that *Bounty* was a "death trap." When he inspected *Bounty*, he concluded that rumor was out-of-date. He decided to be part of the new *Bounty*, where he felt the crew took the job seriously.

Prokosh enjoyed Walbridge's style. And he trusted his crewmates and felt a lot of qualified sailors were on board *Bounty*. He was relying on the officers to assure that the ship was correctly maintained. He assumed that was the case.

The second deckhand on B-Watch was John Jones. He had been aboard since San Juan, had been one of the sail handlers with Scornavacchi. Even though Jones, twenty-nine, didn't spread himself around thick—his wasn't one of the names mentioned first by the rest of the crew—he'd earned a nickname: the Dudester.

B-Watch was seasoned, but the thing it alone could not do—had not done—was keep *Bounty* afloat. One man could be credited with doing that, and it wasn't even Robin Walbridge. Indeed, when Walbridge first became her captain, *Bounty* was nearly sinking at the dock in Fall River, Massachusetts, where she was taking on thirty thousand gallons of water an hour—the volume of water contained in a large in-ground swimming pool. But then in 2001, the ship was bought and money began flowing into *Bounty*'s coffers and her leaks began to be plugged.

Robert E. Hansen Jr. had taken some of his employees on a team-building sail on another tall ship, the *Rose*, and was enthralled with that vessel. When he learned that the City of Fall River was prepared to sell *Bounty*, he bought it.

A decade or so earlier, the HMS Rose Organization, a charitable, nonprofit corporation, had lusted for *Bounty*, wanting to add the rival ship to its fleet. The group was going to run it like *Rose*, as an inspected sailing-school vessel. But at the time, the organization's finances were spread thin simply for operating *Rose*.

Richard Bailey, *Rose*'s skipper then, recalled that in 1994 *Bounty* "was in pretty hard shape." She still had old fuel tanks with a capacity of sixteen thousand gallons that had been installed for her 1960s trip to Tahiti. The condition of her hull was unknown. There had been so many repairs that the hull—far from being sleek—looked as if it were made of bricks, Bailey said.

The ship's condition hadn't improved when in 2001 Hansen became sole owner, with his new company, HMS Bounty Organization LLC, as the documented owner. But at the time, Hansen was seeing promise, not problems.

"We want her on the tall-ship circuit," Hansen told the online site of *Long Island Business News* on February 23, 2001. "It's a sin to let her sit."

Although most tall ships are owned by nonprofits—and all sail-training ships by law have to be owned or operated by nonprofits—the business newspaper reported that Hansen saw *Bounty* as a moneymaking operation, envisioning its use for corporate events, private parties, and tourism-related appearances.

At the time, LIBN.com reported, Hansen had a coinvestor in *Bounty*, an executive from his firm Islandaire Inc. The men told the website that they estimated their start-up cost at $2.25 million. "They are seeking a $2 million loan from the Bank of Smithtown for renovations," the website reported. "Later, the venture hopes to land $1.3 million in long-term financing from the Long Island Development Corp., with backing from the federal Small Business Administration."

"This boat is a publicity magnet," Hansen told the website. "Wherever we go, the cameras will follow, as well as the people."

Later, *Bounty*'s future expanded in Hansen's imagination. He was reported as thinking of the ship's role in "seaside festivals, corporate outings and sponsorships, tall ship gatherings, a movie set, television commercials and teaching 18th century seamanship skills" as part of "her almost limitless possibilities."

Then Hansen began to deal with the reality of owning a tall ship. He hired Maine marine surveyor and naval architect David Wyman to conduct a survey at the dock in Fall River. Wyman hired a diver to inspect the hull. In a word, the condition was "horrible." *Bounty* was leaking badly and had grounded more than once.

Wyman recommended that the entire bottom of the hull be covered in plastic with plywood nailed over it. When that was accomplished, *Bounty* was towed to Gloucester, Massachusetts, where a shipyard refused, due to *Bounty*'s condition, to haul her for repairs.

The towing continued up the Gulf of Maine to Boothbay Harbor, where Sample's Shipyard agreed to put *Bounty* in dry dock.

Joseph Jakomovicz was the yard manager at Sample's, where he had worked since 1978, first as a carpenter and two years later as manager. When *Bounty* came out of the water, Jakomovicz saw her leaking like a colander. He was flabbergasted. Hansen was there beside him, and he, too, was shocked. The bottom planks were thoroughly tunneled with wormholes. Jakomovicz asked Walbridge what had happened. The captain told him that *Bounty* had been in Florida, where worms were a problem, and there was not the money to make repairs.

Now, however, Bob Hansen was there to write checks. He told Jakomovicz to repair the bottom, and the work began. Hansen's plan was to carry passengers, so a coast guard inspector came to examine the ship's condition.

It was agreed that the original white-oak framing was in decent shape. A half dozen pieces of frame were replaced. But the planking was another matter. All of the bottom planking below the waterline was replaced with white oak. Since planks twenty to forty feet long were needed, Jakomovicz had to look outside New England, where the supply of tall white oak had been depleted.

Jakomovicz traveled to Tennessee, where he located a mill that could saw forty-foot planks. He selected the timbers he wanted, and they were sawn to three-and-one-quarter-inch thickness, all of them with their own shapes. The wood was air-dried. Jakomovicz said that you can bend green, fresh oak in a steamer, but you can never bend dry oak. So it was carefully sawn to shape. One plank near the ship's transom twisted from nearly vertical to nearly horizontal.

The oak planking was installed and Hansen wrote the checks, and by the end of that yard period, when *Bounty* left Sample's, Jakomovicz thought it was in much better condition than when it arrived.

All boats need constant maintenance and repairs. Wooden boats—particularly forty-year-old boats—prove this rule. In 2006, *Bounty* was back in the yard, now called Boothbay Harbor Shipyard. Hansen and Walbridge wanted major work done, including replacement of the frames and planking from the waterline to the deck. Partway up from the waterline, *Bounty* had a wale strake—a piece of planking thicker than ordinary—painted yellow. Below the wale strake, the planks were white oak. Above, Smith and Rhuland, the original builders of *Bounty*, had used Douglas fir.

Jakomovicz was not fond of Douglas fir, thinking it more susceptible to decay than other woods. On the positive side, it was available in long lengths. Douglas fir came in two grades, Jakomovicz told Walbridge. To plank *Bounty* with the lower grade would cost $20,000 as opposed to $50,000 for the better grade. The difference, Jakomovicz said, was that the better grade of planks had straight, vertical grain and few knots. Jakomovicz asked Walbridge what he wanted. Because of the knots on the lower-grade fir, the wood won't take a good finish. But Walbridge chose the lower-grade fir for the planking above the wale strake, the job was completed to Jakomovicz's satisfaction, and Hansen paid the bill. In July 2007, *Bounty* was relaunched.

From 2001 until the summer of 2012, *Bounty* visited various shipyards and was hauled five times, according to Jakomovicz's tally. She was hauled in Norfolk and in Tampa, and the 2007 launching was followed by dry dock in Boothbay in 2010.

In 2012, Hansen was looking for a buyer for *Bounty*. He was offering the ship through the broker WME Yachts Ltd. as "a master class example of square-rigged yachting." Hansen's asking price was $4.9 million.

The millions that Hansen had already poured into *Bounty* came, in part, from a company he founded in 1992, Islandaire Inc., a manufacturer of replacement through-the-wall air conditioners for commercial customers such as motels. In 2004, the company had sales of $26 million and employed 120 in its facilities on Long Island, New York.

In 2005, Hansen had sold Islandaire to Fedders Corp., the giant air-conditioning company, for $16 million in cash and preferred stock, according to a filing with the Securities and Exchange Commission. He stayed on as president of the Fedders subsidiary. In 2008, Fedders, having filed for protection in US bankruptcy court in Wilmington, Delaware, sold Islandaire back to Hansen for $7.5 million.

But as early as 2008, Hansen had consulted with New York yacht broker Captain Bernard Coffey and put *Bounty* on the market. As she sailed due south in the early-morning hours of Saturday, October 27, 2012, she had three suitors who had made offers, none of which were "up to par," according to Coffey.

"I think two of the three would come back with something better," Coffey said.

Coffey's firm had brought eight or nine potential buyers to Hansen, he said. Two of them owned ships. A couple of nonprofit maritime organizations were interested. "We had several foreign buyers with resorts. We had a couple of investors that were taking a look at it" who wanted to put *Bounty* into charter service. "All of them had valid plans for it." None of the potential buyers, despite the marketing, were considering *Bounty* as a private yacht, however.

Bounty's condition probably did not help its sale, Coffey said. "I can't recall if we had a true survey of it. That's something that the buyer would normally do if they were truly interested in it. They were taking a look at price. Price was an issue, and then when they put it [price] into their business plan, that's what generally caused them to take a second notice of it, to make sure it was what they wanted it to be.

"All of them wanted it. It certainly had appeal," the broker said. "But on top of appeal, it's got to produce break even or better. Most of them were having a hard time putting that together."

Robin Walbridge knew that Bob Hansen wanted to unload *Bounty*. And he himself had reason to think getting rid of the boat was a good idea.

CHAPTER TEN

A LEAKY BOAT?

I just spent six months in a leaky boat
Lucky just to keep afloat
—"Six Months in a Leaky Boat" by Split Enz

Jessica Black rose from her bunk at five o'clock Saturday morning to begin preparing breakfast. She found that overnight the seas had built.

C-Watch was on duty, and Joshua Scornavacchi, on boat-check duty, had some trouble keeping a prime when he ran the bilge pumps. Dan Cleveland, the watch captain, noted that one of the generators was spitting smoke, its engine producing a surging sound.

Little things.

And in the Nav Shack, the barometer had begun to fall. In small increments. Steadily. When the ship's officers met at eight o'clock, they believed that Hurricane Sandy was behaving as predicted, and that Captain Walbridge's plan was still valid: sail south by east and then veer to the west to get on the slow side of the storm and have a straight sail for Key West and the turn north to St. Petersburg.

The crew aboard *Bounty* was confident that all the work they had finished a week before in Boothbay Harbor had put their ship in good shape to face what lay ahead. Few, if any, of the crew were aware of the emphatic warning Robin Walbridge had heard back in the shipyard.

Bounty had arrived in Boothbay in mid-September following its final public appearance of the season in Eastport, Maine. There, at the edge of the Bay of Fundy, where tides range up to twenty-one feet from high to low, there had been a small incident.

While docking, the port quarter—the rear of the ship on the left side facing forward—had made less than gentle contact with the pier. The obvious result was damage to some of the planking. The crew was uncertain if the damage extended to the framing below the planking. Repairs were needed when the ship was hauled.

On September 16, *Bounty* was in place in the water next to the Boothbay Harbor Shipyard. The author of the *Bounty Blog*, posting the following Thursday, re-created the scene. With the crew wearing winter hats donated by volunteer AB Doug Faunt, the blogger wrote, "A 700-ton railway system slid into place around us and a diver blocked and wedged our keel into place. By noon, after the crew had feasted on delicious, greasy pizza and [had] unsparingly 'oiled' the deck, *Bounty* was ready for haul out. A great chain pulled her up the sloped marine railway system until she was in dry dock. Now, we can walk all the way around her and beneath her to re-paint her hull and to caulk leaky seams. When we look across the deck, no longer do we see the ocean—instead, there are houses on the starboard bow! I wonder what our new neighbors think.

"A day in the shipyard begins before the sun is fully up and lasts until dinner time. In just a few days, we have demolished crew quarters, removed four 900 gallon tanks, and scrubbed barnacles off the hull. I am constantly amazed at the amount of work our tight-knit crew can accomplish. I just hope that the first blizzard of the season doesn't come in October, like last year."

The blogger skipped past the damaged quarter, but it was on Walbridge's mind when *Bounty* arrived at the shipyard. Earlier, in a phone call, the captain mentioned the damage to Todd Kosakowski, the current yard manager, when the two were preparing a punch list of work to be accomplished in what both felt would be a short haul-out. In fact, except for normal maintenance work including recaulking seams, Walbridge told Kosakowski that the damaged quarter was his only concern.

When *Bounty* rode up the rails that Monday, Kosakowski, who had some tall ship experience of his own prior to joining the yard six years earlier as a carpenter, had a good first impression. The hull looked clean and fair—smooth—with tight seams and no "weeping" of water where it should not have been.

The shipyard had assigned five of its workers to do certain of the jobs. The rest of the labor was to be done by *Bounty*'s crew, under the supervision of the ship's officers. This included recaulking those seams that needed work, moving the large fuel and water tanks farther back on the lower deck, replumbing them, and rewiring other parts of the ship. The aft crew quarters would then be moved away to just forward of the tanks.

Every large ship, old or new, steel or wooden, is unique, and *Bounty* was no exception. It took some time to learn all of her parts, her nooks and crannies, and where specific gear was stored, especially on the lower decks. On the tween deck, the chain locker—where the anchor chain was stored—was farthest forward. After that came Jessica Black's workplace, the galley, and beside it the forepeak, including a storage area for the galley, a pantry, and the cook's freezers. The toilet, called the head, was also in this forward area of the tween deck, along with two showers and a sink. A bulkhead separated this lavatory area from the next compartment, the wide and long saloon, a large open area that nevertheless housed some enclosures, such as the main companionway up through the Nav Shack and separate sets of steps descending to the aft crew quarters and the tank room. On the sides of the saloon forward were dining tables hung by ropes, a paint locker, and another locker for spare lines. At the rear end of the saloon, along the ship's sides, were small cabins. Some volunteers, including Doug Faunt, were assigned individual cabins. Robin Walbridge used the cabin farthest aft on the port side. His office was opposite on the starboard side. Other cabins on the starboard side, across the wide-open saloon, were used to store immersion suits—the neoprene "Gumby suits" that crew members would wear if they ever had to abandon ship.

Farthest to the rear was an open space with no doors but with windows in the ship's rear wall, the transom. This was the Great Cabin, where the officers met every morning.

Unlike the tween deck, where the crew was free to move from the bow to the stern without significant impediments, the lower deck, above the bilge, was divided into distinct compartments, some unreachable from others.

The chain locker descended through the tween deck to this lower area. Next aft was the forward tank room, where tanks collected sewage from the head and dishwater from the galley. Crew members could reach these tanks through a trapdoor in the tween deck sole and a ladder.

Stairs led from the tween deck down to the next space aft on the lower deck—the fo'c'sle. Here were found the forward crew quarters, to port, and storage areas, some used for canned food. The aft wall of the fo'c'sle had a big, flat, metal, watertight door that was opened by turning a wheel. The door led aft to the bosun's locker, where three aisles crossed the ship between stacks of shelves holding various boat supplies. There was no passage farther aft from the bosun's locker. A bulkhead there crossed the width of the ship.

Beyond this bulkhead, a new aft crew quarters was to be installed during the Boothbay Harbor yard period. This space had its own ladder down from the tween deck.

The next space was to become the redesigned main tank room during the yard period, with four large metal fuel tanks and four large plastic water tanks.

Next aft was the engine room, reached from the tween deck by its own ladder. A piping manifold was mounted along the bulkhead on the forward end of the engine room. Valves in the manifold could be turned to drain bilge water from individual compartments, forward and aft. On the starboard side of this bulkhead were two water makers for turning seawater into drinking water. A fire hose was stored in the same area.

The major machinery here—the four diesel engines—were mounted beside one another. The two propulsion engines were on either side of the center of the room. The engines that ran the electric generators were outside these, one to port, the other to starboard. Narrow walkways separated the engines and generators.

Finally, at the far end of the deck, to the rear of the engine room, was the lazaret, directly under the Great Cabin. The officers' quarters were here.

Once *Bounty* was hauled, most of the crew was set to work on board the ship. Third Mate Dan Cleveland spent his days in the boatyard woodworking shop, however, shaping new yards, the horizontal spars from which square sails are hung on the mast, and helping boatyard employees with projects laminating wood. Cleveland was not a professional shipwright. He had learned from Walbridge how to scarf two boards together by cutting each one on a long, tapered slant and gluing the faces of those two cuts together. At his skipper's side the past five years, he had also learned how to make a dutchman—a small piece of wood shaped like a bow tie—to join together two boards edge to edge or to repair a crack. He could employ these unique skills making the yards, so his time in the woodshop was valuable.

On board, some jobs required no specialized skills, only sweaty labor.

Until now, *Bounty*'s fuel had been held in four nine-hundred-gallon galvanized-steel tanks, next to the rear crew quarters. The ship's freshwater had been held in four stainless-steel tanks. Second Mate Matt Sanders was in charge of updating the tank system, with the assistance of newly arrived engineer Chris Barksdale. Sanders sketched out some ideas that would connect the new tanks and some of the old, black iron piping with PVC—plastic—piping. Adam Prokosh, Drew Salapatek, and Mark Warner were assigned to the heavy lifting.

The four old fuel tanks were removed completely, as were the four water tanks. Two of the water tanks were then moved aft one compartment and became replacement fuel tanks. Two new stainless-steel tanks were installed for fuel as well, retaining the ship's thirty-six-hundred-gallon fuel capacity. All the water tanks were replaced with circular plastic tanks.

In addition to the four large fuel tanks, two, smaller, day tanks in the engine room each held four hundred gallons. Among Barksdale's engineer duties was to fill the day tanks at eight o'clock each evening. On the side of each day tank was a "sight glass"—a vertical glass tube with a valve at the top and a valve at the bottom. With the valves open, the glass showed the level of the fuel inside the tank. Each watch stander making boat checks had, among his or her duties, to take note of the level of the day tank by looking at the sight glass. Failure to do this could result in an engine's running out of fuel. This was a critical duty on *Bounty*.

While the heavy lifting was going on in the old and new tank rooms, other crew members were busy on *Bounty*'s hull, recaulking seams that needed it. Bosun Laura Groves was in charge of this work.

Groves, on board for three seasons now, had learned her caulking skills on *Bounty*. Her teacher was Dan Cleveland, the crew member she replaced as bosun. Her crew included Jessica Hewitt, who told Groves that she had caulking experience, and green crew members Anna Sprague and Claudene Christian, as well as Mark Warner and John Jones.

In Groves's opinion, 5 percent of *Bounty*'s seams below the waterline needed recaulking. First on her agenda was teaching the four inexperienced hands how to apply seaming compound where the edges of the horizontal hull planks met. Groves thought that 20 to 25 percent of the underwater seams needed new seam compound on top of the existing caulking.

Above the waterline, two planks needed to be recaulked, one on each side of the ship. One of these Groves felt unqualified to handle, and she turned the work over to the shipyard employees.

But Groves and Hewitt took on the caulking under the curve of *Bounty*'s hull. One held a caulking iron—a chisel-like metal tool, used to wedge cotton and then tar-soaked oakum twine into a seam once the old caulk had been removed. The other swung the beetle—a wooden mallet with a long head—against the end of the iron. When they did the job right, the iron rang a musical note similar to one that would sound if the solid wood of the hull had been under the iron.

These were not big women. Groves stood five feet four inches tall, Hewitt perhaps somewhat taller. They didn't need to be muscle-bound to be good caulkers.

"I've watched qualified caulkers who were five foot four, one hundred pounds," said Jan Miles, co-skipper of the square-topsail schooner *Pride of Baltimore II*, a wooden replica of a vessel from the War of

1812. "It's about the swinging of the mallet, the alignment of the iron. You can create an environment without overexhausting yourself."

Miles said that in the past he used an underwater seam compound, but he now uses "a bunch of waxes blended together. [The former compound] wasn't setting up fast enough for us." Miles said he "wouldn't consider . . . at all" using what *Bounty* gave Groves and her team to use in their caulking.

Under Walbridge's direction, the crew used two products that were cheaper than marine seam compound: DAP caulk purchased from a home center, and another product called NP 1. Miles dismisses the latter, a product that, he says, does not remain bonded to the wooden planks when submerged.

Groves had no problem using DAP and NP 1. They were used when she arrived in 2010, and all her knowledge came through Robin Walbridge.

"Oh, indeed, caulking is a specialized skill," said Miles. It "takes time to learn the niceties of the process. It can be injurious to the caulker if they don't understand the power that's needed. It does take discipline."

When the work on the fuel and water tanks was completed, more heavy work had to be done. Walbridge wanted to trim *Bounty* more toward the stern, to put the rudder deeper in the water to improve steering, and to raise the bow. He directed that movable lead ballast ingots weighing twenty to forty pounds each be shifted from under the water tanks to the lazaret and the new tank room. Anna Sprague was recruited for the job. The ingots were eight inches long and three inches thick. Sprague worked with the cook at that time, a woman named Morgan.

Todd Kosakowski and the yard crew tended to the items on the punch list assigned to them, including the repair of the port quarter where it had struck the dock in Eastport. The damage was centered on the last planks aft of the side windows that ended at the transom. Kosakowski preferred to replace the full length of each plank, but Walbridge wanted a less expensive solution. So the yard removed the damaged ends of the existing planks and glued and nailed new three-foot end pieces in place, a cosmetic patch but one that lacked the strength of Kosakowski's preferred traditional solution.

While he oversaw the yard work, Kosakowski checked what the *Bounty* crew were doing. He found their work adequate.

On closer inspection, he thought the planking from near the keel to the waterline was in better-than-average shape. But from the waterline up, he saw the seam compound spitting out of the seams from what he believed was either the movement of the planking or excessive drying. The topsides were in rough shape. Those planks—the lower-grade Douglas fir that had been installed in 2006–7—should have been in better condition.

Some of the planking, which was attached to the underlying frames with three different types of fasteners, was decaying from the inside out. Rot had gone two-thirds of the way toward the outside. Cracks across the planks weakened the wood.

Walbridge had asked Kosakowski to investigate two topside planks, one on each side of the hull, each covered by plywood when *Bounty* arrived at the shipyard. The framing under those planks was soft and damp, Kosakowski found, and it showed the same cross-grained cracks as the planking.

To Kosakowski, this did not look like typical rot. It was dry or burned or charred-looking. He knew that cross-grain cracking is not typical of rot. The only way to deal with the problem was to remove the bad wood and replace it.

But *Bounty*'s stout construction included not only planking on the exterior of the hull, but interior planking, called ceiling. The vertical frames were sandwiched between the two horizontal courses of planks, making inspection impossible without removing planks.

Kosakowski told Walbridge the entire boat should be inspected to see how far the rot went. Then the most severe rot should be dug out and replaced with white oak.

Walbridge was both shocked and furious. Six-year-old wood should not be in this condition. He called Robert Hansen, his boss, who shared the captain's anger and whose first thought was that HMS Bounty LLC should sue Boothbay Harbor Shipyard for inferior work.

In a brief visit to the shipyard office, Walbridge told Kosakowski what Hansen had said. But Walbridge assured the yard manager that he would defend the shipyard when talking with Hansen.

Walbridge said the time-consuming and costly search for wide-spread rot would have to wait for the next yard period, in 2013. He told Kosakowski that he would have the crew paint over the places where rot had been discovered.

Having had his advice soundly rejected by Walbridge, Kosakowski nevertheless told the skipper that he was more than worried about what he had found under *Bounty*'s exterior. Walbridge replied that he was "terrified." Kosakowski later said that he had urged Walbridge to avoid heavy weather wherever *Bounty* went after leaving the yard.

Before he left Boothbay Harbor, Walbridge relayed to Kosakowski the message he had given to his boss, Hansen:

"Get rid of the boat as soon as possible."

CHAPTER ELEVEN

FROM TRUCKS TO TALL SHIPS

Bounty Update . . . Bounty is currently 250 miles due east of the Chesapeake Bay on a Southwest course at 6.8 knots. The Captain reports that Bounty should be encountering weather from the storm sometime this evening.

—*Bounty* Facebook entry, 9:44 a.m., Saturday, October 27, 2012

Bounty's AIS (Automatic Identification System) transmitter recorded the ship's position at 1:21 p.m. on Saturday as N 36° 55', W 70° 25'. Earlier, Robin Walbridge had emerged from his cabin and given the order to change course. *Bounty* had gone far enough to the east and was at the same latitude as Virginia Beach, just south of the mouth of the Chesapeake Bay.

The skipper told his chief mate, John Svendsen, that the hurricane was going to track up the Gulf Stream and not make landfall south of Cape Hatteras, so he wanted to cut across the top of the hurricane's path. (At that moment, *Bounty* was south and east of the Gulf Stream.)

The southwesterly course, he let the crew know through Svendsen, would put the wind on *Bounty*'s port quarter, and the ship would track into the storm's northwest quadrant, where the slower winds should be.

Having delivered the order, Walbridge would normally have returned to his cabin on the tween deck on the port side, the farthest aft of seven officers' cabins on that side. Or he might have gone to his office, directly across the deck from his cabin, also the last of seven cabins, on the starboard side. Everyone who sailed aboard *Bounty* knew Walbridge as a traditional captain, one who delegated the hour-by-hour running of his ship to his officers and who did not otherwise mingle with the crew.

This fit Walbridge's personality, his quiet, taciturn nature, his penchant since childhood for keeping his plans—and his life—closed to the outside world. His personal life was so shuttered that even his most trusted subordinates, who had sailed with him off and on for years, did not know that he had an older sister, Lucille, and another sister, Delia Mae, a year and a half younger, who lived in Poland.

As a young man, Walbridge had devised a long-term plan for securing his financial future. The details of this, too, were private. They involved thrift and effort. His effort was channeled into long-haul trucking. He invested his trucking income in property, whose rents gave him more income even while the value of the real estate appreciated. Some of his property was in Florida. Perhaps only he knew where else he was a landlord or property owner.

When he was in his thirties, he announced that he had retired from trucking.

About then, Walbridge moved to the Suwannee River, on the bend between Florida's peninsula and its panhandle, and took a job at Miller's Houseboats. At first, he lived aboard a small sailboat. One of his jobs was teaching folks who rented houseboats from Bill Miller how to operate the vessels. The Suwannee winds seventy-five navigable miles from its headwaters in the Okefenokee Swamp to the boat rental property, a mile from the Gulf of Mexico.

When he arrived at Miller's, Walbridge was calling himself Robin, and no one was contracting that into a nickname. Everyone at Miller's liked the new guy and appreciated his skill—shaped in his teens when he rebuilt all those old cars—as a mechanic.

Bill Miller's evaluation of his employee was the kind that makes for a good résumé: "He was a very, very smart individual. There wasn't much he couldn't do, and there wasn't anything he wouldn't try to tackle."

In his time at Miller's, Walbridge even dove into the political muck keeping the Suwannee from being dredged, Miller recalled. Walbridge had no success. The river still needs dredging, Miller complained.

In time, Walbridge moved out of his boat and into a house trailer, but while he was living aboard, he acquired a pet parrot. His boat was small. His parrot was smart. Walbridge wanted his ship to remain tidy, so he taught the parrot to go outside to relieve itself. This was a fatal error.

One day, Walbridge climbed his mast and was working up there with a scrub brush, Miller said. The bird, having learned its hygiene lesson, came outside. Walbridge lost his grip on the brush, which plummeted toward the deck. It reached the parrot first, Miller said, and there his bird tale ends.

In the off hours, Walbridge and Miller played chess. The former trucker dominated these contests, and when his time at the houseboat-rental business was over, Walbridge had allowed his boss to win precisely once. Miller chuckled at the memory.

In the late 1980s, the man who as a boy had no use for a classroom other than as a place to sleep began teaching adult-education classes in the area of Cedar Key, Florida. He took his lessons west along the coast to Apalachicola, Florida, where he offered night courses to commercial-fishing-boat captains. The idea was that when they earned a captain's license, they could take paying customers aboard and increase their incomes.

Kristin Anderson, a Northerner, had come to Florida in 1985 to escape the cold. In Wisconsin, she had sailed on other people's boats in the short sailing season. In Florida, she bought a used foam-and-plastic sailboat, got a life jacket and a bailing bucket, and, with a jug of drinking water, set out to learn to sail.

Someone challenged Anderson to take the captain's course, and when she did, she discovered Robin Walbridge was an excellent teacher, who feasted on the success of his students. They became friends.

In 1990, when Anderson helped in an effort to bring the *Governor Stone*, a Gulf Coast schooner, to town, Walbridge became a volunteer captain. He moved to Apalachicola for a while, bought some houses, renovated them, and filled them with paying tenants.

"He'd blow into town once in a while and call on me," Anderson recalled. On one visit, Walbridge took Anderson and another woman out on the *Governor Stone*. It was tied at the land end of a thousand-foot-long pier. Walbridge began teaching the women how to dock the boat. His teaching was deliberate. His explanations were clear. His voice was calm, never raised, and he almost never took the helm but stood back and pointed out the waving of a flag, the effect of the wind atop the masts.

"We spent the entire afternoon and we never got beyond the end of the pier," Anderson recalled. "It was fantastic. He was such a good teacher."

In 1993, Walbridge returned to Cedar Key as the skipper of the schooner *New Way*, a vessel operated by VisionQuest. The goal of the group, one newspaper reported at the time, was "to teach youngsters how to break out of a cycle of failure and become successful by taking risks and trying new activities." The first lessons Walbridge taught were the names of all the lines on the *New Way* and how to tie mariner's knots.

Later, Walbridge was skipper aboard the *Heritage of Miami*, an eighty-five-foot schooner used by the Boy Scouts of America in its High Adventure program. The boat sailed from Islamorada in the Florida Keys to the Dry Tortugas, seventy miles west of Key West, on weeklong tours every week.

Barbara Maggio, whose husband, Joe, was the well-known force behind the schooner, was amazed at what Walbridge accomplished each week. She was particularly impressed the week the son of Vermont's first director of the state's Division for the Blind and Visually Impaired took a group of blind Scouts sailing for an entire week.

Schooner sailing was fine, but like any tall ship enthusiast, Walbridge was looking forward toward the next, bigger vessel. He got his opportunity in 1993 when Joe Maggio told Richard Bailey, skipper of the square-rigged ship *Rose*, about Walbridge.

Bailey was a year younger than Walbridge, and the age difference would usually have concerned Bailey. "His résumé was what made me accept his candidacy. He was a little old for a tall ship. You imagine the mates will be only marginally older than deckhands, who are eighteen," Bailey explained. "I had previously had the experience of finding that deckhands of age twenty-five or thirty had a hard time interacting with mates younger than them." But he found Walbridge not only fit but "he was also personable, a very agreeable kind of guy."

Walbridge held a hundred-ton master's license when he arrived aboard *Rose*. He wanted to get some time on bigger ships to upgrade his license, Bailey said. The captain of less complex schooners, Walbridge happily began his life on a square-rigger as an able-bodied seaman, just a regular crew member. "Within a few months, he moved up through the ranks. I think we may have bumped him up to first mate in '94 when I was gone," said Bailey.

Walbridge quickly demonstrated that he had immense aptitude as a sailor and equally immense aptitude for anything mechanical. "We came to rely on him for his opinions about mechanical issues. The second year, we put a piston rod through the side of an engine, and he got it fixed in forty-eight hours," Bailey said.

In the summer of 1994, Bailey got to know something about *Bounty*. He had taken leave from his helm—and promoted Walbridge to first mate—and was asked to run *Bounty* for short trips here and there. In the fall of that year, *Bounty*—owned by an offshoot of the Fall River, Massachusetts, Chamber of Commerce—needed someone to skipper the ship to St. Petersburg. Bailey assembled a crew and took *Bounty* as far as Wilmington, North Carolina, where it was to stay for a few weeks.

"While it was laid up in Wilmington, they asked me if I knew someone who could be the ship keeper while it was there," Bailey said. "I knew Robin was available. I called him and he came down and familiarized himself with the ship." Then Walbridge became *Bounty*'s caretaker. The job was lent some adventure when, during the night, someone cast off *Bounty*'s dock lines, and Walbridge, alone on board, managed to get his drifting charge back alongside the dock.

Rose had been Robin Walbridge's only schooling in tall ships before he took over *Bounty* in Wilmington. There were differences. *Rose* was fourteen feet taller than *Bounty*, with a bit greater tonnage. But the biggest difference was the type of hull. *Rose* was a replica of a frigate, a naval gunship. As a ship designed to haul coal, *Bounty* was round and strong, and Captain Bligh's mentor, Captain Cook, had chosen the collier over the frigate because it lacked the frigate's array of gunports, openings through which heavy seas could wash over the vessel.

Bailey often joked that *Rose* was like a horse, *Bounty* like a cow. But when the chance came in 1995 to become master of the bovine *Bounty*, Robin Walbridge committed himself to a long-term relationship.

CHAPTER TWELVE

AN AGING ACTOR

Riding the Storm Out . . . Day 2

I'm sure that Bounty's crew would be overwhelmed by all the prayers and best wishes that have been given. Rest assured that the Bounty is safe and in very capable hands.

Bounty's current voyage is a calculated decision . . . NOT AT ALL . . . irresponsible or with a lack of foresight as some have suggested. . . . The fact of the matter is . . . A SHIP IS SAFER AT SEA THAN IN PORT!

In the next few posts I will try to quell some fears and help to explain some of the dynamics that are in Bounty's favor.

—*Bounty* Facebook entry, 11:30 a.m., Saturday, October 27, 2012

Bounty had crossed the Gulf Stream sometime before Robin Walbridge ordered the course change Saturday morning. She was sailing in warmer water southeast of the stream, even as she headed southwest, back toward the East Coast. During the afternoon, she was making a speed of seven knots on the GPS that was mounted in the Nav Shack. That was about the same as her average speed since leaving Long Island Sound. The ride was still comfortable, even in the building seas and winds that had reached twenty-five knots. That wasn't a surprise to the crew, but might have been for others.

Some detractors who knew little about *Bounty* dismissed her as a "movie prop," but her construction was anything but throwaway. On his occasional stints aboard *Bounty* during the 1990s, Richard Bailey, skipper of the *Rose*, found her "stoutly built by Nova

Scotia craftsmen who knew what they were doing. A lot of effort and thought went into building her."

Bounty had needed her young strength because MGM was intent on filming its movie *Mutiny on the Bounty* on location in Tahiti. They asked a naval architect to design a ship capable of the voyage halfway around the world. *Bounty* left Lunenburg, Nova Scotia, sailed through the Panama Canal, and crossed much of the Pacific Ocean before it was on scene.

The reality of life at sea then was substituted for by the imagination of Hollywood. It is somewhat instructive to compare the portrayal of William Bligh—played by Trevor Howard—in that movie with *Bounty*'s skipper in 2012, Robin Walbridge.

In MGM's version of the tale, *Bounty* set sail in 1787 from England, a ship in the Royal Navy commissioned for a commercial venture. She was to take on a cargo of breadfruit harvested in Tahiti and deliver it to the Caribbean, where plantation owners wanted to experiment with the plant as food for slaves. Breadfruit had replaced rice in the Pacific as the crop of choice. Up to two hundred of the grapefruit-size, coarse-skinned fruit grew on one eighty-five-foot-tall tree. The implications for the Caribbean, where plantation owners were apparently seeking a better profit margin through the stomachs of slaves, were promising. Thus far, MGM's film dealt with fact.

But then the plot took liberties, creating a despotic Bligh against whom audiences could jeer and a handsome, sensitive Fletcher Christian—Marlon Brando—whom they could cheer.

Filming in Ultra Panavision 70 for the first time, the cameras—powered by large generators in *Bounty*'s hold—framed Bligh in a series of wrathful acts.

First, he snatches more than his share of cheese, and when he's confronted by an ordinary seaman who accuses the skipper of the pilferage, Bligh orders the man whipped for showing disrespect to a superior.

Brando's Christian is offended, but Bligh states, "Cruelty with a purpose is not cruelty, it is efficiency."

Bligh—who had served with Captain Cook in his earlier expeditions—has choices of routes to get to Tahiti. The longer route is east around Africa's Cape of Good Hope. He attempts the shorter, more treacherous route, around South America's Cape Horn, but after failing to make the rounding and wasting precious time, Bligh eventually takes the eastern route and pushes the crew to get back on schedule, cutting their rations rather than stopping to resupply.

All may not be forgotten by the crew when they reach Tahiti, but they become preoccupied with the willingness of the local women. Even Christian falls for one, the daughter of the local king.

Bligh, however, is stewing. The breadfruit plants are dormant and not ready for harvest, and while his crew frolics and three members attempt to desert—they're stopped by Christian and imprisoned by Bligh—the captain's fury grows.

Once the breadfruit is finally harvested, Bligh loads the hold with twice as many plants as planned. That means that water that should have been shipped for the crew must now be used to water the plants, and the new water rations add fuel to the crew's displeasure, leading one crew member to attack Bligh, who orders the fellow keelhauled and killed.

Then Bligh discovers Christian giving a sick seaman water and strikes his mate, who returns the blow. Bligh issues a death sentence, to be carried out at the next port.

So Christian—Brando—leads a mutiny, sets Bligh adrift in a boat with the crew members loyal to the captain, and steers *Bounty* back toward Tahiti and its ladies, whom the mutineers take to the Pitcairn Islands, where they hide from the British authorities.

Walbridge was unlike the fictional version of Bligh, in most respects. Quiet, calculating, and self-assured as he was, Walbridge seldom if ever disputed another crew member's ideas. He simply had ideas of his own. Five years before Walbridge assumed *Bounty*'s helm, the ship starred in a second movie, *Treasure Island*, starring Charlton Heston as Long John Silver. The film was the product of Turner Network Television and was meant for cable-television distribution. The film was panned by critics, so Walbridge was well served to have missed it.

Now the ship's days in a starring role were over. *Bounty* was thirty years old, well beyond middle age in ship years. So her future roles were in the supporting-actress category. She was not selected for the first *Pirates of the Caribbean* movie. But she played the role of the *Edinburgh Trader* in *Pirates of the Caribbean: Dead Man's Chest* and *Pirates of the Caribbean: At World's End*. She also appeared in the opening of *The SpongeBob SquarePants Movie*.

Walbridge, the captain who eschewed attention for himself when visitors came aboard *Bounty*, was pleased with his ship's movie roles. In August 2012, he told Ned Lightner in Belfast, Maine, "I actually have to say for myself personally I really like the movie industry. I find everybody in the industry really respectful. One of the big questions I hear all the time is 'How much damage did they do to the ship?' Things like that. I find them very, very respectful of the props, of the ship, of the people."

Lightner asked Walbridge's opinion of *Pirates of the Caribbean* star Johnny Depp. Walbridge gushed, "He was extremely nice, he was very, very easy to work with, very humble. For somebody of his status, he was just a great person to work with."

Walbridge said he was most impressed by the effort moviemaking took. "We're shooting probably like a twelve-hour day, and if they can get ninety seconds of screen time, they consider they've had a very good day," he told Lightner.

Bounty had made her mark in films because, like an elegant Hollywood beauty, she had good bones. The shipwrights in Lunenburg, Nova Scotia, had provided them.

The owners of the Smith and Rhuland shipyard put out a call in early 1960 for workers for their new project. The owners had signed a contract with MGM for $750,000 to build what, at the time, was the most expensive movie prop ever. They had hired a naval architect to use the plans for the original *Bounty*—plans held by the British Admiralty—and expand them by about 50 percent to create a replica that could house everything the movie crew would need to sail to Tahiti and film the movie.

Gerald Zwicker, then about twenty-four, had just returned home to Bridgewater, Nova Scotia, after spending time working with his brother in Marlborough, Massachusetts, as a carpenter. He was listening to the radio and heard about the shipyard jobs. He applied and the next day was on the payroll. The keel was being assembled, and Zwicker was on the crew that drove galvanized bolts an inch in diameter and four feet long through the keel timbers.

Next, Zwicker was put to work assembling the ribs—the vertical wooden frames that would give *Bounty*'s hull its curved shape. It was heavy work, and where a job might take six men, only three were assigned to this particular task, making the task even heavier.

Smith and Rhuland, Zwicker felt, was a good company, so unlike some of his colleagues, he didn't complain about the hard labor. Each morning, Zwicker drove the fifteen miles from Bridgewater to Lunenburg, picking up five other workers as he went. In their eight-hour day, they took on whatever work the yard needed. When the ribs were done and shaped with sharp adzes, the men started attaching the planking, using squared, six-inch, galvanized nails and trunnels—thick dowels driven into slightly smaller holes drilled through the planks and into the frames.

Zwicker would see the 1941 Dodge truck, driven by an older man, arrive at the yard with a load of wooden pegs for the trunnels. The man harvested the wood locally in a stand of hackmatack, a tree now called tamarack. At the shipyard, workers shaped the pegs into cylindrical trunnels.

"The planking was maple and ash and birch," Zwicker recalled. "It was all good hardwood. Had to be put in a steam box and steamed. As soon as you took 'em out, you had to put them on. When we put them on and fastened them to the ribs, they had to be tight on the inside. [Planks were] beveled on the outside," to allow for caulking, he said. "Douglas fir on deck had a bevel on top because that all had to be caulked."

Zwicker had work that he preferred: "The laying of the planking of the deck was a lot easier than putting the ribs together and fastening that. Even planking the sides wasn't near as hard as putting the ribs up."

Zwicker, now seventy-seven, recalled, "Once they had the ribs all in and the bowsprit put on, you could tell pretty well what the shape of the boat was going to be. Of course, we had all kinds of tourists in there in the summer. Sometimes they got in the way. Of course they had to ask all kinds of questions. What was this? What was that made out of? The fellow from MGM was there every day. He wasn't Canadian. He didn't get in the way. He'd just come through and look around and maybe talk a minute or two. It went pretty smooth. The head fellows, they knew what they were doing. They had everything pretty well organized."

While the rough carpentry was in progress—during the warmer months—the shipyard had a crew of about eight older men working in a separate shop, making yachts and cabin cruisers. But once *Bounty*'s hull was enclosed, that crew was brought inside to finish the ship's interior.

The whole project took about a year, and then some of the yard crew were signed on by MGM as *Bounty*'s crew. The voyage to Tahiti then began, and *Bounty* sailed into Hollywood history, a legend.

But now, in 2012, unlike an aging actress, *Bounty* could not get by on her old bones alone. Wardrobe couldn't hide her defects. Cosmetics only went so far. She needed constant attention. She was high maintenance. Walbridge knew that, knew that she had her weaknesses.

And now, as darkness overcame the Atlantic and Saturday, October 27, drew to a close, the captain was preparing to put those weaknesses to the test.

CHAPTER THIRTEEN

PAST HER PRIME, LOST HER PRIME

LOCATE THE LOW AND GO AWAY FROM IT!
The need to be able to navigate is critical for the safety of the Bounty. . . . Even Physics has it in Bounty's favor.

—*Bounty* Facebook entry, 11:50 a.m., Saturday, October 27, 2012

Jim Salapatek wasn't worried about his son, Drew, on board *Bounty* as the ship sailed on a route across the path of an oncoming hurricane. But from the traffic on Facebook, he knew that others were worried. He talked with *Bounty*'s shoreside office manager, Tracie Simonin, about what they both were reading on Facebook, and then he decided to take action.

"I told Tracie, 'I'll put a positive spin on this. Try to bring some hope to it.' That's where it started with the post 'Riding the Storm Out . . . Day Two,'" Salapatek recalled.

Except for what he'd learned through his son's experiences on *Bounty*, Salapatek was a complete novice in nautical theory. But he was reading commentary in Internet forums on such websites as gCaptain and WoodenBoat Forum.

"Some were saying they can make it," Salapatek recalled. "I spent quite a bit of time reading this. There were two factions. The guys who said you could do it, they're explaining how you can do it. So that's the reason I posted those up on the twenty-seventh."

When Walbridge emailed Simonin, Salapatek said, "I just cut and pasted that." Otherwise, Salapatek had no more idea what was happening aboard *Bounty* than any of his readers could deduce. None of them knew, for example, that dinner Saturday evening was a curry dish.

The aroma washed from the galley in the forward end of the tween deck, seeped down to the lower deck, and occasionally wafted up through the Nav Shack to the weather deck. *Bounty* crew had never before had cuisine so good. Two "gourmet" meals in two days, some shipmates declared. Jessica Black, the cook three days into her job, was making friends beyond her galley walls. Her closest friend there, however, was a jack line running athwartships—from side to side—by which she kept her balance. The seas had built all day and now ran near twenty-five feet, blown by a forty-knot wind. *Bounty* was rolling from side to side, creating a couple of problems new for the 2012 season, if not unique in the ship's fifty-year life.

Having spent the whole season in relatively placid waters, the planking above the waterline was dry, not swollen with water and pressed together, each plank against its neighbors. The dryness allowed water to enter *Bounty*'s hull when the ship rolled enough to rock its dry topsides beneath the waves.

The second issue was a bit more mysterious. It was the same one Drew Salapatek had noticed on Thursday morning when he was assigned to wash down the deck. Something was wrong with the ship's pumps, the machinery that removed any seawater that came aboard and settled in the bilge.

More water than usual was boarding *Bounty*. The pumps designed to remove that water were whimpering slackers.

Bosun Groves noticed the pump problem during the day on Saturday when she volunteered to help by standing watch. She was doing a lot of galley cleaning and boat checks and noticed that the captain—who seldom strayed from his cabin except for musters—was in the engine room manning the bilge pumps. To Groves, that indicated that *Bounty* had too few crew members. She offered to relieve Walbridge.

Groves discovered then that the electric pumps, attached to a piping system that ran fore and aft to the eight compartments on the lower deck, were weak. They could not hold a prime. That is, the pumps would start sucking water from the bilge but suddenly suck air instead. Then Groves had to work a series of valves to attempt to restore the suction.

Groves was only the latest crew member to notice the lack of prime in the pumps. She thought it might be explained by the rolling of the ship, which caused bilge water to wash up the interior planks—the ceiling—on one side and then the other. She had been in twenty-five-foot seas aboard *Bounty*, though, and had never experienced such a significant loss of prime in the pumps.

Doug Faunt, AB on the A-Watch, had felt there was a problem during the voyage earlier in the week from Boothbay Harbor to New London. It took longer than usual to pump water out of the bilge, even though the amount of bilge water during that passage was minimal. But even with a decent supply of water in the bilge—in the engine room, for example—he had problems getting a prime. It just didn't feel right.

Faunt had reported his concerns to John Svendsen, the chief mate, and to Captain Walbridge. Faunt had heard the skipper acknowledge, "Maybe we have some problems." Faunt thought his concerns were taken seriously, but he wasn't certain how seriously. Like most of the other crew members who questioned their own judgment when compared with the skipper's, he didn't pursue the matter.

While he waited for the ship's officers to take action during the trip to New London, Faunt, technically oriented, fiddled with the pumps and found that when he ran both simultaneously, he could get a prime.

On Thursday, when *Bounty* left New London, Faunt still had concerns about its bilge pumps and still had seen no action taken.

Now it was Saturday, and the pumps still performed poorly. Joshua Scornavacchi found that, when C-Watch was on duty and he had boat-check responsibility, the two electric pumps lost their prime every twenty to thirty seconds. On each hour of boat check, he had to spend half his time in the engine room, attempting to pump the bilge. He spent much of the rest of the time on watch checking the strainers at the ends of the piping system to see if they were clogged. He found no clogging at all. But even in the engine room, where normally the pumps would drain the water completely, they failed to keep pace.

Scornavacchi reported the problem to his watch captain, Dan Cleveland.

On his next watch, Adam Prokosh found the same issue. He thought through the problem analytically. Were changes made to the pumping system in Boothbay Harbor? No. He reviewed logs kept in the engine room and found that it was taking nearly twice as long as normal to clear the bilges. Prokosh, too, checked the strainers and found nothing. He raised the floorboards to see if the strainers were all underwater when the ship was level. They were.

Something was amiss, and Prokosh did his duty, reporting the poor prime up the chain of command, even mentioning it directly to Robin Walbridge. Then he told Matt Sanders, his watch captain. Later, he again brought the poor prime to Walbridge's attention, and the captain said, "I'm thinking about it." Prokosh believed his captain and assumed that the issue would be addressed by the officers.

But on Saturday, October 27, when Prokosh and his B-Watch were about to go off duty, his watchmate Jessica Hewitt was unable to get a prime on the starboard pump, even though plenty of water was in the bilge. She thought back to the short voyage from Boothbay Harbor to New London, recalling that even then she'd had problems with the prime. Now the problem remained unsolved, even if in some quiet corner of *Bounty* the officers and captain had considered it.

As B-Watch turned duties over to C-Watch, Prokosh told Anna Sprague she could expect to find the bilge pumps difficult to prime. Sprague checked the strainers in the bosun's locker and the aft crew quarters. They were underwater and unclogged.

Only one crew member was aboard *Bounty* on this voyage who could remember a problem that threatened *Bounty* fourteen years earlier. Robin Walbridge was the skipper in 1998 when *Bounty* was passing by the coast of the Carolinas about fifty miles offshore in modest seas and a flooding began.

It was Walbridge's fourth season as *Bounty*'s skipper, and he was sailing his vessel from Fall River, Massachusetts, to Florida for her winter berth when, at nine thirty on an October Saturday night, his crew radioed the coast guard for help.

This was in the days when *Bounty* took on thirty thousand gallons of water an hour sitting at the dock in Fall River, its pumps running regularly to keep the ship afloat. Of the three bilge pumps then, one was diesel-powered and mounted on the tween deck with a pickup pipe going straight down to the engine compartment, Cliff Bredeson recalled.

At that time, there were no bulkheads below the tween deck. Any water that made it into the bilge could be sucked up and pumped overboard from that one pipe in the engine room.

The two smaller, electric pumps in the engine compartment were meant as backup for the diesel pump. They were both powered by one diesel generator and were mounted less than a foot above the engine-room floorboards, Bredeson said.

The main diesel pump on the tween deck stopped working, and *Bounty*'s crew couldn't act fast enough to get the electric pumps working. The bilge water rose above the engine-room floorboards and shorted out the electric pumps. Now, *Bounty* was at the mercy of the sea.

A helicopter, two coast guard cutters, and two navy ships were joined by a commercial tugboat, all of the vessels responding to *Bounty*'s location, delivering five portable pumps to the *Bounty*'s crew of twenty-two, according to a newspaper report at the time. *Bounty* was boarded by a navy damage-control team, which helped pump *Bounty* enough that the crew could steer her into port in Charleston, South Carolina, the newspaper reported.

"Investigators say the ship began taking on water after it ran into a storm and caulking between the planks was loosened," the news report said.

"'It was not a phenomenal storm,' said Lt. Jeff Carter, a senior investigating officer with the Coast Guard. But the weather was rough enough to bang it around," the newspaper reported. "'After the caulking loosened, water began to seep inside. The main dewatering pump, which operates on diesel fuel and had evidence of wear, failed."

Bredeson remembered that once *Bounty* was in Charleston, a series of steps were taken to replace the existing bilge system. After Robert Hansen bought *Bounty* in 2001, Bredeson said, at least six bulkheads were built, dividing the space between the tween deck and the bilge deck "just to stop water from running from one section to the other with no restrictions at all," said Bredeson, who last sailed on *Bounty* in 2009. On that transatlantic voyage *Bounty* had pumping problems of another form.

Bounty's bilge pumping system had been thoroughly revamped and was in the same configuration that it would be in 2012 when she left Halifax, Nova Scotia, for Londonderry, Northern Ireland. It had two diesel engines powering two electric generators that each ran its own electric bilge pump. And it had two hydraulic pumps that ran off the main propulsion engines, one fixed in place in the engine room and operating through the manifold system that could pump individual compartments separately, and the other hydraulic pump somewhat portable.

Before the 2009 voyage, Bredeson said, "We had flooded the ship intentionally just to see what our dewatering system would manage. It was within our expectations."

But problems arose once *Bounty* was at sea.

"The shipyard had left a great deal of garbage in the bilges and that affected our pumping ability" by clogging the piping, Bredeson said. "That was just a cleaning job, cleaning out the pumps and the filters and that sort of thing. That went on for several days."

While cleaning the debris made for a rough trip, Bredeson said, "that was an education for us, for sure. I know this time [in the shipyard in 2012] they cleaned bilges every day so the bilges were very, very clean. I was impressed with the bosun's effort to clean it."

Still, there was that trip to Puerto Rico in 2010, the very next year, when *Bounty* hit rough weather, took on water, and had difficulty keeping the bilge pumps—the same ones it had in 2012—primed. The problem then was the rough weather, the rolling ship, the dry topsides dipping down into the ocean with each roll to the side. Most experienced wooden-ship sailors might have anticipated this scenario, particularly when they were accustomed to offshore sailing.

The same scenario had caught one coastal captain by surprise a few years back when he piloted his modest schooner out on Long Island Sound for a short delivery. Eric Van Dormolen, the captain of the *Mary E*, sailing out of Essex, Connecticut, had a charter scheduled in New York City, about 110 miles to the west, an opportunity to make some money for his boat, a restored Maine coastal schooner, and what Van Dormolen calls the UPS truck of its day.

In its day, the *Mary E* was made for offshore work, and every day its planks would get wet and stay swelled, Van Dormolen said. But in the charter service on Long Island Sound, that seldom happened.

"I was sailing from Greenport [Long Island] going toward New York City, and I had some dirty fuel. So I shut the engine down. It was very rough out. What was happening was the boat was not used to seeing swells, eight-foot swells. Every time we would go underwater, a little bit of water would spray in [between the dry planks]. That would weight the boat down. Every wave we hit, we would go under a half an inch."

Van Dormolen called the coast guard and then managed to sail the *Mary E* into New London harbor with just two other crew members.

"If the engine didn't die, I wouldn't have had an issue," Van Dormolen said.

But the engine did die, and although he lost the New York charter, the skipper and his schooner dodged a much greater problem: sinking.

In 2012, caught in the leading winds of Hurricane Sandy, Robin Walbridge hoped he could still make the couple of events planned at his destination. But water was coming in and his bilge pumping system wasn't keeping up. The problem was enough to pull the skipper out of his quarters. If he did not resolve these issues, he would have to write off those events.

Or worse.

CHAPTER FOURTEEN

MUTINY IN HER BLOOD

Normally, the ship's engineer would have filled the day tanks in the engine room at 8:00 p.m. on Saturday, October 27. Each John Deere diesel engine that turned one of the two large propellers beneath *Bounty*'s hull got its fuel directly from a four-hundred-gallon day tank, which had to be pumped full once a day while the ship was at sea. But on Saturday, October 27, Chris Barksdale had filled the day tank twelve hours earlier than scheduled. That timing might be explained by his being new aboard the ship and not yet accustomed to the engine room routine.

The odd timing might also explain why, when Claudene Christian, having just taken her place on the A-Watch at eight o'clock that night, checked the day tank, she recorded its level as "low," not "half-low," which it should have been.

The timing of Barksdale's replenishment was but one possible explanation of why the level of the sight glass was low. At Captain Walbridge's command, both engines were running as hard as anyone had ever seen them run. *Bounty* was racing to the southwest, attempting to pass across the projected path of Hurricane Sandy, and consuming fuel at an extraordinary rate as the ship's bluff bow banged against the growing seas.

The noise in the engine room was deafening, and it was hot in there. No doubt, Christian had a reason to get the boat check completed and move on. And that may explain why Christian missed the real explanation for why the fuel level in the day tank appeared to be low.

There was every reason to believe Christian was an observant and conscientious crew member, since in the past month she had been promoted from volunteer to paid crew. Proof was found in another observation she made in her boat-check notes. Water was coming into the engine room through an opened seam in *Bounty*'s side, Christian wrote. Bosun Laura Groves, not on boat check, had seen the problem around the same time.

Little things were happening, and Claudene Christian, if she wasn't yet voicing doubt, was becoming concerned. This would not have been out of character. Her mother, Dina Christian, saw Claudene as a bit of a worrier, even a cautious person.

Christian's concerns might have been calmed if, in the five months she'd been aboard *Bounty*, she had come to know the boss better. She'd told her mother earlier in the year that she wasn't close to Walbridge, that he was standoffish. More recently she'd reported that the skipper "seems to be coming around. He is interested in me helping him raise money for the ship because I'm in promotions."

When this trip was over, Christian told her best friend, Michelle Wilton, she would get off *Bounty*. But she did hope to land a shoreside job with HMS Bounty Organization LLC, Robert Hansen's holding company. It would be a chance, she told her college friend, to get her life back on track.

Once again, when thinking about *Bounty*, Claudene Christian had big ideas, grand plans to go along with the perpetually bubbly personality that everyone saw and that had disguised a promising life sidetracked by too many disappointments.

Her early life and success was well and publicly documented. Christian, who back in Boothbay Harbor had celebrated her forty-second birthday, was born in 1970 in Anchorage, Alaska, where, in 1987, she won the Miss Alaska National Teenager pageant. She was on her high school track team, competing in the pole vault. She was a gymnast whose specialty was the horse. And she was a cheerleader. At the same time, she participated in plays and performed as a singer. In 1988, she was in an opening act when singer Marie Osmond performed in Anchorage.

Then she enrolled in the University of Southern California,

where the five-foot-one-inch blonde majored in sports information, and she joined a sorority, where, as in the past, her personality had drawn friends to her side.

Wilton was one of those friends. Christian became her roommate, and Wilton, who was not a cheerleader, found she was living with "the most fun person I'd ever met in my life."

Christian simply seemed to enjoy living. She was "one of those type of people that everybody wanted to be around. You'd meet her, you'd automatically become one of her friends."

Wilton saw Christian as unpretentious, nonjudgmental, outgoing. The cheerleader held no grudges, never spoke ill of others.

At USC, Christian sang with a number of local bands and at fraternity parties, and taught herself how to play the guitar. Her mind was always seeing possibilities. Christian became a limited partner in a Hermosa Beach bar called Dragon.

For her LinkedIn résumé, Christian listed "Promotions Manager, Church Hill Downs/Hollywood Park Racetrack, 1993–2001." Although she still listed herself as "Owner, Cheerleader Doll Company, 1989–Present," by the time she boarded *Bounty* in May 2012, all of her business efforts had long since come tumbling down.

Claudene Christian had briefly sailed on the replica of Columbus's ship the *Niña* but had no other time aboard a tall ship when in May she arrived at *Bounty*'s dock in a heat wave in Philadelphia. Her inexperience showed.

Christian was dressed all in pink and white and, towing a suitcase with wheels, not toting a seabag, looked very much like one of her fashion dolls. When she was assigned a cabin, she filled it with clothes, and not the sort meant for swabbing decks. And among her many, many personal items was a hair dryer.

Looks were deceiving. Christian, once she knew what was expected of crew, threw herself into her role as a deckhand. She told Wilton that she wanted to prove herself, so she worked her butt off.

Bounty was nothing like her life immediately before May 2012. The girl from Anchorage, Alaska, where the sight of salt water was within a short walk; the young woman from Southern California, where the suntan beach was just to the west; this person felt landlocked living in Oklahoma, stifled and bored.

Bounty, she told Wilton, was so different. For the first time in a long time, Christian felt at peace and happy.

Her shipmates noticed her attitude. Dan Cleveland saw her always smiling while she was working, saw the attention she paid during muster.

In Boothbay Harbor, Christian was under the hull working for Bosun Groves, getting dirty with the caulking. Her effort was rewarded by the warm embrace she got from the rest of the crew.

Christian's birthday arrived while *Bounty* was up on the rails in Boothbay Harbor, and she was treated to the same intense celebration when she turned forty-two as other crew members got on their birthdays, if not the same precise means of attention. For example, Anna Sprague, youngest aboard *Bounty*, was thrown into the water when she turned twenty and that night got her wish to sleep in a hammock high in *Bounty*'s rigging.

Christian's wish for dessert on her birthday was wine and cheese. The cook at the time got cheese and red wine, Christian's favorite, and everyone drank with her. Then the entire crew went to a Boothbay Harbor bar that served pizza. There the crew sang with Claudene, the professional singer; danced; and performed with a karaoke machine.

The West Coast party girl had many more opportunities with her shipmates to revel. At one port, the photographer, Kannegiesser, bought a drum set, Scornavacchi played, and the whole crew held the *Bounty* Bash on deck, inviting aboard the crews from other ships. In Nova Scotia, most of the crew went camping ashore at some seaside cliff caves, where they had a bonfire and sang sea shanties.

But there was more than mere parties for Christian aboard *Bounty*. She told her mother that she'd found romance.

This apparently was not uncommon aboard the ship. Laura Groves's father, Ira Groves, introduced her and Dan Cleveland to his Florida yacht club members as a couple. Anna Sprague's father said she and Mark Warner were an item. And Jim Salapatek said that his son, Drew, was dating Jessica Hewitt.

Christian's boyfriend, she told her mother, was Second Mate Matt Sanders. Dina Christian believed that her daughter was on good terms with all of her ex-boyfriends, but one relationship—the previous one—had, as Wilton understood it, driven Claudene back to live with her parents. So dating Sanders was perhaps a leap of faith.

On that Thursday afternoon in New London, when Walbridge offered his crew members the chance to go ashore before the ship sailed, Christian had one strong reason to sail—Sanders. But Jessica Hewitt knew that Christian also had some strong reasons to skip the voyage, so before Walbridge addressed the crew and before the dock lines were dropped, Hewitt asked Christian what she was going to do. Christian said she wanted to see the voyage through.

By that time, Christian had already felt some pressure from her family, who urged her to quit *Bounty* in New London. Her father, Rex, called and said, "Look, they have that boat up for sale so I don't know how much upkeep they are doing. So don't do anything you don't feel safe doing."

To a friend also named Rex she had sent an email: "Pumps are not the most reliable and I'd hate to be out at sea and something happens."

Dina knew about Hurricane Sandy and assumed that *Bounty* would not sail. But Thursday afternoon, even before Walbridge announced his decision at the capstan, the mother sent a text message to her daughter while she was touring the submarine *Mississippi*: "Why don't you ask one of the guys if you can stay on the submarine during the storm. You will be nice and safe. Your Dad can come and get you."

Christian had made her decision, however. She replied, "*Bounty* loves hurricanes, haven't you heard? The Captain has thirty years' experience. All will be ok. We will go as far east as we can. We may be half way to Europe to get around it."

Once *Bounty* was under way but before the ship was far out to sea, Christian looked up more information about the hurricane on her phone. When she saw Jessica Hewitt, she repeated her earlier thought: "The storm looks like it will be so enormous we are going to have to go halfway to Europe."

Then she called her mother. Dina Christian was busy and asked if she could call back.

Claudene sounded frantic. "No! We are out on the ocean and I'm afraid I'm going to lose reception. I gotta tell you how much I love you. I really do." A little later, a text message appeared on Dina Christian's phone: "If I go down with the ship and the worst happens, just know that I am truly, genuinely happy."

Now, two days later and hundreds of miles offshore, Claudene Christian had reason to be less than thrilled with her ship. Many little things had happened. Not all, she thought, was well.

The seas, which at eight o'clock in the morning had grown to eight to ten feet with twenty knots of wind, began to build even more. At noon Saturday, with the winds at thirty-two knots—gale force—and the seas reaching fifteen feet, Chris Barksdale, caught by the violent and unpredictable rocking of the ship, lost his balance and, in the attempt to catch himself, injured a hand.

Barksdale also discovered that the nuts on the engine mounts of the port generator had turned loose, allowing the engine to move. The crew turned off that engine and its generator, and Drew Salapatek turned on the starboard generator at two o'clock in the afternoon.

By four in the afternoon, the bilge pumps were losing the battle with rising bilge water. The level was not yet critical, but the indications were of a mounting problem. Walbridge ordered the hydraulic pumps put into service.

At the same time, Jessica Hewitt was becoming seasick—headache only, no vomiting.

When the crew began working with the hydraulic pumps, they found them corroded and inoperative. At least until they could repair these pumps, the bilge water would continue to rise.

At eight o'clock, after the evening meal had been served, the wind had reached forty knots—not an unusual offshore wind—and the seas were close to twenty-five feet when Claudene Christian began her rounds of boat checks. She saw seawater squirting in through the seams of the planking in the engine room, putting the condition in her report. She reported that the fuel in the day tank was low, but as events would make clear—perhaps due to the inexperience she shared with at least half of the crew—she failed to notice the problem causing the low fuel level, a detail that was right before her eyes.

It would be another three hours before anyone discovered the problem.

THE *PATH* OF **BOUNTY** AND ITS *INTERACTION* WITH *HURRICANE SANDY*

1. Thursday, October 25, 2012: Departing from New London, Connecticut, *Bounty* begins its journey to St. Petersburg, Florida. Sandy becomes a Category 1 hurricane.

2. Friday, October 26, 2012: The crew prepares the ship for rough weather as the engines pump furiously to complete the three-hundred-mile southern trek to the same latitude as Cape Hatteras, where Captain Walbridge hopes to catch favorable winds. Sandy escalates to a Category 2 hurricane, hitting Cuba with 110-miles-per-hour winds.

3. Saturday, October 27, 2012: Walbridge orders a change in course to the southwest, crossing the Gulf Stream, with the intention to sail across the anticipated path of the hurricane and reach its more favorable west side. The seas steadily reach twenty-five feet, and the wind hits forty knots. Sandy, now back to a Category 1 hurricane, makes a turn for the northeast off the coast of Florida.

4. Sunday, October 28, 2012: *Bounty*, in an eddy on the southeast side of the Gulf Stream, west of Sandy, is rocked by seas of a uniform twenty-five feet and steady fifty-knot winds. At the last known location of the ship before it completely loses power, the crew calls and emails for help. Hurricane Sandy continues moving northward with storm winds spanning over eight hundred miles.

5. Monday, October 29, 2012: The coast guard locates *Bounty* and enacts a rescue in the infamous "Graveyard of the Atlantic."

CANADA
ME
VT
NH
MA
NY
CT
RI
OH
PA
NJ
MD
WV
VA
DE
NC
SC
New London
New York City
Washington, DC
Elizabeth City
Route of HMS *Bounty*
Route of Hurricane Sandy
Atlantic Ocean
Mon. Oct. 29, 2012, 8:00pm
Mon. Oct. 29, 2012, 2:00pm
Mon. Oct. 29, 2012, 8:00am
Mon. Oct. 29, 2012, 2:00am
Sun. Oct. 28, 2012, 8:00pm
Sun. Oct. 28, 2012, 2:00pm
80°
75°
70°
45°
40°
35°

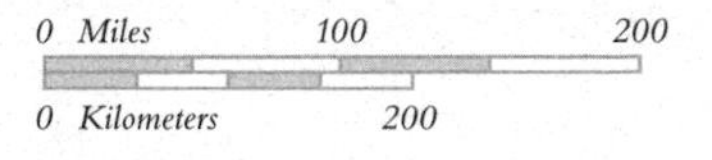

PART TWO

CHAPTER FIFTEEN

ALONE

Good evening Miss Tracie
. . . I think we are going to be into this for several days, the weather looks like even after the eye goes by it will linger for a couple of days We are just going to keep trying to go fast and squeeze by the storm and land as fast as we can.
I am thinking that we will pass each other sometime Sunday night or Monday morning
All else is well
Robin

—Email from Robin Walbridge to Tracie Simonin,
Saturday night, October 27, 2012

The sounds aboard *Bounty* were deafening. Everywhere. With both propulsion engines running, conversation was impossible in the engine room. But with the sea regularly and repeatedly slamming the three-inch-thick planks along *Bounty*'s sides, an endless base-drum thumping accompanied the jarring of the ship. The timbers throughout *Bounty* groaned as the wind, acting on everything above the weather deck—the sails and masts—pushed in one direction, and the weight of the lead ballast in the bilge and the lazaret belowdecks attempted to maintain course in another direction. Above the weather deck, the wind was now howling through those ten miles of rope rigging as midnight came and went and Saturday became Sunday, October 28.

Doug Faunt, exhausted at the end of his watch, descended from the helm to his stateroom on the port side of the tween deck and found that water was raining down from above. Water always came through the weather deck, found paths through the deck caulking even when *Bounty* was moored in port. Faunt had built a plastic tent above his bunk, but his bedding nevertheless was wet.

It didn't matter. Faunt needed sleep, and he would make do.

Jessica Hewitt was on watch now, dealing with her mal-de-mer headache, doing boat checks. Mechanically, everything was running that should have been. The starboard generator was in use, contributing to the engine room cacophony. But Hewitt could not get the electric pump to keep a prime on the starboard side. Then she noticed the day tank was running low. Looking closer, she saw that the sight glass was broken. She told her watch captain, Matt Sanders, who said she should report the damage to the engineer. So Hewitt sought out Chris Barksdale, and his response was remarkably calm.

"Oh, yeah," Barksdale told Hewitt. "Someone must have broken it and not told me." He did not offer any suggestions or say he was working on repairs of the sight glass.

Like other crew members' concerns about the loss of prime in the bilge pumps, Hewitt's report of the sight-glass problem up the chain of command seemed to be received with nonchalance, as if it were not truly an issue in need of immediate action. No crew member reported a diesel odor or saw spilled diesel.

Around this time, Adam Prokosh was passing through the Nav Shack, lit in the darkness by the screens of the various instruments. He noticed one instrument in particular: the AIS, a device something like a chart plotter on whose screen a constellation of dots would indicate the presence of all the commercial ships within a certain range.

The AIS was blank. Not one other ship on the Atlantic Ocean was anywhere near *Bounty*.

Prokosh, a voluble man seldom reluctant to share an opinion or observation, was sufficiently dumbstruck that he did not report his finding up the chain of command. *Bounty* was utterly alone, and Prokosh was at this moment given to understatement. The message from the AIS was, he thought, "a little alarming."

If Prokosh was left speechless by the realization that his ship was alone at sea, seasoned tall ship captain Daniel E. Moreland had been completely shocked a few hours earlier when he'd learned *Bounty* was offshore, headed toward—not away from—Hurricane Sandy. Moreland, skipper of the *Picton Castle*, a steel-hulled, square-rigged ship about the same overall length as *Bounty*, had several days before decided to keep his vessel in port, changing long-established plans.

The *Picton Castle* had been scheduled to sail to the West Indies by way of Bermuda, leaving Lunenburg, Nova Scotia, on October 19. By Tuesday, October 23, Moreland held muster on his ship and told the crew they were not sailing. Instead, he instructed his crew to begin planning for life at the dock.

"A ship and its crew cannot possibly be safer at sea," he said.

Then as the weekend arrived, Moreland learned that his friend Robin Walbridge had left port. *I can't imagine for the life of me why he would leave in those conditions,* Moreland thought. That sixteen mariners were offshore in the same patch of water as Hurricane Sandy was, to Moreland, mind-boggling.

In the tall ship community, *Bounty* was thought to be a bit of an outlier—not really in the same game as the scores of tall ships that were sail-training vessels. Moreland knew that improvements were being made on *Bounty*, that a lot of money was being spent on her. The ship was looking better than he'd ever seen her in the fifteen years he had known Walbridge. And the crew was doing a good job.

Moreland, with forty years of experience on the ocean, many of them on tall ships—some wooden—put it this way: "A car is safer in a parking lot." Being in the North Atlantic in late October 2012 was simply a bad idea. The track of the hurricane wasn't important. There was no safe place out there.

Jan Miles, the "partner captain" of the *Pride of Baltimore II*, learned of *Bounty*'s location late on Saturday. He drew a blank, couldn't understand it. Here was the largest storm in geographic spread ever forecast. So many questions had no answers.

Safer at sea? Miles thought. A navy ship or a large cruise ship, perhaps. One that could make twenty knots and in twenty-four hours would be nearly five hundred miles away.

But a sailboat? *Pride of Baltimore II* had a simple hurricane plan. Avoid them, and don't go to sea when they are out there.

When Hurricane Sandy was approaching, *Pride II* was moved from Chestertown, Maryland, to Baltimore ahead of the storm.

"All of my efforts," Miles would say, "have been to expose the vessel to the least amount of weather possible."

But there was *Bounty*, steering into Sandy. Nobody, *nobody*, was out there going directly at Sandy, Miles knew. Not even the navy with its high-speed ships and not the passenger industry that went out on Sunday. They went the opposite direction.

But not *Bounty*. She and her crew were following their captain's vision and his alone. *Bounty*'s culture was traditional, and traditionally a sea captain's authority was second only to God's. To question such authority was, in the days of sail that Robin Walbridge wished to in some ways re-create, to risk severe—sometimes capital—punishment.

As recently as World War II, the sanctity of a ship's chain of command was in play. Such was the case on board the supply ship *Pollux*. In a small convoy with two other American warships on February 18, 1942, *Pollux* was steaming from Portland, Maine, to Newfoundland in a blinding winter storm.

To evade German submarines, *Pollux* and the two other ships were zigzagging to port and starboard along a base course that would lead them to Placentia Bay in Newfoundland. With so little visibility in the thick and driven snow, the ships' navigators, who had almost no electronics other than rudimentary and unreliable radar, had to rely on taking sun and star sights with a sextant. A severe southeast wind was pummeling the starboard flanks of the ships, driving them to port—north on the compass. In her book that chronicles the story, Cassie Brown related one navigator's reaction:

> Lt. (jg) William Grindley, navigator of the *Pollux*, had had no premonition of disaster as [another crewman] had, but Grindley's own alarm bells were ringing. After years of making landfalls in all kinds of weather, he had developed a built-in alarm clock, an uncanny sense when things were just not right, and he had that feeling now. Something was amiss.
>
> Because of the poor visibility he had been on the bridge for 19 hours, and during this hour before midnight he was definitely

uneasy. Since 1100 hours his best efforts had not enabled him to absolutely fix their position. He recommended to Commander Turney [the officer in command] that they discontinue zigzagging.

Commander Turney had been on the bridge for the past 16 hours and, already harassed by the numerous messages directed at them earlier, he had refused. Worry had triggered disagreement between the two men.

Grindley had gotten three quick star sights under hazy conditions at 0620. It was less than satisfactory, but better than no sight at all. By early afternoon he had caught three sun lines; one, at 1220 hours, had not been an exact fix, and he made a notation on the report: "This position could be five to eight miles in error in any direction due to adverse weather conditions while taking sights. . . . Be governed accordingly."

Grindley caught one more sun line at 1400 hours as they steamed into Newfoundland waters, and radio bearings, although only approximate, established their position.

Knowing approximately where they were was not satisfactory. In midocean, five to eight miles was nothing to be concerned about. Approaching land in bad weather, at night, that distance was something else. Commander Turney was on tenterhooks, but still would not discontinue the zigzag.

In Grindley's estimation the zigzag plan had too many broad changes of course, which made it practically impossible for him to correct the course to compensate for the wind and waves hitting the starboard beam. Since landfall would be made in darkness, it would be more sensible, and assure better dead reckoning navigating, if he had only to plot the straight lines of the base course. It certainly would lessen the danger of a northward drift toward land.

He had bluntly suggested to Commander Turney that they request permission of the escort commander to discontinue zigzagging. Annoyed, Turney had refused. Under Navy rules the senior officer (Webb) [on board another ship in the convoy] was the one who determined what action to take, and no orders had been received from him, [Turney] told Grindley, therefore unless and until he received orders they would continue to zigzag.

Grindley understood his commanding officer quite well. Those needling messages still rankled, and Turney had no intention of stepping out of line and giving the flagship the opportunity to humiliate him further in front of his crew.

The *Pollux* rolled on. Quartermaster Isaac Henry Strauss and the rest of the lookouts rotating on the wings had squinted against the wind, snow and spume, watching to make sure they did not run into the *Wilkes* or the *Truxtun* [the other two ships]. Wretchedly and unspeakably cold, Strauss was torn between keeping a good lookout to avoid collision and hoping they would collide and go down and get the misery over with quickly.

During the compass checks, which had to be entered in the logbook, Strauss was in and out of the chartroom, where the tension between the captain and the navigator was becoming quite unbearable. Once Strauss heard a snatch of the conversation as Grindley maintained that very possibly they were standing into danger.

The navigator was correct. But his superior officer, heeding the tradition of honoring the chain of command, did nothing. Inevitably, the *Pollux*—as well as the *Wilkes* and the *Truxtun*—veered off course until dead ahead they saw snow-covered cliffs rising from the sea. All three vessels smashed onto the rocks.

In the ensuing evacuation, which Brown describes in *Standing into Danger*, 203 seamen died in the freezing seawater when they attempted to make their way from the stranded *Pollux* and *Truxtun* to shore. That was more than half of the men involved. The culture of the maritime chain of command had claimed them as victims.

At its birth, the aviation industry adopted the maritime culture in its cockpits. When in 1979 the National Aeronautics and Space Administration (NASA) found that the majority of aviation accidents resulted from human error, a move was made to change the culture.

"What they had to do is mandate a methodology for charging the captain of the plane to listen and charging the copilot to talk," said Jan Miles. "Then they trained the two officers to listen to each other. Then they created this training regimen. It was important to break down the mythology of vertical command structure."

The training was called Crew Resource Management or Cockpit Resource Management. The goal of CRM is to promote among crew members the willingness to question authority. In the maritime tradition, subordinates were not encouraged to question their supervisors, and supervisors frequently disciplined those who did. CRM attempts to alter this traditional outlook in a manner nonthreatening to either supervisors or crew.

In time, many in the maritime industry adopted a similar policy, called Bridge Resource Management. But not *Bounty*.

The darkest hours for *Bounty*'s crew were when Prokosh looked at the AIS, at a time far from sunset, when dawn seems so distant when looking out at the sea—any sea, but particularly a sea ripped by a storm.

Faunt slept restlessly if at all in his portside cabin on the tween deck. On the deck below, Scornavacchi awoke for his four o'clock watch and discovered that the sole boards in the crew quarters were wet with seawater that splashed up from the bilge. Gripping whatever was in reach so he wouldn't be hurled against a fixed object and injured, Scornavacchi made his way to the weather deck, meeting his watchmates. Then he began boat checks and, in the engine room, found the broken sight glass on the day tank.

He could have been the first to notice because no one from the B-Watch mentioned the problem to him when he took over. But Scornavacchi did the right thing, reported the problem to his watch captain, Dan Cleveland.

Cleveland said, yes, the officers were aware of the problem. Then Scornavacchi passed the information along to his watchmate Anna Sprague, who would do the next boat check.

At this point, green crew members who at times came to the weather deck to experience the storm firsthand were mostly below in their berths.

Jessica Black, who would normally have risen at five o'clock to begin preparing breakfast, got to remain in her berth an hour later on Sunday morning. She had followed Walbridge's advice and prepared meals in advance so that when it got rough, there would be something to feed the crew. For this morning, she had made French toast, which she could simply reheat in the oven.

But when she got to the galley, Black found smoke coming from the oven, which was turned off, and smelled burning plastic. She told the skipper, who flipped a circuit breaker off. The smoke stopped.

An investigation revealed that water was dripping on a switch. Doug Faunt was summoned, and he wrapped the switch with electrical tape, making it water resistant for the moment.

By seven o'clock Sunday morning, the wind was blowing a steady fifty knots and the seas had grown to a uniform twenty-five feet. The bilge pumps were running constantly, but they were still not holding their prime.

Those who could eat breakfast did. But everyone was now suffering from fatigue, and the day was just starting. Walbridge declared there would be no work parties so that those off watch could rest.

This voyage was beginning to have the look and feel of the 2010 trip to San Juan, except this time *Bounty* wasn't overtaken by the weather. Robin Walbridge had chosen it. He had given the orders. He had selected the route, the time to make the turn to the southwest so that *Bounty* could race across the hurricane's track, get on the good side. Alone, he had chosen all of this and assumed, without apparent contradiction, that his plan was well conceived, that doubters were misguided.

Seventeen years earlier, when he'd made the bold decision to step up to the rank of square-rigger captain, there had been no doubters, certainly not Walbridge himself, who by then believed he had acquired enough knowledge for the job. Nor was he surrounded by individuals qualified to independently assess his credentials. Like his current crew aboard *Bounty*, the movers and shakers in Fall River, Massachusetts, who in 1995 sought out Walbridge as their captain knew little about tall ship sailing. They had a few expert advisers to guide them in the hiring. Beyond that, they chose to trust their new captain explicitly.

CHAPTER SIXTEEN

LANDING THE UNQUESTIONED CAPTAIN

Fall River, Massachusetts, is a seaport twenty miles from the ocean, on Mount Hope Bay, at the northeastern corner of Narragansett Bay. It is home to the largest collection of US Navy ships on display anywhere. The city had hosted tall ship festivals, and the Fall River Area Chamber of Commerce—the local business-booster organization—had been a big part of those celebrations.

After the city organized a couple of tall ship festivals, the members at the chamber were sitting around when one of them, Phil Roderick, said, "Wouldn't it be great if Fall River had its own tall ship?"

Collectively, the members imagined the name FALL RIVER on the transom of some handsome tall ship visiting ports around the country. What a promotional tool! Spreading the word about their city on the bay. It was only a daydream, though. In 1992, no tall ship sprang to mind that was capable of filling the bill.

Six years earlier, in 1986, yachtsman Ted Turner, whose sailing credentials included victory in the 1977 America's Cup race in nearby Newport, Rhode Island, had purchased MGM/UA Entertainment Company for $1.5 billion. With it he acquired the company's film and television library, and he got *Bounty*. Turner liked boats, but he was willing to get rid of this now-twenty-six-year-old movie prop. So in 1992, he sent out a request for proposals to about twenty communities that had hosted *Bounty*, including Fall River.

"They were kind of fishing to see who could take it over," recalled Tom Murray, who at the time ran the Fall River Area Chamber Foundation Inc. "When Turner contacted us, we were kind of already primed for it. We had a core crew of guys who went to work on it and put together an operating plan without knowing what they were doing."

But why would Fall River, a somewhat down-at-the-heels mill town past its prime, be attractive to Ted Turner?

If he was thinking about the ship alone, there was the city's protected harbor as well as an organization willing to take the ship.

"Of course Turner would be looking for a tax deduction," Murray said. "We did something nobody else did." The group applied to the Internal Revenue Service for a "private letter ruling." In the application, they placed a value on *Bounty* of $3.5 million. "When that private ruling came through, that guaranteed [Turner's company] would be able to take a $3.5 million deduction on its tax return."

Turner sent his pal Bunky Helfrich to Fall River to make sure the city could handle the ship. The chamber members took Bunky to the city's Marine Museum for a short visit. They couldn't extract him on schedule, but that was okay because now Bunky had "warm fuzzies about the place," Murray said. "Come in with the private letter ruling, it was a slam dunk. They gave us the ship."

Bounty arrived in Fall River on June 18, 1993, under the command of delivery skipper Jay Bolton. It was officially owned by the Tall Ship Bounty Foundation Inc., a charitable nonprofit formed by Murray's Fall River Area Chamber Foundation Inc.

"We were the rookies, as far as owning a ship," Murray conceded. "Our initial plans were to have it as a dockside attraction, with a long-term plan to have her sail to festivals to promote the city. Our early budget was peanuts compared to the long-term plans. We were hoping to do a very aggressive sailing-school program."

Underneath all the plans was a simple, overriding goal: to put the name Fall River on the stern and generate publicity.

The payoff was immediate. Across the country, newspapers large and tiny announced Turner's gift to the city: a total of 7.9 million copies of various newspapers ran articles mentioning both Fall River and *Bounty*.

"And that's what we were looking for, because the ship wherever it went was a front-page story. That's why we did it, a very selfish purpose why we did it," Murray said.

The chamber was prepared to send *Bounty* off to distant ports now, but they were also thinking beyond that to a sail-training program. They began that first year with a program for adults and had a sail-training program for youth in the works.

"So that became the single-minded focus of the group. The gold standard would be to have it as a sailing school," Murray said. The chamber envisioned the young people aboard *Bounty* learning life lessons because the ship doesn't discriminate. "You make a decision and the ship responds. Whatever they [students] do, the ship's going to hold them accountable."

Jay Bolton was only *Bounty*'s delivery captain. In the next two years, the Fall River owners continued to sign fill-in captains whenever they wanted to send the ship on a tour. Richard Bailey, captain of the *Rose*, was one. But they needed a full-time captain. On their board they had a couple of seasoned tall ship skippers to help guide their search. Ernst Cummings had been the captain of the coast guard's tall ship, *Eagle*, when he was in uniform. Another adviser to the chamber members was Hugh Boyd, the Lunenburg, Nova Scotia, seaman who took *Bounty* on her first voyage to Tahiti. While most of the chamber guys were not tall ship guys, they believed they could rely on Cummings and Boyd to give them good advice in the hiring of a new captain.

Bounty stayed in Fall River her first winter, 1993–94. But even in a protected port, winters can be rough on a wooden ship. The following year, *Bounty* was sent south, with Richard Bailey as fill-in skipper, to Wilmington, North Carolina. There, Robin Walbridge took over as dock captain and caretaker until the ship sailed to St. Petersburg, Florida.

Phil Roderick—the chamber member who had first dreamed about having a tall ship with FALL RIVER on the transom—owned a winter home in St. Petersburg, and he boarded *Bounty* every day when she was tied to the city-owned pier. Roderick negotiated the dock rentals and any other needs *Bounty* had, and in that role he met Walbridge. When Murray visited St. Petersburg, Roderick introduced him to Walbridge and then vetted the aspiring skipper's credentials. He discovered Walbridge had worked for the

Adventure Scouting program in Miami, where the owners had high praise for him.

Walbridge had more tall ship experience than any other potential candidate except Ernst Cummings, so he was brought to Fall River to meet the board of directors. He didn't ask for a high salary, which appealed to the chamber, and so he became *Bounty*'s full-time captain.

Murray found Walbridge likable, smart, pleasantly amusing but not at anybody's expense, a clever guy who was easy to talk to.

"I thought he was competent," Murray said. "He and I would talk regularly, oftentimes every day. I was the office guy. Robin was stellar to work with. It was a full-time job and he always had the best interest of the *Bounty* at heart. I thought he was very agreeable with the crew, and I thought he was very pro-education."

Walbridge fit in perfectly with the chamber's sail-training plan for *Bounty*.

In the spring of 1995, Robin Walbridge became *Bounty*'s captain, and he steered his ship as its owners wanted, becoming an asset to the organization. The chamber was already sold on sail training and its use as a way to spark investment in *Bounty*. Sail training had a wholesome ring that could appeal to financial backers. The historical skills could be taught and the tactics of how a ship was run, Murray said. All to the better.

"But really, it was about, number one, getting the city promoted."

Unknown in Fall River at the time of Walbridge's selection, *Bounty*'s new and vibrant path was about to be joined with that of another legendary tall ship. In Boston, a new commander took the dormant helm of the USS *Constitution*, Old Ironsides, the ship made famous for her defeat of eight British ships in the War of 1812. Michael Beck had commanded *Pegasus*, the navy's fastest ship, before seeking the helm of *Constitution* in 1995. When he was interviewed by a retired vice admiral for the job, he said he wanted to sail *Constitution*, and when—at the same time that Walbridge was becoming *Bounty*'s permanent captain—he took command, Beck announced that *Constitution*, a commissioned naval vessel built in 1797 and last sailed in the 1930s, would sail on her two hundredth birthday in 1997.

Of course, Beck had some issues to address. First, the navy brass didn't want *Constitution* to sail. She'd been a museum for decades. Second, she had no rigging, no sails.

While Beck set about to resolve those issues, he had a couple more problems. He had no crew capable of sailing a square-rigged ship, and his own sailing experience was limited to time spent aboard Naval Academy yawls before he graduated in Annapolis in 1977. Beck's most recent background was aboard a relatively small, heavily armed naval vessel that could make over forty-eight knots. He had traded that "stinkpot" for a "rag bagger" with no rags, no crew, and no competent captain.

In fact, *Constitution* had a crew of tour guides. In the fall of 1995, Beck sent them to Jacksonville, Florida, where they boarded the coast guard tall ship, *Eagle*. "Their assignment was to learn [tall ship sailing] but also to write me a letter to tell me they could sail *Constitution*," Beck said. "Every one of those kids when they took *Eagle* from Florida to New London, every one said, 'We can do it.'"

Now the question was, could Beck do it? He invited what he thought were eminent tall ship captains for a meeting in Boston. A handful arrived. He presented them with his idea of sailing *Constitution* for the first time in decades. They found old drawings, brainstormed how to set up the ship, how to use the rigging, and what sort of ship would provide a similar sailing experience for training. "*Bounty* was, quite frankly, the closest," Beck said.

Bounty was at her winter berth in St. Petersburg when Beck first saw her. He had asked to visit in order to learn what he needed to know. He went up the gangplank and reported aboard. The first mate told him the captain had given the order to get under way immediately.

"There was a guy in a hammock at the stern of the ship and I didn't know who that person was," Beck recalled. "I assumed the first mate had authority to get under way. When we got out into the water and needed to set sail, Robin came up to me and tapped me on the shoulder and said, 'This is where you're going to learn.' The process of learning was [to become] an ordinary seaman and following commands."

Beck said, "In that week, I learned an awful lot." He trusted

Walbridge, who never showed him arrogance, but only displayed a sense of competence. "He struck me as professional, and he did it in a way that was unassuming. My life was always oriented around 'How do you build trust in a crew?' I was very much aware of anyone who had a similar approach to teaching their sailors through building trust. That's what Robin was all about."

When the week was over, Beck asked Walbridge to come to Boston to train *Constitution*'s mast captains and deck officers. *Bounty* was one-third *Constitution*'s size but had the same three-mast sail plan. Each mast had a mast captain, responsible for giving orders to the sail handlers up on the rigging. The captain would give the first mate an order regarding the sails. The first mate would pass along the command to the appropriate mast captain, who would pass it along to the crew on his mast.

On board *Bounty*, Beck had learned that the mainmast—the middle of the three—had to be set first to maintain a balanced ship. A navy man with two decades under his belt, Beck knew none of this. Walbridge was his teacher. Beck loved him as a good student would.

And so, with a certain reverence, Beck invited Walbridge on board *Constitution* for the celebratory sail in Boston Harbor on July 20, 1997. Among the invited dignitaries were Massachusetts senators Ted Kennedy and John Kerry, and legendary television anchorman Walter Cronkite. In the shadows was Robin Walbridge. Beck had assigned him as his backup. If for any reason Beck was incapacitated, Walbridge was to sail *Constitution*.

The two-hundredth-anniversary sail was a highlight in Walbridge's career. It was also a golden opportunity for the chamber members from Fall River. Tom Murray was on board, surrounded by captains of industry, the sort of men whose largesse he coveted. Murray was shaking hands and passing along the message from *Bounty*. Sponsorships were available, for a fee.

Fall River could count on a donation from the state government, but only if the chamber could raise a substantial portion of their costs themselves. Murray did his best, attempting to convince Fortune 500 executives aboard *Constitution* that sail training was a great investment.

He failed. "I couldn't convince anybody to kick in one hundred thousand dollars," Murray said. Nor could some other chamber members who traveled in loftier financial circles than Murray find any fat cats to help keep *Bounty* afloat.

The expenses were vastly more than the chamber guys had anticipated when they'd accepted the wily Ted Turner's gift. They couldn't afford to haul *Bounty* every two years for repairs. They couldn't do the work needed to assure the ship's survival.

Murray broke the news to his friends: "The jig's up."

In the next year, the chamber guys had an offer of $2 million from one potential buyer, but they believed *Bounty* was worth $3 million. So the ship stayed tied to big aluminum pilings in Fall River.

The crew was dismissed, and Walbridge, who had met and married a local woman—Claudia McCann—was unemployed but still in town, checking on *Bounty*.

At one point, the wave action on Mount Hope Bay slammed *Bounty* so hard against the aluminum pilings, padded with old tires, that she suffered a hole in her hull. Water came in faster than the bilge pumps could discharge it, and a Fall River fire truck was called to pump out the bilges.

But then an angel of mercy arrived—Robert Hansen—and for what a chamber of commerce member characterized as a bargain price, he bought *Bounty*.

On March 15, 2001, Tom Murray boarded *Bounty* and raised an American flag to mark the final day of Fall River's ownership.

The next day, Hansen was the owner. And Robin Walbridge once again was her captain. Now, of all the square-rigger captains in the world, he was the one whose credentials had the US Navy stamp of approval. It appeared to almost everyone who met him that to understand how a tall ship operated in the day of sail, one only had to learn from Robin Walbridge.

But, as Tom Murray noted earlier, the ship doesn't discriminate: it's going to hold you accountable.

CHAPTER SEVENTEEN

QUESTIONING THE CAPTAIN

Bounty Update 10/28 . . .So far so good! Bounty's move to the east avoided all the storms up the Atlantic Coast. Bounty has now positioned herself to pass on the west side of Hurricane Sandy.

—*Bounty* Facebook entry, 9:39 a.m., Sunday, October 28, 2012

French toast was heating in the galley oven when Laura Groves got up on Sunday morning. She helped herself to a serving, and then, making her way the length of the tween deck while *Bounty* rocked, slammed, and groaned, she joined her fellow officers for the morning meeting in the Great Cabin. A chart lay out on a table, and the officers took note of their position and that of the hurricane.

Although Sandy was still quite a distance to the southwest, it was clear that at the moment, *Bounty* was crossing directly in front of the approaching weather. It was like crossing railroad tracks and seeing the train coming a mile away. The crossing wasn't a problem if they didn't linger or stall.

The explanation for Walbridge's move from an easterly course to a southwesterly one would be obvious to a sailor, who would know that a hurricane's winds rotate counterclockwise. The winds on the right side of the path are going in the same direction as the center of the storm. If the winds are sixty knots and the storm is traveling at fifteen knots, the cumulative effect on the right side of the storm's path is seventy-five knots of wind. But on the left side of the storm's track, the same fifteen knots—blowing opposite the direction the storm is traveling—is deducted, giving wind speeds of forty-five knots.

It is sound practice if caught at sea with a tropical cyclone or hurricane to get on the slower side. Based on *Bounty*'s position and that of the approaching hurricane, Walbridge calculated that he had time to make it to that favorable left side of Sandy.

Walbridge had outlined his plan two days earlier in an email to *Bounty* headquarters on Long Island.

"We are headed S x E waiting to see what the storm wants to do," he stated in the message to Robert Hansen and office manager Tracie Simonin. "I am guessing it wants to come ashore in NJ/NYC. We are running trying to stay on the east side of it. Bad side of it until we get some sea room. If we guess wrong, we can run toward Newfoundland. If it turns and wants to tangle with us that means it is pretty far off shore and we can turn and go down the west side of it. I need to be sure it is well off shore before we can take advantage of the good weather for us. Right now I do not want to get between a hurricane and a hard spot. If you can send us updated track info (where it is projected to go) that would be great. We know where it is, I have to guess (along with the weather man) where it is going."

About ten hours later, on Friday evening, he continued in another email, "We are still heading toward the storm and waiting for it to make up its mind as to where it wants to go. I am hoping it heads a little further out to sea so we can sneak down the west side of it. Otherwise we will be heading to Newfoundland."

Now, thirty-six hours later, Walbridge had another option. He could yet aim for a safe harbor. As the officers met in the Great Cabin, *Bounty* was almost due east of the entrance to the Chesapeake Bay, with the harbors around Norfolk within hours. The wind was coming from the right direction to blow him there, and *Bounty* was making good speed. And—as had been the case even before *Bounty* left New London—the ship clearly had issues that could better be addressed in protected waters.

One of those problems was a hydraulic pump. A-Watch was on duty, and Doug Faunt was in the engine room, attempting to drain the bilge with the portable hydraulic pump, which had been serviced and was now working.

But this so-called portable pump could not be moved from the starboard side of the keelson—the longitudinal beam that rose from the bottom of the bilge up to the sole boards of the lower deck—to the port side. Faunt discovered that at some point in *Bounty*'s history someone had made a modification that trapped the pump's hose in place.

Chris Barksdale, the engineer, whose job was to handle the ship's mechanical needs, was seasick and not immediately available. So Walbridge, Second Mate Matt Sanders, and deckhand John Jones descended the engine-room ladder and attempted to move the pump. They failed.

While this crew was working in *Bounty*'s bowels, another was up in the rigging. Eager and adventurous, Joshua Scornavacchi had come off watch at 8:00 a.m. and learned that the captain had canceled work parties for the day. So he went to his berth in the aft crew quarters and had just lain down when there was a call for all hands on deck.

With no time to put on foul-weather clothes, Scornavacchi was wearing ragged trousers, a T-shirt, sneakers, and glasses. He scrambled back to the weather deck and saw that the fore course sail—which had been set with the fore staysail as storm sails but then had been furled—had blown out of its furling. All the deck officers and several of the deckhands now scrambled up the rigging. This required them to climb up on the bulwark—the three-foot-high wall at the outer edge of the deck—and then step around the ropes that slanted from there to halfway up the foremast. Now on the outside of the rigging, with only their hands to secure them, the crew members climbed the ratlines—the webbing between the slanting shrouds. As the boat rocked, the climbers found themselves at one moment looking down across the deck into the sea below, then up into the sky, their backs free to fall straight down into the ocean.

Everyone made it up to the second yard, where the fore course was whipping and snapping, adding its own racket to the ocean's roar and the wind's howl.

Once at the yard, they stepped away from the mast and, like acrobats on a high wire, onto a single footrope. A back rope was behind them, and they each had on a climbing harness that they clipped to the nearest fixed rope.

But now they were face-to-face with the fore course—a large, white spread of fabric that, driven by fifty-knot winds, viciously slapped their faces. At the same time, flailing lines—buntlines used to furl the sail—whipped at the crew. Scornavacchi's arms were cut repeatedly as he struggled with the sailcloth, which ballooned before him, stretched so tight he could not get a grasp. As soon as he would get a grip and begin to pull the sail in, the wind would yank it from his grasp.

"Punch it!" yelled John Svendsen, standing on the footrope beside him.

Scornavacchi punched, the balloon collapsed, and he was able to grab a fistful of fabric.

Punching again and again, Scornavacchi over time gathered most of the port side of the sail and had it furled.

While *Bounty*'s crew wrestled with the fore course, Coast Guard Sector North Carolina, located in Wilmington on the Cape Fear River, was keeping an eye on Sandy. A year earlier, Hurricane Irene had hit the Outer Banks, and a repeat in 2012 was the biggest concern.

The folks at Sector North Carolina didn't yet know that a vessel was at sea in their neighborhood. They did know that Sandy was a massive weather system, a large hurricane that stretched 800 to 860 miles across, taking up a lot of real estate.

The district search-and-rescue coordinator, Commander Jimmy Mitchell, had alerted the eight small boat stations along the Outer Banks and the bays. As usual, those units were monitoring VHF Channel 16, the hailing and distress channel, and high-frequency communications—ham radio and single-sideband. The radio room also kept touch with the coast guard's Rescue 21 system, which has ten send-and-receive towers along the North Carolina coast that can receive marine distress calls and locate the position from which a call is sent. Rescue 21 "takes the search out of search and rescue," Mitchell would say.

The coast guard's primary search-and-rescue assets in the mid-Atlantic area—its helicopters and fixed-wing aircraft—are stationed at Elizabeth City, North Carolina, just south of the Virginia border. But on Sunday, October 28, the winds had been blowing for a full day too fiercely for a C-130 aircraft to take off and land from that airfield. So all the fixed-wing planes had been moved inland, to

Raleigh, North Carolina. They could fly from there if necessary. The agency's helicopters—which have a substantially shorter range than the fixed-wing craft—were ordered to remain "on deck" and ready in Elizabeth City.

Bounty's rub rail—its deck level—was getting submerged from time to time in the building seas as the ship heeled thirty degrees to starboard. Occasionally, her cap rail at the top of the bulwark was underwater. Moving about any deck was a serious challenge. This was the sort of sea that Scornavacchi had been looking for when he signed on *Bounty*, and now, when he had no chores, he was on the weather deck, filming the chaos and violence.

The evidence of the storm was belowdecks, too. The port generator and the port engine had stopped running. The starboard generator was working, powering the bilge pumps. But the pumps were increasingly ineffective.

Meanwhile, in the galley, Jessica Black was struggling. She attempted to boil water in a pot, and the pot flew into a bulkhead. She held her personal jack line with one hand while with the other she cooked hot dogs and macaroni and cheese for lunch for a crew that was exhausted and losing its appetite.

An entry on *Bounty*'s Facebook page at 10:41 a.m., Sunday, October 28, revealed the conditions at sea, the source of crew fatigue:

> *Here are some readings from a weather buoy 150 miles east of Cape Hatteras, which is close to Bounty's current position.*
> *Station 41001*
> *. . . NDBC*
> *Location: 34.561N 72.631W*
> *Date: Sun, 28 Oct 2012 14:50:00 UTC*
> *Winds: ENE (70°) at 36.9 kt gusting to 48.6 kt*
> *Significant Wave Height: 29.5 ft*
> *Dominant Wave Period: 12 sec*
> *Mean Wave Direction: E (84°)*
> *Atmospheric Pressure: 28.87 in and falling*
> *Air Temperature: 75.9 F*
> *Water Temperature: 79.9 F*

Interpretation: The seas were nearly thirty feet high, the winds gusting close to fifty knots.

About fifteen minutes later, at around 11:00 a.m., Sunday morning, Robin Walbridge appeared in the engine room. Above the roar of the starboard engine and generator, he heard the news from Barksdale. The ship was taking on even more water than before. The level in the bilge had risen to thirty inches, the top of the keelson, double what it would normally be.

Walbridge remained silent. But as noon approached, Barksdale was certain that more water was entering *Bounty* than the bilge pumps were removing.

Barksdale, nauseated but not vomiting, could stand the hundred-degree engine-room heat only so long before he needed to breathe fresh air. He was becoming dehydrated. After fifteen minutes, he would have to go topside. But while in the engine room, he saw water flowing in sheets down the inside of the hull. When he saw Chief Mate Svendsen and Third Mate Cleveland, he mentioned these waterfalls inside *Bounty*'s hull. They wondered whether it was not simply water that had washed up the side of the boat when *Bounty* rolled. "No," Barksdale said. "This water is coming in through the hull."

Barksdale knew that not only the ship was taking a beating. He had already wrenched one arm and badly bruised a leg in falls.

Barksdale went to the tween deck for a break and found Walbridge in the Great Cabin. The two men were alone in what might have been the most quiet spot aboard *Bounty* when, without warning, the ship lurched, catching Walbridge off guard, catapulting him through the air, backward. A solid table bolted directly to the deck met Walbridge's spine, halting his flight and dropping him to the floor. The table didn't move. Barksdale was amazed that Walbridge did. He rose to his feet, but he was clearly injured.

Instead of retiring as he normally would have to the solitude of his stateroom, Walbridge descended again into the engine room. There was work to be done, machinery to be fixed. Everyone on board was needed. The mechanic who had kept all those houseboats running back in Florida and who, with amazing speed, had rebuilt a blown diesel aboard *Rose* could no longer delegate. Injured or not, he and his hands were needed, too.

CHAPTER EIGHTEEN

OH, THE WATER

Bounty Update 2 for 10/28 . . . Bounty looks to be sailing thru the tail end of the rain storms.
Last reported coordinates as of 2 PM EST
N 34 degrees 22' W 074 degrees 15'
Speed 10.3 knots

—*Bounty* Facebook entry, 1:52 p.m., Sunday, October 28, 2012

Jessica Black had the hot dogs and mac and cheese ready on the tween deck at noon Sunday when the A-Watch ended its shift. The four watch standers turned the helm over to their replacements on the B-Watch in the shrieking and howling of the rigging and the rearing and plunging of the bow and went below to the thundering inside the ship's hull.

Bounty, which had earlier been making ten knots—double her normal cruising speed—was now getting by on one engine, the starboard unit, because the port engine had stopped running. The starboard generator was powering the bilge pumps. The ship was heeled to port more often than not since she was on a starboard tack.

Doug Faunt, a retiree who could have been anywhere he wanted doing anything that he pleased, was feeling his age when he got off watch. He grabbed some lunch, but then, ready for some rest, he headed across the Great Cabin to his stateroom on the port side, just aft of amidships. It would be an uncomfortable nap. His bunk was soaked.

Anna Sprague, once baptized by her father in the Savannah River, had just gotten up at noon, having napped since eight o'clock, when her morning watch ended. She got a bowl of mac and cheese and, hearing no work parties were scheduled, settled in to await her next watch at four o'clock in the afternoon.

Jessica Hewitt woke just before noon for her next watch. She talked with Claudene Christian, who told her the electric bilge pumps were running constantly, as was the portable hydraulic pump. Hewitt knew the pumps were finicky and she didn't feel she was competent with them. If there was a problem with the pumps, she would hardly recognize the issue, so she was not particularly alarmed. She joined Adam Prokosh on the helm, which now, in the towering seas, required the strength of two crew members.

The seas seemed to be getting worse by the hour.

At about this time, Christian, whose cabin was near Faunt's, approached him. The normally ebullient woman was serious. She had noted problems—basic machinery problems—on board, but, she told Faunt, when she tried to raise her concerns with the ship's officers, she felt ignored.

Faunt attempted to assure Christian that their leaders were aware of the problems and were seeking solutions.

Joshua Scornavacchi had several hours to wait before his next watch, and although Walbridge had told the crew there would be no work parties, the young outdoorsman saw work to be done. He climbed down the ladder to the engine room and set to work removing debris from the bilge so the pumps wouldn't clog. The many wood chips might have been causing the pumping problems. But when Scornavacchi inspected a strainer at the end of one bilge hose, he didn't see any blockage.

On the weather deck, Prokosh and Hewitt were at the helm and looked up and saw the fore course—the same sail that the crew had furled earlier—ripping down the middle. Prokosh yelled an alert that brought the injured Walbridge to the deck. A call for all hands went out as the captain relieved Prokosh on the helm and began assembling a team to deal with the flailing canvas partway up the foremast.

Laura Groves was in her cabin in the lazaret when she heard the call. She scampered to the weather deck, joining in the shouting that rang through *Bounty*'s cabins as each crew member called out the message. It was near two o'clock in the afternoon. The wind was now blowing at fifty knots, howling through the rigging, although in the engine room, all other sounds were overwhelmed by the hammering of the diesels. Scornavacchi, working down in the bilge area, was only aware of the loud protests of the ship's timbers. They screeched like enormous rusty hinges when, as the ship rolled side to side, the bulkheads worked against the deck. But over all this, Scornavacchi heard, from above, the latest call for all hands. He began hollering, "All hands! All hands!"—as he had learned to do during his six months aboard. Anytime anybody said an order, crew members were required to call it back to assure they had heard it. For serious events, such as man overboard, the rule was to call it out loud over and over. That was happening now. The alarm was being broadcast.

When Scornavacchi arrived on the weather deck, Walbridge was selecting crew to go aloft as he and Hewitt wrestled with the helm. He wanted only the most experienced men aloft, he said. He chose Drew Salapatek, John Jones, Josh, and Adam, and they scurried across the slanting deck to the starboard rigging and began to climb.

Hewitt was offended. Walbridge had limited his call to men. But she joked instead, "What about me?"

The wind was hitting sixty knots in the rigging. It had caught a fold in the furled sail and created a bubble and was pushing the sail, adding strain on the mast and the steering.

As the men climbed the rigging and looked out from the ship, they saw waves towering thirty feet, twice as high as the height of *Bounty*'s cap rail above the water while docked. Spindrift was everywhere, a white lace of blowing foam that streaked from the breaking wave tops in long tendrils into the deep troughs between the peaks. Looking out, the climbers saw waves, and beyond them, more waves, grayness and froth marching away from them on the lee side toward the horizon.

The wind was at their backs, and they didn't have to hold on with their hands because the wind was plastering them against the rigging. But if they turned and tried to look into the wind, they were blinded by driving rain. It felt like hail, stinging needles of rain.

They couldn't see because of the wind and they couldn't hear. The wind roared and howled, and there was no chance at communications.

Once they reached the fore course, they couldn't hold on to the sailcloth. As they pulled at the cloth, the wind would yank it from their grip. The sail rebelled against their touch, jerking hard enough that they felt they would be flung from their tenuous perches on the footrope.

The men had taken extra gaskets with them—lines to tie the sail tight against the yard. But they lacked the strength to secure the sail, and eventually they let it go and the wind ripped the heavy fabric as if it were cheap toilet paper.

Dan Cleveland was down on the deck, overseeing the men's work high in the rigging. He signaled the crew to return to the deck. It was getting dangerous and they had no hope of corralling the ripped fore course. Looking down, they saw Cleveland look aft and then run toward the stern. Following his path with their eyes as they descended the shrouds, they saw what had drawn the third mate. The spanker, a fore-and-aft sail mounted on the aft side of the mizzenmast and used to stabilize the ship's track, was flailing out of control. The sail was mounted on a wooden boom at the bottom and a wooden gaff along its top. That gaff had broken in two places, making three sections of gaff, each with a piece of sail connected to it. All three were flying like kites just above the aft deck. By itself, the spanker and its broken gaff was not a serious hazard, even in these conditions. But wooden blocks—pulleys—were attached by ropes to the gaff and were swinging in lethal arcs like medieval weapons.

Once on the deck, the four climbers crouched and scampered back to the mizzenmast, where the whole crew was now gathered in an attempt to control the treacherous spanker gaff. Scornavacchi grabbed a line—called a vang—designed to control the gaff. The wind gusted, lifting the scrap of sail attached to the gaff, hauling light, wiry Joshua Scornavacchi up off the deck. Adam Prokosh, heavier than his mate, grabbed the vang, too, and he also found himself suspended in the air over the deck. Four other crew members grabbed the vang, and finally, with Scornavacchi hooking his toes under the lip of the doghouse roof over the Great Cabin, they pulled the shattered rigging to the deck, where they tied it down.

Two sections of gaff were still unrestrained. Cleveland climbed the shrouds on the port side—*Bounty*'s low side—and lassoed the remaining sections. Sçornavacchi, wearing a helmet camera on a headband, had caught the whole adventure on video. He was having a blast, with the sort of excitement that he had until now experienced only in his dreams.

When the excitement subsided, Scornavacchi climbed down the forward stairs from the tween deck to the fo'c'sle and then, spinning the wheel on the steel door, into the claustrophobia-inducing bosun's locker. He found water three inches above the sole boards in the locker, and when the boat rolled, if he did not have a grasp on a fixed object, he would feel his body rise in the air, seeming to float, or he would smash into a bulkhead. He collected tools and climbed back to the tween deck.

Laura Groves went aft to the lazaret to resume her nap with her bunkmate, Dan Cleveland. He got a wake-up call at three forty-five to go on watch, but she remained in her bunk. At about four o'clock a large wave slammed into *Bounty*'s rear corner, near where she was napping. It was loud, like a dump truck hitting a house, and water was coming in the Great Cabin windows. Groves went on deck to report this problem to Cleveland.

Around this time, Walbridge had given the order to turn to a port tack to put the bilge water on the starboard side, closer to the bilge pump strainers. Jessica Black began serving more macaroni and cheese for the dinner meal. Contained in bowls, the food had a chance of being eaten as the seas built even larger and the crew struggled to remain upright. Their efforts were aided when Walbridge went to the watch and directed Cleveland to heave *Bounty* to, a maneuver that would hold the ship relatively in place, facing into the seas, putting the ship on a more even keel. Walbridge wanted to take a break from moving, not for the convenience of diners, but to allow the crew to solve some of the mounting problems.

The starboard generator—the only one operational by midafternoon—was surging, and the electrical current throughout the boat was uneven. Walbridge ordered all nonessential electrical circuits turned off.

Meanwhile, the fuel filters on all of the engines needed to be changed, and the crew discovered that the filters supplied back in New London would restrict the fuel flow too much or did not fit in the ship's engines.

Cleveland brought *Bounty* around into the wind, instructing his watch to set the remaining sail so that the wind would blow the bow in one direction while the helm was turned to steer in the opposite direction. When the maneuver was completed, *Bounty* settled in this attitude and, now on a somewhat more even keel but rocking in the big waves, began slowly drifting with the still-violent wind and seas.

Sometime after the B-Watch had been relieved by the C-Watch, Matt Sanders went into the engine room to see what he could do. He found Svendsen and Walbridge there. The captain, seriously injured several hours earlier, nevertheless worked with the pumping systems, attempting to keep the bilge water below the sole boards, which it had already reached. Sanders had never seen that much water in the bilge. He made up his mind to remain in the engine room as long as it took to dry out the boat.

An hour later, Sanders found debris in the screen of the hydraulic pump, which was struggling to get water out of the engine room. He cleaned it, removing some old line that was wrapped around the pump's impeller—the paddle wheel that moved water through the pump. Twenty minutes later, he had to clear the pump again. Sanders was also opening and closing valves on the electric-pump manifold and finding that when the boat rocked, which it did regularly in these seas, the pump lost its prime.

Oh, the water. It continued to accumulate, and Chief Mate Svendsen was more than concerned. He went to Walbridge and suggested that it was time to let the coast guard know about *Bounty*'s condition. Walbridge told him he felt it was more important to focus their efforts on getting the machinery running.

Svendsen went on deck with the ship's satellite telephone and attempted to call home base on Long Island. He seemed to have a connection. He thought maybe he was talking with Robert Hansen. But the wind roared and he could not be certain. So he shouted out *Bounty*'s coordinates several times. Then he called some telephone numbers that the ship had for the coast guard. Svendsen knew *Bounty* was in distress. He hadn't been able to convince Walbridge. He didn't know whether he had reached anyone on the telephone. He hoped for the best.

The call had gone through. Tracie Simonin had heard John Svendsen's voice, had recorded *Bounty*'s coordinates, and by eight thirty, she had called a coast guard number and relayed the message.

The ship was ninety miles off Hatteras, floating in an eddy of cold water on the southeast side of the Gulf Stream.

No one ashore knew the exact nature of the ship's distress. In fact, few aboard *Bounty* knew everything that was happening on *Bounty*'s various decks. The string of small events that had been accumulating all day was growing into a tangled ball as darkness overcame the ship on Sunday night.

Simonin and *Bounty* still had email contact. The coast guard told the office manager to tell the crew to activate their EPIRB, and she followed those instructions. Soon an electronic signal was radiating from the ship, triggering a passing satellite, which relayed the ship's position to antennas ashore. Now the coast guard had a live indication where *Bounty* was—and that she was still floating.

At nine o'clock Sunday evening, Robin Walbridge finally sent an email acknowledging problems aboard *Bounty*.

"We are taking on water. Will probably need assistance in the morning. Sat phone is not working very good. We have activated the EPIRB. We are not in danger tonight, but if conditions don't improve on the boat we will be in danger tomorrow. We can only run the generator for a short time. I just found out the fuel oil filters you got were the wrong filters. Let me know when you have contacted the USCG [coast guard] so we can shut the EPIRB off. The boat is doing great but we can't dewater."

Tracie Simonin got that message and again called the coast guard. Just a few minutes later *Bounty*'s electronics started to fail—like everything else on the ship—and communication was sporadic. The only way to reliably communicate with the vessel would be through its battery-operated, handheld radio, whose range was limited to just a few miles.

Commander Billy Mitchell, the Response Department head for Sector North Carolina, faced his first big decision. He thought: *We've got a vessel out in a hurricane, taking on water with no power, and that is about all we know. We need to get direct, reliable communications with the vessel to find out just how bad the situation is. But to do this we need to be on scene, and the safest and quickest way would be to send out a C-130.* Mitchell didn't like his choices. To send out the C-130—the coast guard's fixed-wing aircraft used for searching—would be dangerous, but to wait for improvements in the weather might be too late for the *Bounty*. *If only we knew exactly what was happening on the ship. Why does the captain think they can make it to morning if they are taking on water in the middle of a hurricane? Is he underestimating the seriousness of their situation?*

Mitchell and his team teleconferenced with the officers at the Fifth District and at Air Station Elizabeth City. They immediately activated the AMVER (Automated Mutual Assistance Vessel Rescue) program, which allowed them to locate and identify any ships registered in the system that might be near *Bounty* and could offer assistance. The program originated after the sinking of the *Titanic*, when the need for a coordinated effort by ships to help one another became clear. AMVER has been incredibly successful, saving thousands of lives, particularly when an emergency occurs far from coast guard resources. But in a hurricane as well forecasted as Sandy, most large ships were far from the storm. Just one ship, a thirty-thousand-ton Danish oil tanker, the *Torm Rosetta*, was anywhere near *Bounty*, and it responded that the seas were so bad it would be unable to assist in the rescue.

No coast guard cutters were at sea in the area, and sending one to *Bounty* would take many hours. Besides, with conditions the way they were, the cutter itself could become a casualty of the storm. After much discussion among SAR officials regarding the risks versus the gains of launching a C-130, the decision was made. They would launch the aircraft and let the pilot judge the winds firsthand and see how close he or she could fly to *Bounty* and try for direct communications.

C-130 commander Frank "Wes" McIntosh was sprawled on the bed in his hotel room watching Sunday-night football. His aircraft had been prepositioned at Raleigh-Durham International Airport, where potential crosswinds would be less troublesome than at Elizabeth City. He and his crew of six were staying at the Courtyard Marriott Hotel adjacent to the airport so they could get to the plane quickly. But the thirty-three-year-old pilot with the mild Southern accent thought it might be a quiet night. With the hurricane dominating the news for the last three days, he surmised all vessels would either be in port or far away from the swirling storm.

When his phone rang at 9:15 p.m., Wes realized he was dead wrong. On the line was the Elizabeth City operations duty officer, Todd Farrell.

"Hey, Wes," said Todd, "we got a case for you. The HMS *Bounty*, a one-hundred-and-eighty-foot-tall ship, is reportedly taking on water and having generator problems about ninety miles southeast of Cape Hatteras. Communication with the vessel has been lost, and we're probably going to need you to fly out and establish comms with them. So start mobilizing."

"Okay, we'll get ready."

Wes McIntosh seemed destined to be a pilot. Growing up in Beaufort, South Carolina, he watched F-18 military jets fly to and from the nearby Marine Corps Air Station, wondering what it would be like to be in one of those planes. His family also attended Blue Angels air shows, and he pictured himself in a cockpit, guiding a streaking aircraft across a cloudless sky. So it was no surprise when, a few years later, after graduating from Georgia Tech on an ROTC scholarship program, he accepted a commission in the navy and immediately started flight school. Once he earned his wings and graduated, he started flying E-6Bs—modified Boeing 707s whose primary mission was to function as a communications platform in case of a ballistic missile attack on the United States. After three years of flying E-6Bs, Wes went on to be a flight instructor in military training aircraft, logging fifteen hundred hours of training sorties in three and a half years. At the end of that tour he had a choice: stay with the navy in a series of nonflying roles of increasing management responsibility or transition to the coast guard, where he could continue flying. The decision was easy—he wanted to stay in the sky, and in 2010 Wes joined the coast guard as a pilot of C-130s.

Now, with orders to mobilize his crew for a night flight to *Bounty*, Wes was glad he had already flown on several coast guard search-and-rescue missions. None of them, however, involved flying into a hurricane.

Once at the airport, the crew began getting the aircraft ready, while Wes went to the Flight Planning Room for one last conversation with SAR officers and his command at Elizabeth City. His final instructions were to proceed, but to stay away from the worst part of the storm, and to try to communicate with *Bounty* without putting the plane and his crew in extreme danger. It was up to Wes to determine just how far into the storm he could fly before the hurricane winds overwhelmed both aircraft and crew.

Fortunately for the crew of the aircraft and of *Bounty*, the Lockheed C-130J Super Hercules is one tough aircraft. The C-130J was a newer version of the C-130, but most aviation professionals referred to it as the C-130. First manufactured over fifty years ago, the four-engine turboprop was originally designed and used as a transport. With a wingspan of 132 feet, a length of 97 feet, and a weight of seventy-six thousand pounds, the C-130 looks almost too large to fly in extreme weather. But the coast guard has found the aircraft to be extremely durable and reliable, and the C-130 has became the primary fixed-winged aircraft used for search and rescue, as well as reconnaissance and patrol.

On the flight to *Bounty*, Wes McIntosh would be the aircraft commander, and Mike Myers his copilot. They were supported by five other crew members: flight mechanic Hector Rios, mission system operators (MSOs) Joshua Adams and Joshua Vargo, drop master Jesse Embert, and basic aircrewman Eric Laster. The flight mechanic sat directly behind the pilots, and the mission system operators, who work with a variety of electronics such as navigation and radio systems, were stationed just aft of the cockpit. The drop master and basic aircrewman occupied the spacious cargo compartment and, during the search, scanned the ocean from their perches at two side windows. If Embert or Laster were fortunate enough to make visual contact with *Bounty*, their responsibility was to deploy any needed equipment, such as rafts, dewatering pumps, survival suits, radios, or flares, all housed in floating, watertight containers. The two men would do so by opening the ramp door at the rear of the aircraft, where they could push the equipment out. In light winds they would attach parachutes, but Embert and Laster knew that in the hurricane the gear went without parachutes to avoid its sailing hundreds of yards from the intended target. Should they need to deploy a data-marker buoy, which measured drift rates and gave location fixes, this could be done through smaller side doors. Dropping any equipment, however, would not be easy, because to do so required both men to be on their feet as the plane passed through turbulence.

By 10:00 p.m. the crew were on board the idling aircraft, anxiously wondering just how bad the winds would become once they entered the enormous reach of Sandy. Prior to launch, a warning light blinked, alerting them that the anti-icing element on the propellers had failed. Wes thought: *Well, this isn't the ideal way to begin a flight into a hurricane.*

The pilots conferred, and Wes announced over the internal communications system that they would fly out toward *Bounty* at seven thousand feet but no higher, to avoid icing.

As they barreled down the runway and the aircraft climbed into the black sky, a bit of rain splattered on the windshield. Wes and Mike Myers, both wearing night-vision goggles (NVGs), guided the plane to the southeast. Usually a bit of chatter could be heard on the radio, but that night was eerily quiet.

Then an air traffic controller from Raleigh-Durham broke the silence, asking, "Hey, are you guys heading into Sandy?"

Wes responded in the affirmative.

"Well, good luck to you."

The commander thought about how theirs was the only aircraft heading in that direction—everyone else was either sitting on the tarmac or flying the opposite way. Another system malfunction abruptly interrupted Wes's rumination, this time the weather radar. He immediately tried to get a screen shot in the ground-mapping mode on the system, but it came up blank, causing the commander to curse to himself. Then he informed the mission system operators sitting behind him that he would be relying on them to use a different system—one Wes and Mike could not see—to assist them during flight.

They continued cruising, now over the open ocean, and Wes thought, *Well, at least the malfunctions aren't serious enough for us to abort, but there better not be any more. Not tonight.*

CHAPTER NINETEEN

PROBLEMS EVERYWHERE

The entire crew on *Bounty* were diligently working—some individuals focusing on a single problem, others freelancing from one emergency to another as their effort was needed. There was now no orderly watch system, no organized work party, no sense of command except that within each member of the crew; their motivation was to save *Bounty*, to save themselves.

At nine o'clock at night, the second mate, Matt Sanders, had been in the heat and noise of the engine room since his last watch ended at four o'clock. He had gone there to keep the bilge pumps running, but instead of bringing the flooding under control, he was wrestling with various mechanical problems even as the level of the water rose.

When the starboard generator began surging and its power output fell—the port generator had stopped working long ago—it was decided that the fuel filters needed to be changed. Sanders, a tall, athletically built man, took on the job.

The filter on the starboard generator's diesel engine was on the back side. To get to it, Sanders had to wedge himself behind the hot engine and get in a position where he could twist the filter free.

But first, the generator had to be shut down. This meant the ship had no electrical current, and except for flashlights *Bounty* went dark.

The starboard propulsion engine was running well, still driving *Bounty* forward enough to hold it in place, hove to. That meant the portable hydraulic pump, which ran off the power takeoff shaft of that engine, could be operated, although it was only taking water from the engine room. In all the other bilge compartments, water was accumulating unchecked.

Sanders got into position and removed the old filter. Then Chief Mate Svendsen handed him a replacement filter. It took a while for Sanders to get the new filter seated properly. He had never replaced this filter in his time aboard *Bounty*, so the whole process may have taken up to forty minutes. Sanders lost track of time. Nor did he pay attention to the water that rose up the planking and soaked him when *Bounty* rolled to starboard. He was focused on his work.

With the new filter in place, Sanders was able to get the generator running. It started right up. Finally, something mechanical had responded the way it was supposed to.

But in the time it had taken to replace one filter, the water had risen to two feet above the engine-room floorboards, within a foot of the elevated generator.

His success restarting the generator freed Sanders to return to work on the bilge pump manifold. He was not alone. A parade of crew members—Svendsen, Jones, Salapatek, Faunt—came and went, performing other work in the engine room and along the lower deck. Occasionally, Robin Walbridge visited the engine room, too.

And the water rose, inch by inch, until it was thigh to waist deep on the starboard side and shorted out the starboard generator. Sanders went to the tween deck, where he found Walbridge. The diesel was still running, but a dangerous electrical current was in the water. Sanders asked permission to shut down the generator.

Permission granted, Sanders returned to the engine room and cut the fuel supply, stopping the engine and its generator.

Once again the ship was dark. The only hope was to get the port generator back in action. Sanders now changed the fuel filter on the port generator, bled the air out of the fuel system, cleaned the fuel injectors, and tried to restart the engine.

Nothing. The engine turned over but wouldn't ignite.

After consulting with Walbridge, Sanders went to the engine control panel and disabled an electrical switch, and this time, when he tried to start the engine, it fired up. The lights went on inside *Bounty* for the first time in more than an hour.

Sanders had been in the engine room for more than six hours

now. He began transferring fuel to the port day tank—the one with the broken sight glass—and still the water rose. By now, it had reached the computer module for a mechanism that turned salt water into fresh, and blue arcs of electricity were visible. Moreover, the engine-room sole boards were floating and slamming from side to side as *Bounty* rolled. The water was waist to chest deep on Sanders, who felt the atmosphere was unsafe. He left the engine room.

Looking for a place to be useful, Joshua Scornavacchi had descended to the engine room in the early evening. Walbridge, Barksdale, Faunt, and Sanders were working on the starboard generator. The bilge water was at Scornavacchi's shins, and the bilge alarm was sounding, its warning rising above all the other thumps and groans and screeching inside *Bounty*'s hull. In the engine room, he dove into the work of removing debris that was floating on the surface below his knees. He worked for an hour, and the water rose six inches.

Scornavacchi knew the source of the water. He saw it coming through the ceiling planks. Every time *Bounty* rolled, water flowed in sheets down the starboard side. The farther the ship rolled, the more water came in. The starboard topsides were underwater. The dry planking was not sufficiently swollen to keep the water out.

Adam Prokosh was in the engine room as well, using a colander from the galley to scoop debris. He gave the colander to Scornavacchi and climbed the engine-room ladder, heading for the galley to get another colander.

Shortly, there was a call for help on the weather deck. The Zodiac inflatable dinghy had broken loose. Scornavacchi scrambled up the engine-room ladder and dashed up the two flights of stairs through the Nav Shack, where he met Salapatek, Anna Sprague, and Third Mate Cleveland.

Leaving Sprague in the Nav Shack companionway to keep watch over them, the three men stepped onto the weather deck in winds reaching ninety knots and saw the problem. The Zodiac was flattened bottom-first against the starboard shrouds.

Crouching and waiting for the best moment, Cleveland and Salapatek made their way to the starboard side, grabbing the nearest fixed object to hold themselves in place. Scornavacchi crawled on hands and knees up the steep deck to the port side and waited to make his way forward to a railing at the mainmast where a line had been stored.

Wait, move, grab, then wait for the roll of the ship and the next opportunity. Slowly, they crept forward until Scornavacchi was high on the deck, above the dinghy and his crewmates. Then Scornavacchi tossed the line toward his mates, who tied it to the dinghy.

It was dark and dangerous, but all three hands were calm, focusing on the job at hand. The two men climbed the deck to join Scornavacchi, then all three pulled the dinghy back to its place on deck and secured it.

Time had passed. No one could be certain how much time. Time, events, were surreal. Scornavacchi headed back toward the engine room, and passing through the tween deck.

The water was too high in the engine room now, though—maybe five feet deep. The sole boards were slamming around down there, and Scornavacchi saw that the place had been abandoned.

So Scornavacchi went to his cabin in the aft crew quarters—down that solitary ladder from the center of the tween deck—to grab some tools and flashlights, things that might be needed later. In passing, he saw that Walbridge, Sanders, and Barksdale had a small gasoline pump—the crew called it a trash pump and it had never been used but was stored wrapped in plastic for an emergency. They had placed a hose from the pump running aft thirty feet to a Great Cabin window. Another hose went from the tween deck down into the engine room.

But the trash pump wasn't working yet, despite the efforts of the three officers.

Earlier, when the spanker gaff had been brought under control, Adam Prokosh was feeling pretty confident. But then the power went out and the lights went off and he was saying to himself, *What the hell is going on?*

He went to the engine room, where he found Walbridge, Sanders, and Barksdale—what he considered the entirety of the ship's engineering skills. It crossed Prokosh's mind that the high bilge water was finding all the nooks and crannies in the bilge, and that this flooding would flush out any leftover yard debris, disgusting muck. If the guys in the engine room were successful, then the strainers in the pump system would need to be kept clean. He went to the galley and asked to borrow a colander from Jessica Black. Back in the bilge, he began scooping.

Then Scornavacchi joined him in the bilge and asked how he could help.

"You can take over this job and take this colander and I'll grab another," Prokosh replied. He climbed back to the tween deck and asked the cook if he could borrow another colander.

"Use whatever you need," Black said.

Now Prokosh followed Black out of the galley, heading aft in the vast, open saloon, toward the engine-room ladder. The cook—only four days into her tall ship career—was holding on to the long jack line that had earlier been strung the length of the cabin. Prokosh, one step behind and talking with Black, had the colander in one hand but wasn't holding the jack line with his free hand when a huge wave slammed into the side of *Bounty* and the ship rocked violently to starboard.

Prokosh was airborne. An unguided missile, his body flew toward the low, starboard side, where his head and back smashed into an arms chest bolted to the floor. He collapsed in a heap where he landed. Black thought concussion, and she raced to find the chief mate.

Other crew members found a mattress, and Prokosh rolled onto it, still on the low side.

The damage was extensive. Prokosh had suffered a compression fracture in a vertebra, three broken ribs, a separated shoulder, and head trauma. He would be of no further use in the effort to save *Bounty*.

Jessica Black had no duties other than to keep the crew fed. From time to time, she got reports from crew members about the breakdowns, the flooding, the injuries, even before she heard Adam Prokosh behind her slamming into the furniture. Much of her information came from Claudene Christian, who visited the galley frequently to keep Black in the loop. Scornavacchi called Christian the crew's "spy" because all season long she had been spreading news, listening in to conversations among the officers in particular, and delivering their private thoughts to her crewmates.

Black was focused on getting meals out, though. Gossip was fine, but she had to prepare dinner early Sunday evening. Once again, due to the instability of the boat, the food had to be something that could be served in a bowl. Mac and cheese was her choice for a second time. But she wanted there to be a vegetable, and she chose frozen peas. They could be heated in the microwave, a good thing since the boat was on a constant heel of twenty-five to thirty degrees. The glass-topped stove wouldn't work.

The microwave was on the port—or high—side of the galley, which was in the bow. The bow was still pounding up and down, even when the boat was hove to. And the microwave door opened to the lower, starboard side.

Black warned the crew: Don't open the microwave. If they did, the peas would go flying. Then she turned on the microwave.

Sparks shot out. There was smoke. Black had her own small disaster right there in the galley. There was an arc, like lightning, but no fire. Doug Faunt was summoned, and he solved the problem and dinner preparations continued.

Normally, there were three shifts for meals, one from each watch. But on Sunday night, there were few diners. Someone told Black that there were so many problems that people didn't have time to eat on schedule.

She had seen some of the action herself before she began cooking. She went on deck to see the excitement of furling the torn sail and corralling the flailing spanker gaff. Faunt was on the helm then, and she asked him whether it would be appropriate for her to film the action. The masts were going from port to starboard to port as the ship rocked, looking as if they would touch the water on either side.

Faunt said it would be terrific if Black recorded the action, so she began making a video. That was much earlier, and all had ended with success.

Now, though, it was different. A few crew members came for dinner. A lot didn't. So Black made up bundles of bottled water and snacks and began delivering them to crew members immersed in their work.

As she circulated, Black saw little of the bane of a ship's cook—seasickness. Only Chris Barksdale, the engineer, was afflicted. She found him struggling with the trash pump at the top of the engine-room ladder.

With her work for the day completed, Black stopped to help the ship's engineer, holding the trash pump for well over an hour while Barksdale tried to get it started.

CHAPTER TWENTY

UNSEEN PUNCHES

After half an hour of flying in turbulence, the crew of the C-130 became uncomfortable. Buffeting winds caused the plane to suddenly drop ten to twenty feet, leaving everyone feeling as if their stomachs were somewhere north of their eyeballs. No one talked, and several crew members tried to fight off nausea.

After another twenty minutes of flying, Wes tried to raise *Bounty* on the radio.

"HMS *Bounty*, this is coast guard C-130 on Channel Sixteen. How copy? Over."

"C-130, this is HMS *Bounty*, we read you loud and clear."

Startled by the immediate response and the clarity, Wes gave a thumbs-up to copilot Mike Myers, thankful that the ship was afloat and its battery-operated radio was working.

"This is C-130. Request to know position, number of people on board, and nature of your distress."

Wes assumed he was talking to the captain, but it was Chief Mate John Svendsen. In a calm and professional voice John gave the commander their position and explained that sixteen people were on board, that the generators were down, and they were dead in the water. He then added, "We have six feet of water on board and are taking on an additional one foot of water per hour."

Wes and Mike exchanged glances. This news was worse than they expected.

"What is your plan of action?" asked Wes to *Bounty*.

"We think we can make it to dawn. If we don't have assistance at seven thirty a.m., we will abandon ship in the daylight."

The C-130 was still approximately fifty miles away, and although the wind strengthened with each passing mile, the commander felt it was well within the capabilities of his aircraft. Wes had flown in worse. Now he worried that if *Bounty*'s battery-operated radio died, he needed to be close enough to get a visual on the ship to make sure it was still afloat.

Through his night-vision goggles Wes could see the tops of clouds, and they didn't appear to be the cumulonimbus type known as thunderstorm clouds. Although the winds rose to eighty knots and the turbulence worsened, Wes didn't think the weather was convective—the type that could sheer the plane's wings off in the blink of an eye. He guided the aircraft ever deeper into the storm toward the foundering ship, asking his mission system operators if they could see *Bounty* on radar. They answered no, the waves were simply too big. Wes then asked Mike to take over the controls and to slowly descend toward the location of the ship, while the commander radioed Sector North Carolina, giving them a complete briefing.

As Mike decreased altitude, the wind eased to sixty knots, yet the gusts became more frequent and severe, causing the plane to shudder and lurch. The autopilot had long since been switched off, and Mike flew by hand controls. Descending through walls of clouds, the aircraft yawed violently to the left as the wind shifted direction. As Mike countered to get the plane back on track, the clouds released their load of rain, pelting the windshield so hard the pilots felt as if it could shatter at any moment. Despite wearing noise-canceling headsets, the pilots clearly heard the roar of the pounding and now knew they really were in the grips of the monster hurricane.

With the rain, the turbulence increased to yet another level, and the C-130's wings flexed up and down by as much as four feet, as unseen punches rocked the plane. Anything not strapped down hurled across the cockpit and the cargo area.

Suddenly, a gust of wind, stronger than anything yet experienced, hit the plane on the nose, shooting it upward two hundred feet. Then, as soon as the gust passed, the aircraft plummeted four hundred feet before Mike could bring it back under control. Anyone feeling nauseated earlier was now vomiting. Torrents of rain made for zero visibility, and the crew in the back could only sit tight and put their faith, and their lives, in the hands of the two men in the cockpit.

The *Bounty* crew was ecstatic to learn that a coast guard plane had made radio contact with John Svendsen and was just a few miles away. It gave them hope at a time when conditions were deteriorating fast. Maybe the plane could drop pumps, maybe it could find a commercial ship to assist in a rescue, but most important, they were no longer alone in the storm.

In the meantime, there was still a battle to be fought on board the ship.

Doug Faunt found himself working in the engine room and at any other jobs where electrical issues called for his expertise. He was summoned to turn off the bilge alarm. Everyone knew the water was high. The alarm contributed nothing but noise.

Faunt was the onboard expert with radios. He attempted to use the single-sideband unit. It failed. He knew it had not been checked before *Bounty* departed New London. That would have been his job and he was busy installing electric lights in various cabins. There was no way of knowing now whether the radio had been functional when Walbridge announced his decision to leave the dock.

The crew tried the satellite telephone, with little success. They had been able to send email through their Winlink system. But the older satellite telephone was not functioning.

Laura Groves had spent time nailing boards over the Great Cabin windows that had blown out earlier. She organized a crew—Claudene Christian, John Jones, Anna Sprague—that gathered tools and battery chargers from the bosun's locker and secured five-gallon paint buckets there. But then the sole boards began floating, moving, threatening injury or worse. Groves and her crew took everything they had gathered to the tween deck, storing some of it in the galley.

Although there was no official proclamation, the bilge and the lower deck were surrendered to the rising water well before midnight.

Up in the C-130, Wes still had on his NVGs and hoped he might see the ocean when the plane descended to a thousand feet, but the cloud ceiling was lower than that. He took the controls back from Mike and put the plane in a racetrack pattern, coaxing the C-130 slowly downward toward a five-hundred-foot altitude. Going lower than that was not an option, not with the aircraft rising and falling precipitously with each sudden wind gust. He had been told *Bounty*'s masts were approximately 150 feet tall, and he didn't want to verify that information the hard way.

Suddenly through a break in the clouds the commander saw waves, large waves, some cresting at an astonishing thirty feet. But what really got his attention was that the waves were coming from all directions, as if the giant rollers were battling one another for supremacy. The night-vision goggles made the scene especially eerie: the waves and sky were a dark green, but the streaking foam and churning wave tops were bright and clearly visible, clashing and smashing into one another. Wes wondered how in the world any vessel, much less one taking on considerable water, could stay afloat in such chaos.

Up ahead and off to the right, a beam of light rose from the ocean, and Wes carefully banked the plane in that direction. A sailor on *Bounty* was shining a handheld flashlight at the aircraft. Mike, sitting in the right seat, saw the ship first and with awe in his voice said, "There she is."

The ship was out of Wes's line of sight, and he asked the copilot what it looked like.

"Well," said Mike, "it looks like a big pirate ship in the middle of a hurricane."

As the C-130 roared past *Bounty*, Wes made a wide turn to bring the aircraft back over the ship. This time Wes had a perfect view of the vessel, and he thought how Mike's description was perfect. The ship was listing about forty-five degrees to starboard, and enormous waves smashed into her, sending spray up into the sky, where it was snatched by the wind. *This is surreal,* Wes thought, *the ship looks like it's part of a movie set.*

His glimpse lasted only a couple seconds before the aircraft zipped past *Bounty*, but Wes had seen enough to know that the ship was in far worse trouble than merely taking on water. It seemed to the commander that the very next wave might put the vessel completely on its side.

CHAPTER TWENTY-ONE

THE DANGEROUS HOURS

Midnight came, and in the blackness off Cape Hatteras, North Carolina, it was Monday, October 29, 2012. *Bounty*'s entire crew was gathered on the tween deck. The water was six feet or more above where the engine-room sole boards, now floating, once made a floor. Giant, lethal waves sloshed within the fore and aft crew quarters, the bosun's locker, the lazaret, and all the other compartments at that level. Everywhere below, sole boards slammed into bulkheads and interior walls, unrestrained.

On the weather deck, conditions were worse. *Bounty* heeled steeply to starboard, her deck slick, as if greased, with salt spray, her bow bucking up and plunging down. There was no need to be on deck. There were no sails to man, no forward progress to threaten a collision.

Everything that could be salvaged from the compartments below the tween deck had already been brought up. It was piled in heaps in the galley and to the rear of the stairway leading up to the Nav Shack and the weather deck above.

The only work left was to man the trash pump, and only a few hands were needed in that increasingly futile endeavor.

Everyone was exhausted. Sleeping had been difficult to impossible for more than twenty-four hours, and the situation wasn't going to improve. Walbridge gave instructions for everyone who had no duties to get some rest.

If no one had announced it, almost everyone knew: *Bounty* was doomed.

The coast guard had told the ship that although the call had gone out, no ships were closer than eight hours away, and none were headed toward *Bounty* bringing dewatering pumps. The old collier was on its own, and the water kept rising. Robin Walbridge acknowledged the fate of the love of his life, if only obliquely. He let the crew know that when—not if—the water rose to the tween deck, everyone would be required to get into an immersion suit.

It was a tribute to Walbridge's foresight that *Bounty* had at least thirty of what are popularly called survival suits—neoprene, red Gumby suits that provide flotation and warmth and visibility—in a deck box on the weather deck or stored in a cabin on the port side of the tween deck, aft of the Nav Shack stairway. The small suits—the ones to fit Claudene Christian, who stood five feet one inch, and Laura Groves, five-four—were in the red bags, medium in orange, and large in green. No one was assigned to a specific suit, but there were more than enough to choose from.

While the water was still below the tween-deck sole, Chief Mate Svendsen told Bosun Groves to distribute seasick pills to the crew. She began making the rounds, offering a pill to each crew member. Walbridge, who was having trouble walking but was still mobile, declined. Barksdale, already seasick, took one and vomited.

Then the bosun, who had earlier organized a crew to collect essential goods from the lower deck, organized another crew to locate safety gear. They brought all of the life jackets from a cabin and tied many of them together so that, thrown into the water, the orange fabric of the jackets would make a large, visible target for possible rescuers. They filled plastic construction bags with bottles of water, canned food, personal dry bags, and tied them closed so they would float.

The power was failing and then returning, so the work was conducted under the light of individual headlamps. Almost no one was napping. Barksdale was still working on the trash pump, aided by a couple of crew members. Prokosh was still lying on a mattress on the starboard side of the Great Cabin, forward from the Nav Shack stairs. Third Mate Dan Cleveland was keeping watch in the Nav Shack companionway, and Svendsen and Sanders were taking turns manning the VHF radio, keeping communications alive with the circling coast guard C-130.

People were vividly aware of their precarious situation, and fear was unsettling the once-happy crew.

A few hours earlier, Joshua Scornavacchi had been having fun. The fore course had ripped and he was up in the mast, rain like hail blinding his vision, wind driving his arms and body against the rigging. It was thrilling, awesome.

Now was different. Scornavacchi was nervous, uncertain, although the situation was clear. The water was almost to the tween deck, and the time was almost at hand when the crew—and he—would pull on the immersion suits he had helped bring out of storage from a tween-deck cabin. But when would it happen, the evacuation? He didn't know.

Most of all, though, Scornavacchi was tired. Thinking was difficult. The morning before, the captain had promised a day without work parties. But then, things began happening, events that demanded work. Man the pumps constantly. Climb the rigging. Steer the boat until it was hove to, and then, as the boat rocked and tilted, give the hard physical effort demanded for even the smallest movement across a deck.

That was Sunday, all day. Now on Monday morning the work was ongoing. Scornavacchi still did not nap. He went to help with the trash pump.

Meanwhile, some water accumulated on the low side of the tween deck, where Prokosh lay on a mattress. Claudene Christian, who had been visiting him regularly, giving him updates, helped him to his feet and supported him as he climbed the sloped deck to a cabin on the port side. There he was put in a bunk somewhat drier than the soggy mattress.

At about three o'clock in the morning, Walbridge called his crew together near the Nav Shack. Standing on the stairway and looking down—as he had done four afternoons before from the Nav Shack roof in New London—he asked them to brainstorm, to answer a question: At what point did we lose control?

One thing was clear to Laura Groves: two seams in the topside planking were open. One was in the engine room on the port side. The other was above a mop closet above the waterline forward on the starboard side. For hours on end, water had been squirting and hissing through those seams, water that remained inside *Bounty*'s groaning hull while the bilge pumps sputtered ineffectively. She knew this, but she did not attempt to answer Walbridge's question.

Nor did anybody else offer Walbridge an answer. Indeed, most of the crew were so mentally wasted that few even knew a question was being asked.

The meeting broke up, and many in the crew, unwilling to embrace sleep, gravitated to the only place with some action still: the trash pump. Now the pump was on the weather deck, and Barksdale and others worked feverishly, yanking the pull cord, attempting to start it. Suddenly, the pump sputtered to life.

The crew cheered wildly.

Thirty seconds later, the pump—and then the crew—fell quiet.

Now the muted conversations on *Bounty* centered on one theme. The crew would wait until daylight, then conduct an orderly transfer into the two twenty-five-man life rafts mounted at the stern on a grating just in front of the aft caprail.

Scornavacchi, waiting in the area where he had helped pile the immersion suits, looked into the last cabin on the port side—Walbridge's state room. He saw the captain holding a picture, staring at it. It seemed to be a portrait of Claudia McCann, his wife.

Walbridge was in his late forties when he found McCann, the woman who would earn his trust, who could accept life on his terms. For most of his first four decades, he had been rebelling against the most significant woman in his life, Anna Palmer Walbridge, his mother. For many years, he thought she was the worst of mothers, a person who was too far removed from her own childhood to comprehend what it was like to be a child or to be her son.

Robin Walbridge remembered that when he was a child his mother had once gotten him up before daybreak to see a circus train arriving in town, watch the elephants raise the big top, and eat frozen peanut butter sandwiches she had made in haste. He resented her for disrupting his sleep when he was ten to watch the Sputnik satellite pass overhead. He carried a grudge because, when he was sixteen, she had made him promise he would finish high school.

He believed his childhood was a miserable one, and when he left home, he did not return to see her. But then, in his late thirties, a woman he was seeing asked him why he hated his mother.

He realized he had no good answer, and so he invited his mother to visit him. It had been so long that he didn't recognize her at the airport.

There the bitterness evaporated, replaced by a warmth that always had been in the captain's heart, a warmth subsequently fanned by monthly phone calls. When he stopped hating, he began using his native talent for analysis, coming to realize that his mother had her own issues and, as a mother, she did the best she could raising her children. If he had children of his own, he would want to give them the same good experiences that his mother gave him because she shaped him into an adult who liked himself.

This was the man whom Scornavacchi saw gazing at a photograph of a woman. He did not intrude on the skipper's private thoughts. He moved on.

Moments later, Prokosh, who had been in the bunk on the port side for only a few minutes, got the word that Walbridge had issued the order: Put on your immersion suits. He crawled across the slant of the deck to a suit and, lying in pain from his injured back, shook it from its bag, unrolled it, and began pulling it over his shoes.

His pain was too intense for him to stand, so Prokosh waited for the water to actually rush into the tween deck—waited lying on the deck boards while, around him, the rest of the crew milled about like a race of obese beings in their ridiculously bulky suits.

The officers pulled on the legs of the suits and zipped the fronts up to their waists, leaving their hands free to help the rest of the crew, who now assembled by the Nav Shack stairs, the only reasonable place to leave the tween deck when encumbered this way.

Each crew member selected from the pile of suits one that fit him or her. Scornavacchi, who would have fit in a small suit, chose a medium to be sure that Claudene and Laura were well suited. The crew members helped each other stretch the neoprene to stuff their hands into the gloved arms. Even now, calm prevailed. There was no urgency to get on deck. *Bounty* was riding evenly, if on a severe tilt, with the water now at least ankle deep on the high side of the tween deck, deeper to leeward.

As was often the case aboard *Bounty*, word spread among crew members, this time suggesting that climbing harnesses and life jackets were to be worn outside the immersion suits. The coast guard, circling above now in the C-130, routinely asks a vessel in distress whether its occupants are wearing life jackets. In this case, jackets would be redundant since everyone aboard was inside the greater protection of a Gumby suit. There was no direct order from Walbridge to don a life jacket, but most crew members heard the spreading word. At the same time, the explanation circulated that harnesses would allow them to clip together once they had abandoned ship. They could bring along personal "ditch" bags, shackled to the harness, so they could save possessions they felt were vital.

Getting into harnesses and life jackets once the crew members were inside the immersion suits was cumbersome and demanded more cooperation. One crew member had a multitool that had a set of pliers. He used this to help tighten harnesses that the wearers were unable to adjust on their own.

Doug Faunt, in his cabin forward of Walbridge's, put on an extra layer of warm clothing before he got into his suit.

Claudene Christian, in the next cabin, stepped into a size small.

Jessica Hewitt reminded people around her to strap the legs tight with the Velcro straps around the ankles so that walking would be easier.

Scornavacchi felt lost in his massive medium-size suit.

But it still was not time to climb up to the dangers of the weather deck. That moment came after three o'clock in the morning, when the crew was shin deep in sloshing water.

Wes and Mike continued guiding the C-130 through the turbulence, hoping that each time they tried to reach *Bounty* the ship would still be afloat.

"*Bounty*, this is the coast guard C-130, do you copy?"

"This is *Bounty*, we hear you loud and clear."

"We can finally see you, and we are going to relay your predicament back to headquarters. In the meantime we're going to see about getting pumps to you and locate ships that can head to your position."

Wes played through the procedure of dropping pumps to a vessel taking on water. Normally that is done from an altitude of two hundred feet, a height from which the pump has a realistic chance of making it to the vessel. The pump is in a watertight canister with a long trailing line. If all goes as planned, the pump lands in the water and the line lands on the vessel's deck, where a sailor can grab it and haul the pump to the ship.

Wes factored in the sixty-five-knot winds and the enormous waves and quickly concluded that with *Bounty* a pump would have small chance of being recovered by the crew and would probably add a whole new element of danger for everyone involved. If Wes took the plane down to two hundred feet, he risked getting his entire crew killed, and he immediately dismissed that notion. He might get lucky by releasing the pump from five hundred feet, but if a *Bounty* crew member scrambled out on the steeply angled deck to retrieve the line, very possibly the sailor would be swept overboard. "I worried the pump would make things worse," recalled Wes. "The seventy-pound pump might plummet directly onto the deck like a missile, crashing through the planking and opening yet another spot for water to enter the vessel." Adding to his concern was that the heavy rain made visibility of the ship impossible until they were directly over it.

Wes made another pass over the ship, and when it briefly came into view, he noticed that the starboard-side rail was now completely submerged. He made up his mind about the pump. Because *Bounty* was taking on a foot of water an hour, Wes knew it needed a much larger pump than he had on the plane and probably several, operating simultaneously, to make a dent in the incoming water. Dropping one small pump would barely have an impact, and it wasn't worth risking the life of a *Bounty* crew member's racing out onto the pitching deck to grab a line. Wes relayed his decision back to Sector North Carolina, and they agreed.

"*Bounty*, this is CG C-130, how copy?"

"Loud and clear."

"In these winds it would be next to impossible to get a pump to you, and even if we got the trailing line on your deck, retrieving this one small pump would put the life of your crew members in jeopardy."

"Roger, we understand."

"What are your plans?"

"We are in survival suits. We have multiple EPIRBs and have two large life rafts. We hope to make it until daylight, when we can more safely get in the rafts. Each raft will have an EPIRB and a handheld VHF radio, but we can't guarantee they will work if they get wet. Are there any ships on the way?"

Wes had to tell them the truth. "Negative."

After an awkward silence, Mike Myers spoke with Svendsen, reviewing the plans for abandoning ship safely.

When the conversation was over, Sector North Carolina asked Wes for his ORM (Operational Risk Management, a numerical score to determine the risk factor to the aircraft and crew if they stayed on scene). Before Wes responded, he used his internal communication system to ask the entire crew how they were feeling. Dead silence. Wes suspected the crew were having difficulty with the turbulence, but their temporary silence confirmed it. Then one crew member said, "Sir, I know a few of us are feeling pretty sick."

"Roger," said Wes. "We're going to climb back up in altitude where the gusts are not as powerful. We will still have excellent comms with the sailing vessel."

Wes notified Sector that his risk analysis was that the crew and aircraft were taking a beating, but that they could continue the mission. His numerical score, based on factors such as airsickness, fatigue, visibility, turbulence, and the flight time, put him "in the red," which was cause for concern. Sector then confirmed that because the vessel's command thought they could make it to morning, it would be best to have the helicopter launch just before dawn. It was simply too dangerous to send a helo into Sandy at night. "Roger," said Wes. "But remember, we are going to need at least two helicopters, with sixteen people in life rafts."

Mike eased the aircraft back up to seven thousand feet and continued the racetrack pattern over the *Bounty*. Every now and then either Mike or Wes would ask *Bounty* for an update. Conditions were more stable at the higher altitude, and Wes hoped his crew, who were being knocked around in the belly of the plane, would get a better handle on their motion sickness. He knew they weren't going home anytime soon.

Bounty under sail was a handsome ship.

A view of *Bounty*'s deck and some of the rigging.

The Great Cabin belowdecks at the stern.

Captain Robin Walbridge, who made the fateful decision to leave New London, aboard *Bounty*.

On October 25, 2012, the day *Bounty* set sail on its eventual clash with Hurricane Sandy, Claudene Christian was on deck with the visiting sailors from the submarine *Mississippi* as they attempted to learn *Bounty*'s complex and elaborate rigging.

Doug Faunt was the most senior crew member on board.

These seas, encountered during *Bounty*'s November 2010 voyage to Puerto Rico, were, according to survivors of the final voyage, in the range of those that took her down during Sandy in 2012.

A few hours after *Bounty* rolled to her side, her masts began to rise as water spread throughout her hull.

The third coast guard helicopter arrived on the scene later in the morning and found *Bounty* in this position.

Rescue swimmer Daniel Todd was in the second helicopter to arrive on the distress scene.

C-130 pilot Wes McIntosh flew into the hurricane at night. Here he is receiving an award from Commandant of the Coast Guard Robert Papp.

The first helicopter to arrive on the emergency scene was crewed by (*left to right*) Randy Haba, Steve Cerveny, Jane Peña, and Michael Lufkin.

The second helicopter crew (*left to right*): Daniel Todd, Jenny Fields, Steve Bonn, and Neil Moulder.

After fifteen or twenty minutes, the commander decided it was time to descend to five hundred feet for a visual on *Bounty*. He hoped to see the ship listing at the same angle as before, but instead the vessel was farther on its side, with more green water sweeping over the deck. The ship's three massive masts were not all that far from the tops of the waves.

Wes became increasingly anxious about *Bounty*'s chances of making it to morning. Adding to his concern, Svendsen asked if any helicopters had launched. Wes responded that the helicopters would arrive in the morning if possible, that the hurricane winds were extremely dangerous for a helo to fly into at night and try a rescue.

It was now about 4:00 a.m. and the commander felt that conditions were deteriorating on *Bounty* faster than the sailors had anticipated. Wes decided it would be prudent to call Air Station Elizabeth City and tell Todd Farrell at the Operations Center exactly what was going on and paint a complete picture of the conditions so the helicopter pilots would have as much information as possible.

To Wes's surprise a helicopter copilot named Jane Peña picked up the phone rather than Todd. Wes explained, "Things are getting worse on board the vessel; before too long there will probably be people in the water."

He had Jane's full attention—she was part of the ready crew that would launch if need be. Wes described the powerful wind gusts and the three-story waves crashing in confused seas. As they ended the conversation, Wes added, "We are going to need another C-130 out here. We're running low on fuel. They should launch as soon as possible in case the worst happens."

Jane hung up the phone and looked at both Todd Farrell and Lieutenant Commander Steve Cerveny, who were standing next to her, listening to her side of the conversation. "Wes thinks the sailors might have to abandon ship before dawn. And he needs another C-130 out there ASAP."

While Todd got busy coordinating the next plane to launch, Steve said to Jane, "Well, I hope *Bounty* can make it to morning, but let's get our aircraft and crew ready to go at a moment's notice, just in case." Jane gave a tense nod. This would be her first major helicopter rescue, and the flying conditions would be unlike anything she'd ever remotely experienced. She could feel the excitement and anticipation building in her and hoped they would launch soon.

On board the C-130, Mike Myers talked with Sector. He was asked to relay a message to *Bounty* and picked up the radio:

"Another C-130 is coming. Would two P-100 pumps be enough to dewater the ship and keep it afloat?"

Svendsen responded with a sense of humor, "Two P-100s would be nice, but two P-250s would even be better."

Myers sensed that behind the gallows humor Svendsen was deadly serious that only the largest of pumps could even have a chance at saving *Bounty*. Myers's heart went out to the mariners, and he stayed on the radio, talking and trying to keep the sailors' spirits up. Although Mike had only just been qualified to fly C-130s for six weeks, he did have thirteen years of experience flying helicopters, and this offered him a unique perspective of the different emotional involvement that being in a C-130 had compared to a helo. The helicopter crews usually have a much shorter interaction with those in distress: the helo would arrive on scene, locate the target, and execute the rescue as quickly as possible. But now, on board the C-130, Mike would be on scene for hours and had already formed an emotional connection with the crew. "It was painful," Mike later recounted, "to experience their highs and lows."

CHAPTER TWENTY-TWO

A RUSHED AND URGENT CALL

Doug Faunt was in the Nav Shack when he heard Walbridge give the order. *We only have one way to get on deck,* the captain noted, *so as many as possible should be on deck.*

Faunt didn't need more prompting. He began climbing the starboard flight of steps in the companionway.

Hewitt was right there with him. She had been uncomfortable—feeling trapped—in her immersion suit belowdecks. Adam Prokosh, despite his pain, was with her, climbing.

John Svendsen was in the Nav Shack, and as his crewmates passed, he called out their names: "Prokosh on deck!"

One by one, they filed to the weather deck with little hysteria. Still wearing their suits halfway, Cleveland and Groves stood on deck at the Nav Shack entrance, directing traffic toward the windward deck—the high side—some going forward to brace themselves on structures in front of the Nav Shack, others heading aft, toward the life rafts.

The wind had abated some, to perhaps forty knots, still strong enough to make the rigging sing and roar, to stifle conversation with its volume. But the seas were still huge. With her bowels filled with a heavy ballast of salt water, *Bounty* rode smoothly. A full moon above lit the edges of the racing clouds, enough light that the crew could see their ship leaning forty-five degrees to starboard, see the waves all around them, as if they were sitting deep in a valley with dark mountains on every side and only the silvery sky above.

As they made their way to the weather deck, some of the crew members formed a line and handed up the gear that the bosun had assembled in plastic bags, the life jackets that were tied together in orange rafts.

Walbridge and Svendsen remained in the Nav Shack as the exodus continued. Then the captain asked Anna Sprague, one of the last to go on deck, to help him into the top of his survival suit. He followed her to the weather deck, which slanted up like a steeply pitched roof, and sat down on two yards that had been lashed there to the deck, near his bosun, Laura Groves, waiting for morning to arrive, the time when he would dictate an orderly departure.

Moments later, Svendsen came on deck. He had been watching the starboard rail. It had dipped under the waves. With so much water in her, *Bounty* was leaning farther and farther on her side. The chief mate knew his captain wanted to avoid abandoning ship during the night, hoped to conduct that final desertion of his beloved *Bounty* when daylight would make it safer. But now the caprail was submerged, and Svendsen sensed that the time was at hand.

Despite the roaring wind, Laura Groves heard it clearly.

"It's time to go," Svendsen told Walbridge.

The captain did not respond, so the chief mate waited a half minute and repeated his suggestion, his plea.

Again Walbridge ignored the warning.

When for the third time in two minutes Svendsen asked Walbridge to order the crew into the life rafts, the captain agreed. Svendsen returned to the Nav Shack to alert the C-130 flying above. The word began to spread across the ship. The crew would launch the two rafts and attempt a controlled descent from the deck.

It was too late. With a suddenness bordering on petulance, the ship leaned hard to starboard, as if in response to the skipper's betrayal, dropping its masts in the ocean, bringing its deck to vertical. Anyone not thoroughly braced instantly fell into the sea. Others clung to the nearest fixed object, desperately trying to postpone their own baptism.

Laura Groves had just helped Dan Cleveland into the top half of his immersion suit when *Bounty* lurched. There was no space in her awareness between her efforts to secure Cleveland's safety gear and the instant when she found herself in the ocean.

Joshua Scornavacchi had settled on the port side of the fife rail around the mainmast, his feet braced on the rail, his back lying on the tilted deck. Claudene Christian was beside him, and she smiled at him. Then she scampered aft, toward another group of crew members. Scornavacchi closed his eyes, and a moment later when he opened them, he saw his fellow sailors hanging like so much laundry from various lines and railings. Scornavacchi himself was standing on the now-horizontal balusters of the fife rail, the once-tilted deck a vertical wall behind him. He worked his way down the deck toward the water and then jumped.

Prokosh, at the stern behind the helm, saw the big wheel go under the water and thought, *This is where I get off.* He allowed himself to slide down onto the helm and then jumped toward a clear patch of water, hoping to avoid getting entangled in the rigging.

Jessica Hewitt had fallen asleep near the helm. She awoke to see water directly before her.

Jessica Black heard someone yell "She's going!" and sensed what was happening. She wanted to be in control of her destiny, so she let go and fell into the sea.

Svendsen, still in the Nav Shack calling the coast guard, was caught by a flood of sea, a waterfall coming into the companionway. He fought against it, made it to the deck. Before him he saw Robin Walbridge, a life jacket strapped over his immersion suit, walking aft—walking, not crawling, because while the deck was vertical, there were horizontal surfaces such as the fife-rail balusters.

The chief mate found the nearest mast, now horizontal, and climbed along it, away from the deck, away from his captain, away from *Bounty*.

Just prior to *Bounty*'s lying on her side, Wes and Mike alternated flying the C-130 above the ship, sometimes flying at five hundred feet to get a visual and sometimes at seven thousand to give their team less of a pounding. The two pilots knew the turbulence was considerably rougher on the crew than on themselves. The pilots were so focused on flying the plane and exchanging information with both *Bounty* and Sector that it was easy to ignore the stomach-churning dips and rises of the plane. Most of their crew, however, were in standby mode, waiting to see how things played out. If the vessel stayed afloat until the helos arrived, their role would stay modest, but should *Bounty* sink before dawn, they'd be scrambling with a number of tasks. But for now they had plenty of undistracted time to experience the full nauseating effects of their roller-coaster ride.

Suddenly at 4:45 a.m. Svendsen's voice boomed into the cockpit of the C-130. "We are abandoning ship! We are abandoning ship!"

Wes's heart skipped a beat. All previous calls had been calm and collected, but this one was rushed and urgent. He grabbed the radio. "*Bounty*, this is CG 130, tell us what is happening."

Silence.

Chills went down Wes's back. "*Bounty,* this is CG 130, how copy?"

Silence.

"*Bounty*, are you getting into life rafts?"

Dead air.

Wes switched to another channel. "HMS *Bounty*, this is coast guard C-130, how copy?

No response.

Wes cursed under his breath and made eye contact with Mike. He knew this was not the orderly abandoning of ship everyone had hoped for. Svendsen clearly had just a second to get his distress call out. Something sudden and cataclysmic had happened, and Wes wondered if anyone got off the ship alive.

Adrenaline shot through every vein of Wes McIntosh, and he had to fight back a surge of nervous energy. He had formed a bond with the people on *Bounty*, particularly with Svendsen on the radio. *This whole night it's been just us and the* Bounty *alone out in this black mess, and now it might be all over. It sure didn't sound like they had time to get in life rafts.* Wes was certain the ship had capsized, but the people could be either in the water or trapped inside the ship.

The plane was up at seven thousand feet, and while Mike took the controls and started descending, one of the MSOs radioed Sector that *Bounty* sailors were abandoning ship and communication had been lost.

Then Wes spoke on the internal communications system to his crew: "They're abandoning ship. You know what we need to do now."

They needed to get life rafts in the water immediately. This is where drop master Joshua Vargo and basic aircrewman Eric Laster earned their pay, no matter how motion sick they were. The two men had trained for months with the Air-Sea Rescue Kit (ASRK), which includes eight-man life rafts and survival bags stuffed with water packs, patches for the life rafts, space blankets, whistles, flares, and strobes. Now they had to drag the equipment toward the rear of the plane where the giant cargo ramp could be lowered. The turbulence caused the men to stagger, and when a particularly strong air gust hit, the floor beneath them fell away and they were airborne, lucky to come down on their feet and not break an ankle.

Meanwhile, Wes entered data into a computer to help calculate a release point. The emergency equipment would be useless if it landed far from *Bounty*. The MSOs worked the radio making continuous callouts to the foundering vessel, hoping against all odds for an answer.

Vargo's voice came over the internal communication set: "Mr. McIntosh, we have completed our checklist and have the equipment in place."

"Roger," answered Wes. "We are descending to five hundred feet and are depressurizing the plane."

The C-130 barreled out of the clouds at 150 knots, and *Bounty* appeared below them, lying flat on her side, like a once-proud racehorse that's been put down. Everyone in the aircraft stared out rain-slashed windows trying to pick out survivors. Debris littered the ocean. One of the crew members shouted, "I see a raft!" Then another hollered, "There's a second raft at two o'clock!"

In addition to the two rafts being carried away from *Bounty* on the enormous waves, the crew also saw multiple strobe lights blinking in the water, but they couldn't see people. It was an awful sight for the crew members to take in, especially not knowing if survivors were attached to the strobes or in the rafts. Worst of all, the strobes spread out in all directions around the crippled ship, and soon they would be far apart.

As the plane zoomed past the debris field, Wes banked it to return to the site, trying hard not to grip the controls too tightly as the aircraft groaned and shuddered, battered by varying wind gusts. Keeping the plane in any kind of steady flight was impossible, and the altitude indicator jumped wildly. Wes gave the ocean a wide berth, trying to keep the plane as close to five hundred feet as possible.

Myers radioed Sector, "We've visually confirmed that the ship has capsized, it's on its side. We have seen two rafts, and many strobe lights in the water, but unsure where the people are. We are deploying the ASRK."

Wes gave Vargo the okay to open the ramp door and told him they were circling back to *Bounty*, and Wes would give the command when to drop two rafts.

A thousand feet of line connected the two rafts, with the hope that a survivor could grab the line and pull himself or herself to safety. Vargo and Laster began opening the ramp, and the roar of the wind was deafening. Each man wore a harness with a tether fixed to the aircraft wall. Should they slip and fall, this would keep them inside the aircraft and prevent them from free-falling into the sea. They double-checked each other's harness and tether, just to make sure.

Moving the rafts to the open cargo doorway, the two men fought back their motion sickness as best they could. The rear of the aircraft took the brunt of the turbulence, and the men found it impossible to stand without holding on to the walls of the plane. Nausea got the best of one of the men, and he vomited, causing the rain-soaked floor by the ramp to become even more slippery.

Over the headset, Wes alerted Vargo and Laster that they were coming up on *Bounty* and to get ready. Normally Wes would have his drop master release the rafts about thirty yards upwind of the target, but that's based on twenty-knot winds and an altitude of two hundred feet. Now, at an altitude of five hundred feet with sixty- and seventy-knot buffeting gusts, the commander knew the drop should happen farther upwind. He used the information provided by the computer along with his own experience to estimate the proper distance ahead of the target where the release should take place.

When Wes saw *Bounty* almost directly below them, he waited about five seconds then ordered, "Drop! Drop! Drop!"

Vargo and Laster shoved the first raft out of the plane, counted off two seconds, then pushed the second into the black void. The two-second interval between the rafts was to ensure they did not become tangled. They wanted the rafts to land in different spots with the tether between them. Usually the drop master can see if his drop is accurate, but with pelting wind and darkness the rafts were swallowed by the night before they hit the water. The two men inched back away from the doorway, thankful to have avoided a mishap at the outer lip of the ramp.

Wes circled back around and through his NVGs could see that the two coast guard rafts had landed just where he had wanted them to, near the debris field. But the wind wasn't going to allow them to stay there for long. Although the rafts had drogue chutes designed to drag aft and slow their drifting, the rafts still blew end over end.

CHAPTER TWENTY-THREE

THE FIRST RAFT

Order had turned into chaos. Human voices were shouting where before the only sounds were from savage nature and its assault on the foundering old ship. In an instant, the sea rose from the starboard bulwark, enveloping half the crew, from deckhands to deck officers.

The order that had marked life aboard *Bounty* had vanished. In its place was the bedlam of unrestrained nature.

The drills that had been so much a part of *Bounty*'s order—the practice and repetition that had made it seem to Adam Prokosh that *Bounty* was a finely organized vessel with great communication—all that regimentation evaporated.

Had Walbridge recognized in time the imminence of disaster, perhaps there could have been an orderly evacuation into the life rafts. But the captain with the unquestioned expertise thought he and his crew could make it to daylight. When they could not, all the planning and the practice were worth nothing. If they were going to survive, the crew members now had only themselves and their will to live—and a couple of life rafts that plunged overboard with the rest of them—to give them any hope.

One group of seven would find one raft. A separate group of six would locate another raft. But in the darkness and the tumult—in the utter confusion as each man and woman went from membership in the *Bounty* family to struggling mortal amid thrashing rigging and surging seas—their paths to those life rafts were anything but obvious.

The new yards that Dan Cleveland had fashioned in Boothbay Harbor had been stored on deck, to the port side of the capstan and near the Nav Shack companionway. Several crew members, when they arrived on the steeply pitched deck in their immersion suits, used these long shafts to brace their feet. Anna Sprague and Mark Warner were sitting there, not far from the Nav Shack, as was Second Mate Matt Sanders. Claudene Christian came from the mizzen fife rail, where she had been lying back next to Josh Scornavacchi, and joined Sanders. Cleveland and Laura Groves were in front of this group, near the companionway, and then Captain Walbridge emerged from the Nav Shack and stood with his third mate and bosun. Everyone was settled in, knowing that when the order was given, they would abandon ship.

Then *Bounty* rolled to starboard and the water rose. Sanders saw Walbridge hit the water and watched the captain get washed back and forth by the wave action, but Sanders was unable to move, to give aid. His feet were trapped in the yards.

"What do I do? What do I do?" Christian pleaded with her struggling friend.

"Claudene, you just have to go for it! You have to make your way aft and get clear of the boat!" Sanders shouted, and he watched Claudene make her way to the fife rail. A second or two later he freed his feet, and he, too, headed aft, toward the helm. Claudene was out of sight and Sanders climbed past the big wooden wheel and leaped off *Bounty*'s stern.

Sprague was able to stand on the yards when the deck tilted to vertical. Without contemplation, she jumped in the water, landing in front of where the mizzenmast was in the water. There she reunited with Warner and, moments later, John Jones, and they saw a life raft canister and talked about deploying the packed raft.

Without warning, the mizzenmast began to rise, surfacing directly under Jones, whose legs straddled the spar as the ship rolled to port and the mast hoisted him into the air.

Doug Faunt had been one of the first on deck in his immersion suit, working his way back to the helm. As the water rose around him, he swam away from the ship, but not clear of its rigging. Twice he was shoved under. He feared being drawn under permanently if the swamped ship plunged to the depths. Now things appeared like pictures in a slide show, disconnected except for the setting, coming over what period of time—seconds, minutes, hours—he did not know. He looked up and saw the broken spanker gaff, a ragged sword poised over his head. He saw a life ring that seemed to be still attached to the boat, then a life-raft canister that he could not open. Then he saw an inflated life raft and swam to it. Low as he was in the water, he could not see the raft's canopy. He hung on to it, though, and the raft, riding on rough waters, separated his shoulder.

Jessica Black had come on deck shortly after Faunt. As she passed through the Nav Shack, Svendsen had strapped on her life vest. She ended up with her feet braced against the mizzen fife rail, near Scornavacchi, and then she was in the water, grasping for things to hold on to. She came upon Scornavacchi, who was near a life-raft canister. She tried to rip the raft's tether to deploy it, but she lost her grip and drifted away from the raft and Scornavacchi. She was aware of where one of the masts—probably the mizzen—was slashing into the water and wanted to escape it, so she swam. Then she thought, *I'm clear of the ship, but where's the life raft?*

Some of the waves were bigger than others as Black swam blindly. When she rose to the crest of one huge wave, she looked down and saw before her, as if at the bottom of a hill, a life raft. She still had her life vest, but the waist strap had detached and the vest was beside her. Sighting the raft ahead, the cook stiffened her body and surfed down the face of the wave toward the raft, thinking as she went that if she was not precise, she could overshoot—and lose—the chance for survival that the raft presented.

Her aim was accurate, and when she reached the raft, she found Faunt.

Joshua Scornavacchi had come on deck feeling incredibly restricted in his oversize immersion suit and feeling depleted from the work required to get into it. Just outside the Nav Shack, he encountered Cleveland and Groves, shouting orders, attempting to direct traffic. Their words were swept away in the howl of the wind. He moved to port and aft, waiting for the ship to roll to port, moving when the deck became more level. He moved the short distance to the mizzen fife rail, where he lay with his back on the deck, his feet braced against the rail.

Scornavacchi knew that Claudene Christian had left the Nav Shack behind him, and that she followed him to the fife rail. They had boarded *Bounty* the same weekend in May in Philadelphia, Christian for the first time, Scornavacchi the second. During the five months since, when Scornavacchi would nap on *Bounty*'s deck, Christian would check on him. Now she checked, smiled, and then, crouching, waited for the moment and scurried aft, where some crew were tying all the gathered emergency supplies together in one giant bundle. The heap had over a hundred life jackets lashed with other supplies.

Scornavacchi, who had put some gear in an empty immersion-suit bag and clipped it to his harness, watched Christian until she reached the other group. Around him crew members were in the midst of motioning others toward the stern, the life rafts. Then he looked up at the sky, the racing, silver-lined clouds, and closed his eyes for a moment. When he opened them, he saw the ship rolling swiftly to starboard, bringing him to a standing position on the fife rail. Unfolding before him, the ship and the sea were conducting an uncoordinated evacuation of *Bounty*. Some crew members slid down the deck into the water. Some were holding on to lines or rails and dangling in space. These were not individuals, just red immersion suits. He couldn't tell which suits contained which friends.

Scornavacchi controlled his descent, climbing down to a spot between the mizzen and main masts. Frozen in place, he saw someone already in the water, another jumping overboard. He jumped, too, and when he did, someone—a woman still on the boat, he didn't know who—reached out and tried to grab his hand. Instantly he saw that the sea was littered with ship debris, pieces of wood, trash—a sloshing soup like, he thought, the bowl of an unflushed toilet. He reached to grab some floating debris and it was torn from his grip. In that first instant in the water, he felt himself being sucked under the ship, felt his boots being yanked from his feet inside his suit. In fact, he was being pulled bodily beneath the surface. A snarl of *Bounty*'s lines had wrapped around his ditch bag and was pulling him down. His survival gear was threatening to kill him.

In his work as a white-water rafting guide, Scornavacchi had learned to escape when he found himself getting sucked under by down currents. The technique was to swim while executing a barrel roll. Holding his breath, he tried the maneuver now, but it didn't work because he couldn't get the bag untangled from the ropes that held it and couldn't undo the shackle that fastened it to his harness.

Salt water mixed with diesel fuel in Scornavacchi's mouth. He ran out of breath, started coughing underwater, and involuntarily drew that foul mixture into his windpipe, perhaps his lungs. He felt his muscles quit working and believed he was drowning.

Anger filled him. He had promised his mother and his eleven-year-old brother that he wouldn't drown, and now he realized he would never see them again. Thoughts raced through his mind. If he was drowning, then everyone else from *Bounty* was probably dead. He couldn't understand why they hadn't boarded the rafts sooner. They should have gone to the rafts and paddled away.

Then the voice came. Maybe, he thought, it was God. It said, *It's not your time yet.* At that moment, the ditch bag released itself from his harness and he swam to the surface, where he saw the big mound of emergency supplies. He swam to it, clutched at it with his hands, tried to climb atop it, away from the snares of the sinking ship.

From out of the dark, Jessica Black appeared. It seemed she was asking him what to do. He urged her to climb the pile with him. But just then the mainmast—he knew its bottom section alone weighed over six tons—slammed down on the pile, launching Scornavacchi into the air. When he fell back in the water, Black was gone.

Alone, he tried to swim away, but got another line wrapped around his leg. He removed it, then saw the mizzenmast in the water nearby. He grabbed the spar and tried to pull himself away from the ship along it, to escape the debris, but the mast began to rise from the water as the ship rolled. In rising, it lifted him out of the water thirty feet.

"Jump!" a male voice yelled.

Scornavacchi didn't want to jump but he did, landing in a clear patch of water.

In the distance, he saw a life-raft canister, so he swam as hard as he could and reached it. As he worked to undo the canister, Johnny Jones—the Dudester—appeared and tried to yank the raft's tether to deploy it.

Jones and Scornavacchi worked on the raft canister but couldn't get it open. So they pushed it toward a spot where they thought there might be other crew members. High above, weird-looking clouds raced south and east. Down in the troughs between the waves, it was quiet, a startling absence of sound after the hours on end aboard *Bounty* amid the cacophony of the ship and the storm. Scornavacchi asked Jones if he had seen anyone else. He hadn't. All that was certain was that the two of them were alive.

Then the cook reappeared and grabbed on to the canister. But just as quickly as Jessica Black had arrived, a huge wave snatched her away again.

Now Jones told Scornavacchi that he had seen lights underwater, near where the ship was. They thought of returning to the ship to see if the lights meant other survivors, but they abandoned the idea because they could barely hold on to the canister, and they still were struggling to get it open.

As they fought to open the canister, an inflated life raft floated toward the two men. They swam to it and found Warner and Sprague already holding on to it.

Individually, the four each tried twice to climb into the raft. The opening was too high, and merely closing their hands in fists to hold on was close to impossible, draining all their strength.

While they were clinging to the raft, Sprague heard, from the direction of the ship, a woman calling.

"Help me! I'm caught," the voice pleaded. Sprague didn't know who it was. But the ship was far away. There was no way to get to it, Sprague thought.

Instead, she and her crewmates around the raft thought hard about how they could climb to the safety above the rubber tubes. Someone suggested Sprague might be the lightest. If the three men could push her high enough, perhaps she could crawl into the raft's door. It took time, but it worked. Sprague now pulled on Warner's harness, and although his immersion suit was weighed down by seawater, he clambered into the raft. The two inside the raft hauled Scornavacchi inside, and while they were bringing Jones aboard, Scornavacchi crossed the raft and looked out the far door. There he found Sanders, Faunt, and Black clinging to the side. The work was slow. It took half an hour or more in all. In the end, seven were aboard this twenty-five-man raft, sprawled across the floor.

They knew they were not yet safe. But each thought about the other nine crew members and wondered. Through the open door, they could see *Bounty*. They were being driven away from their ship, and they saw no one else in the water. Were they alone?

"Do you think everybody made it?" someone in the raft asked, the question they all were thinking.

Now Second Mate Sanders took charge: "Yep. They all made it."

Scornavacchi and Sprague now asked everybody to hold hands while they prayed. Then they asked if anyone else wanted to pray.

"I don't have faith in God," Faunt said, "but I have faith in the coast guard."

Now Scornavacchi began singing a sea shanty about going home, one the crew had sung in every port, the "Mingulay Boat Song" composed in the 1930s by Sir Hugh S. Roberton. It begins, "Heel y'ho, boys, let her go, boys."

The sailors would sing and then pray, but the ride was less than peaceful. Suddenly, a huge wave would hit the raft and fold it like a taco, throwing the seven into a heap on one side. Nor was there the silence they had experienced in the troughs. Back atop the waves, the sea was loud, violent.

The raft would unfold as the sailors spread themselves around and resumed casual conversations laced with jokes.

Bang! They were folded into a taco again.

They quickly adjusted to this new maritime routine. Fold, flatten, resume talking, as if nothing had happened.

And every once in a while, over the raft noise, they would find hope in a sound from above: the drone of a C-130.

CHAPTER TWENTY-FOUR

THE SECOND RAFT

Third Mate Dan Cleveland was near the Nav Shack companionway when he heard John Svendsen tell Robin Walbridge that the bow had gone underwater. Cleveland could not then have imagined how he and Laura Groves would find the same haven. But they did.

Cleveland, with his immersion suit zipped up only to his waist to leave his hands free, had been tying a loop in the end of a long line that—according to his plan—would be used to secure each crew member when, during the anticipated orderly evacuation, they transferred from the ship to a life raft. He finished with the loop, and Groves helped him zip up his immersion suit the rest of the way.

In the next instant, he felt the sea rise up and grab him from the deck. He saw his crewmates, who had been making their way aft toward the life rafts, tossed about, assaulted by loose or broken parts of the ship.

Then the third mate was floating in warm water, his gloved hands grabbing something—a wooden grating—his feet kicking, instinctively driving him away from the hostility of the rolling ship. Moments passed uncounted as he struggled against the sea, and then he found Groves. A current seemed to be taking them together forward along the side of the rolling ship, in the direction of the main- and foremasts, which, along with their miles of rope rigging, rose up out of the water, only to come slashing back into the sea, lethal clubs threatening to pummel the swimmers.

Groves had been struggling to keep her face out of the water when, in the moonlight, something—she didn't know what—struck her on the head. Time lost its meaning. There was only survival. Then there was Cleveland, clinging to the wooden grating.

Chris Barksdale, the seasick engineer who couldn't remember a time in his life when he wasn't on the water, was now in the water ninety miles offshore and got caught in the rigging once, twice, and then again and again as he fought to swim away. He struggled until he met Cleveland and Groves.

Adam Prokosh, incapacitated earlier, had made it to the weather deck and then back to the stern, near the life rafts and to port of the helm. When the deck reared to vertical, he let himself slide down to the helm. Then, injured or not, he decided it was time to jump. The boat was moving faster than the disabled seaman. A mast rose, streaming seawater from its rigging, then, like a tree felled by a logger, crashed back into the sea, into the now-littered water where a wooden grating that had washed off *Bounty*'s deck floated. The grating hit Prokosh in the head. Then a yard on the mast slammed him. He was driven under the surface, but managed, even with painful back injuries, to swim up, and when he broke the surface, he found fellow crew members nearby.

Jessica Hewitt had been near the helm. She had chosen not to wear a life jacket. She didn't want to be encumbered. But she and Drew Salapatek had connected their harnesses. Someone had suggested this. She thought that in those winds and seas, she would rather be clipped to him than holding his hand for safety. But then she was in the water and she was connected to no one.

Salapatek was standing on the stem grating when the boat went over. He had also attached a small dry bag to his climbing harness, and he had a life preserver around his neck and strapped behind his back. He was standing on the stern grating when the boat went over. He and Hewitt were able to step onto the now-horizontal side of the cabin trunk over the Great Cabin. Then the cabin side sank, an elevator going down, taking Salapatek and Hewitt below. They seemed to be snagged, perhaps by their harnesses and tethers. Salapatek was being held under the waves and was concerned about his survival. His first reaction was to rid himself of his harness—losing the connection to Hewitt. Still submerged, he curled his legs up and shoved the harness off with his hands.

Once he surfaced, Salapatek was alone in the water for time uncounted before he saw a group of immersion suits. He swam toward them, finding Hewitt and Groves and Cleveland. The three were clinging to the wooden grating when he joined them.

Sometime later, Prokosh and Barksdale joined these four. Then, next to *Bounty*'s hull, someone in the group spotted an inflated life raft. No one on board had deployed any of the rafts, so this one had to have been set free by its hydrostatic release when the deck went underwater. The raft floated toward them, and the six swam to it. But the wind that drove the raft moved it beyond their reach. Soon, they saw a life-raft canister floating nearby. Cleveland had tied a long rope to the canister earlier, and Barksdale found the rope and let the canister float away a distance before he yanked on it. The yanking triggered a CO_2 cartridge inside the canister, opening it and inflating the raft. What emerged was a twenty-five-person raft about thirteen feet in diameter with black rubber tubing and an orange canopy with 25 PERSON stenciled at its peak.

The gloves of the immersion suits were stiff, making it difficult to hold on to the rope, called a painter. Cleveland grabbed the line, wrapping it around his fist, and the rest of the swimmers joined in to form a chain, hauling on the line, drawing themselves closer to the raft.

Catching the life raft was exhausting. The swimmers wanted to take a break before climbing in, but they found no easy way to hold on. A line for that purpose circled the raft, but the clumsy immersion-suit gloves made grabbing it impossible until Groves got an idea and bit the line, pulling it with her teeth away from the inflated tubing far enough to slide her gloved hand up under the line. Then she hooked her forearm over the line and hung there, trying to relax, recover.

Climbing into a life raft might be easy in a swimming pool during training, as several of the crew members had done. Hewitt saw that in thirty-foot seas, there would be a challenge. But she noticed that everyone around her appeared to be calm, and she realized that she was not afraid. She felt safe in her immersion suit, floating beside the life raft far from shore at the edge of a passing hurricane.

Prokosh, injured and in pain, clipped the tether from his harness to the line encircling the raft, then lay on his back, trying to conserve what little strength he had left. The waves pushed him to the end of the ten-foot tether and he had no choice but to float while the rest of the group surrounded the raft with their elbows lopped through the raft's line.

Groves was the first to attempt to enter the raft, and she discovered a new issue. Her immersion suit had filled with water. Too much wet ballast was in the legs of her suit, too heavy a weight for her to climb aboard. Efforts by others to enter the raft failed until Salapatek got his knee onto Cleveland's thigh. It was just enough of a lift to get Salapatek's belly on top of the raft tube. He, too, had water in his survival-suit legs, but with Cleveland and the others shoving from below, he squirmed on his belly and got his torso into the raft.

Salapatek helped haul Cleveland aboard, and soon all were in the raft except Prokosh, who was tethered to the outside and content to stay there for fear of further aggravating his injured back and ribs. But he soon noticed the lifeline encircling the raft was pulling away from the raft. Each wave that hammered him tore the line away, and instead of ten feet from the raft he was now twelve feet away. *One big wave might tear the entire line free of the raft and I'm going to be washed away.* Now he had no choice and called out to the others to pull him in. When they had him next to the raft, several pairs of hands grabbed his harness. Adam gritted his teeth as searing pain shot down his back and through his chest as he was hauled inside.

Now the six of them rode up the faces of monstrous waves and slid down their backs, but they were inside the raft with the orange canopy above them, a fabric door to be zippered shut, with lots of room to move around. Emergency supplies were inside the raft, as well as a lot of seawater. Manacled by the immersion-suit gloves, the crew couldn't open the supplies, so Cleveland stripped down the top of his suit and, with his hands free, opened the supplies. The crew now began looking for a bailer but found none. They spread out to distribute their weight evenly, then opened water bottles within other supplies. When his bottle was empty, Cleveland started bailing with it. Although the seawater was warm, the third mate noticed that he was getting cold, so he pulled the top of his suit back on.

Occasionally, breaking waves would splash through the raft's opening. Although they tried, the crew members couldn't find a way to zip the opening shut. So the view of the sea outside as dawn arrived was a constant, and looking out the opening, they could from time to time see the previously inflated raft. They watched it drift farther and farther away.

Groves joined Cleveland, bailing with a water bottle. She had brought along one of the ship's EPIRBs and had it tied to her. Now and then, she held it out the unzipped raft opening. There was not much else to be done, though. The sailors knew the coast guard was flying a C-130 above. They knew that rescue helicopters should arrive.

So they relaxed, the mood even-tempered, no one noticeably emotional. They shared their experiences back in the water, their struggles against the sea and the rigging and the dark. They even joked about these events. They talked about what they were going to do when they got home.

In the silence between words came the sounds of the storm and, in passing moments, of the circling airplane. The sounds of danger and of hope.

It may have happened when the sea flooded down the top flight of steps into the Nav Shack. John Svendsen had returned there when his captain authorized the crew to abandon ship. He had grabbed the microphone of the VHF radio, pushed the button to talk, and called up to the crew of the C-130.

Then the ship rolled so far that the companionway was underwater, and the flood slammed down the steps, pummeling the chief mate. He fought his way against the flood, escaped to the weather deck, saw Walbridge walking aft along a once-vertical, now-horizontal surface, and finally chose his own, separate path, climbing out along a horizontal mast before he jumped in the water.

In this, Svendsen had suffered numerous injuries—his face was battered, he had trauma on his head and neck, broken bones in his right hand, and chest and abdominal trauma.

In the water, Svendsen was alone. He found an unopened life-raft canister, which he abandoned. Later, he found a strobe light and kept it with him. The strobe flashed in the dark. Daylight arrived and it continued to flash. Buoyed by his immersion suit, his distinctive long hair hidden inside the featureless hood, he floated, a piece of debris on a sea littered with similar trash—empty immersion suits among the timbers and gratings and rigging and, not that far away, the still-floating wreck of *Bounty*.

Unlike the other flotsam, this red dot with the blinking light had a pulse, although that was steadily slowing as hypothermia set in.

Peering out the rain-streaked aircraft windshield, Wes McIntosh turned his gaze from the coast guard rafts to *Bounty*'s rafts and noticed something that gave him a glimmer of hope. Two rafts from *Bounty* were not tumbling, and he thought maybe that was because people were inside.

Fuel was running low, and although Wes knew another C-130 would soon launch, he wasn't sure he could stay on scene until it arrived. Over the headset he instructed the drop master to release a self-locating marker buoy, which would electronically mark *Bounty*'s position for the other aircrews. Once that was done, there was nothing else to drop, and Wes ordered the drop master to close the ramp.

Flight mechanic Hector Rios said on the internal communications, "Mr. McIntosh, why don't we close the ramp using the flight-deck controls. Vargo and Laster are puking their brains out."

"Roger, that." Wes then told Vargo and Laster to move clear of the ramp area because Rios would use his controls to seal the plane, a process rarely used.

Mike Myers was on the radio with Sector, and he turned to Wes and said, "The other C-130 has already launched, and a Jayhawk will launch in a couple minutes."

For the first time since they'd arrived at the distress scene, Wes felt relief wash over him. It would be daylight soon, and if the *Bounty* sailors were still alive, these additional resources would find them and begin a rescue.

During the next half hour the C-130 alternated between flying at seven thousand feet for less turbulence and better communication with Sector and dropping down to five hundred feet to search for survivors. While the crew could still see several blinking strobe lights, which they now realized were attached to survival suits, it was nearly impossible to tell if anyone was in the suits.

It was still dark when the second C-130, flown by Commander Peyton Russell, neared the search scene. Russell was flying with co-pilot Aaron Cmiel, flight mechanic Corey Lupton, Mission System Operators (MSOs) David Dull and Lee Christensen, drop master Jonathan Sageser, and basic aircrewman Austin Black.

While en route, Russell was briefed on the radio by Wes and Mike. They described how *Bounty*'s radio operator had abruptly shouted, "We're abandoning ship!" how the vessel capsized, and that they didn't know for sure where the survivors were.

"There are strobe lights blinking in the water on survival suits," said Wes over the radio, "but it's difficult to tell if there are people in them. We have dropped two rafts, and there are also two rafts from the vessel. Our rafts have blinking beacons and the *Bounty*'s rafts have steady lights."

A few minutes later the second C-130 arrived, and Commander Russell took over as on-scene coordinator and immediately began searching the water for signs of life. Drop master Sageser, using his NVG, surveyed the debris field and couldn't shake the feeling that he was looking down inside a giant washing machine. He had done more than his share of search and rescues, but Sageser had never seen waves so confused, coming from all directions, creating what looked like endless miles of whitecapped mountains. *It's going to be tough to spot anyone in the water. That helo can't get here soon enough. They can hover and get a better look at each of the strobes.*

Wes got cleared to return to Raleigh because of his fuel situation. He first made one last pass over the life rafts and then over *Bounty*, where he saw a strange and haunting sight. To this point the vessel had been lying on its side, its masts battering the ocean's surface into a froth as waves made them rise and fall. Now the masts were straight up, pointing toward the C-130, as if the ship were coming back to life. Wes shook his head, wondering if the plane's wild vacillations were making his eyes play tricks on him. Then he realized what had happened. As the interior of the ship filled with additional water, it spread out more evenly, and the ship righted itself, even though the deck was now several feet underwater.

The MSOs used a night-vision camera that allowed them to

zoom in for a better look, and they had the clearest view. One empty survival suit with a blinking strobe was caught in a mast. All three of *Bounty*'s masts had their top few feet shorn away, but the rigging and shroud lines were still attached to the masts and the yardarms. The lines ran down from the masts and disappeared into the ocean, where they were swallowed up by the foaming white sea, giving the impression that the ship was poking up through clouds. Not an inch of the deck could be seen, yet because the masts and the lines were still intact, *Bounty* had the look of a ghost ship that could rise up and sail yet again.

Wes steered the plane toward the coast. *Are the sailors alive?* he wondered. *If they were in the life rafts, why didn't they fire a flare?* He tried to push a disturbing thought out of his mind: *Did we just witness the deaths of sixteen people?*

PART THREE

CHAPTER TWENTY-FIVE

ONE SMALL STROBE ALL ALONE

Lieutenant Commander Steve Cerveny had had a long night. The Jayhawk helicopter pilot had begun his day at Air Station Elizabeth City at 8:00 a.m. Sunday morning as the ready aircraft commander if he was called upon to fly. It was a quiet day up until Sector had notified him of *Bounty*'s problems in the evening. He and Duty Officer Todd Farrell immediately learned all they could about the vessel and its predicament. At 9:30 a.m. Steve figured he better get some sleep just in case he was called upon to fly, and he left Todd at the operations desk to monitor the situation.

Around midnight Steve called Todd Farrell to get a quick update on *Bounty*. He was told the sailors still thought they could keep the situation under control until morning, but that Wes McIntosh was heading out on the C-130.

Steve tried to get a little more shut-eye, but now his mind was racing, anticipating the sound of the SAR alarm at any moment. The slim, forty-three-year-old pilot, with a touch of gray in his hair, had over twenty years of flying time and had been around long enough to sense that *Bounty* might be in bigger trouble than its captain realized. After all, the ship was in the path of a hurricane that Steve had heard meteorologists begin referring to as Frankenstorm. With Steve's type A personality, he could not simply go back to sleep and block out the possibility that he might be flying into a hurricane at any second.

Steve's career as a helicopter pilot began in the navy when he started flight school in 1992. After almost ten years flying for the navy he transitioned to the coast guard, where he began flying the HH-60 Jayhawk, a ten-ton, sixty-five-foot-long helicopter, used for long-range rescues. Air stations such as Elizabeth City, Kodiak, Mobile, and Cape Cod all have Jayhawks, while other stations have the smaller and shorter-range Dolphin helicopter.

Steve was one of the pilots who flew multiple rescues over several days when Katrina hit New Orleans in 2005. Then, in 2010, Steve had needed to be rescued, after an awful crash on board a Jayhawk. He was the aircraft's copilot and was traveling over a remote, mountainous region of Utah after providing security in a joint US-Canadian operation for the 2010 Winter Olympics in Vancouver, British Columbia. Snow was falling during the flight, and some was sticking to the aircraft, forcing the pilots to activate the anti-icing mechanism. As they increased altitude over higher terrain, another coast guard helicopter flying in tandem with Steve's disappeared into a cloud bank. Somewhere in front of both aircraft was a ridgeline that the pilots knew they had to fly over.

The commander was flying the helicopter from the left seat, and Steve was in the right. As the commander tried to gain additional altitude to crest the ten-thousand-foot ridgeline, the Jayhawk was not responding. Steve called for more airspeed, realizing the anti-icing mechanism was robbing them of power. But the aircraft was sluggish and the commander had no choice except to turn away from the mountaintops. Banking hard to the right, both men were horrified to see the tops of trees emerge from the clouds just a few feet in front of them. The rotors clipped the trees, and in a split second the giant steel bird lurched to a stop and plummeted sideways, crashing through splintering pines and into the snow.

When the helicopter finally came to rest, Steve felt a searing pain shooting through his leg. He looked for the commander, who should have been in the seat to his left. Instead, he saw snow. Steve released his safety harness and tried to stand, then noticed the lower part of his leg was turned inward at a forty-five-degree angle and blood was seeping through his pants.

The commander's head popped out of the snow, but he, too, was injured, and both men were trapped in the steaming, hissing aircraft that could ignite at any moment. In the rear of the helicopter, basic aircrew member Gina Panuzzi was critically hurt with severe internal injuries. Luckily, rescue swimmer Darren Hicks and flight mechanic Edward Sychra were relatively unscathed and started pulling the injured from the wreckage, which was scattered over hundreds of feet, including up in the trees.

The accident had happened so quickly that no emergency call could be made, and the lead helicopter pilots that had been in front of Steve's aircraft didn't know it had gone down. Now, the five survivors were in a race against time; their injuries and hypothermia would sap their strength and soon snuff out their lives.

Flight mechanic Edward Sychra used his cell phone to send a text message to the flight mechanic of the lead helicopter, who texted back that they were alerting authorities and were going to land as close to the crash site as possible. Meantime, Steve's open compound fracture was causing excruciating pain, and the rescue swimmer did his best to help by using a tree branch as a splint. Steve thought to himself, *Well, I'm responsible for getting us into this jam, and maybe now God is going to help us get out of it.* Despite his pain he felt a calmness come over him, and his thoughts turned to the more seriously injured Gina Panuzzi. He knew she needed medical attention immediately.

A short time later the lead helicopter returned, but the Jayhawk was incapable of hovering at that altitude. Pilot Steven Bonn flew to a lower altitude and lightened the aircraft by dumping fuel and equipment. Then he returned and, in an amazing display of skill, somehow guided the helicopter down into a confined opening in the woods, just a couple hundred yards below the crash site. A Med-Flight helicopter also landed nearby, and the injured were whisked off to Salt Lake City. Snowmobilers arrived on scene and took Sychra and rescue swimmer Hicks down off the mountain.

When Steve was identified as one of the injured, authorities called his mother. The pilot's mother had the same feeling Steve did on the mountain: that her son would pull through. The date of the accident—March 3—was significant to her. This was the day her infant daughter had died years earlier. *God's not going to take two away,* she told herself. *Steve is being watched over and will be fine.*

Steve did pull through, but he wasn't fine. He had surgery on his leg, and afterward his orthopedic doctor warned him that the damage was so serious he could still lose the limb. After a month on his back in the hospital, a second surgery was performed, which included bone grafts and the bitter news that he might not ever be able to put weight on his leg and his flying days were likely over.

While recuperating Steve went over the rescue events and counted several things that had had to go precisely as they did for him and the others to survive. First, they landed in an incredible nine feet of snow, softening their impact and reducing the risk of fire. Second, in hundreds of miles of woods they crashed just two hundred yards from a clearing. And third, pilot Bonn managed to maneuver his helicopter into the opening despite it being difficult to hover at such an altitude. Steve considered several other factors, such as had the accident happened at night, they would likely not have been found until morning. He thought how pilots like himself who fly into dangerous situations need confidence, but how in the big scheme of things some factors are beyond control, and how faith can get you through the toughest of times.

For the next several months Steve directed his energy into physical therapy, and with each step he began to realize he might someday fly again. Approximately a year and a half after the accident, in October of 2011, Steve was behind the controls of a Jayhawk and throttled the helicopter off the tarmac and into the sky.

Now Steve was lying awake, wondering what was happening aboard the tall ship *Bounty*. He didn't have to speculate for long. At 3:00 a.m. Todd Farrell called him and asked him to come into the Operations Center because Steve might have to fly out to the ship and drop pumps. Copilot Jane Peña had also been alerted, and all three reviewed the situation with Sector. *Bounty* had not yet capsized, but Wes McIntosh on the C-130 described brutal conditions at the distress scene. That the captain of the vessel thought the crew could hang on until morning suggested to the Operations Center that *Bounty*'s situation was not acute, though potentially volatile. Weighing the safety of their rescue teams against this information, they decided the risks of flying immediately were just too great. But Steve and Jane were ready to fly instantly if the situation changed.

Because Steve had been on duty since 8:00 a.m. the prior morning, a fresh crew would be called in to fly at dawn if *Bounty* stayed afloat that long. Farrell made the calls. Then just a short time later, Sector called and relayed the urgent message from Wes that the people on *Bounty* were abandoning ship. That call changed everything. There was no time to wait for the new crew, no time to wait for safer conditions at dawn.

The SAR alarm sounded its whooping warble, and rescue swimmer Randy Haba and flight mechanic Michael Lufkin ran to the Operations Center to join up with Steve and Jane. Steve explained what was happening with *Bounty*, then described the extreme conditions at the accident scene. He asked each crew member if he or she felt alert enough to do the mission, knowing that all of them were near the end of their twenty-four-hour shift. They responded positively and raced to their helicopter, which was already out of the hangar, fueled, and ready to go.

Michael Lufkin and Jane Peña had only done a couple of rescues and were glad to have been paired with veterans such as Randy and Steve. Lufkin, a tall and lanky twenty-five-year-old, had been in the coast guard for five years serving in different roles, but had only been a qualified flight mechanic for seven months, and it would be his job to raise and lower the cable and help guide the pilots during the hoists. Randy's life would literally be in his hands because Michael, not Randy, controlled the movements of the cable when the rescue swimmer was on the other end. Lufkin would also be responsible for hoisting survivors, which was usually done by basket. In his work, timing was everything; he would need to factor in the wind and the waves to get the swimmer in the sweet spot of the back side of a wave, with just enough slack in the cable to allow the swimmer to maneuver. He would want to avoid putting Haba in the middle of a breaking wave where he could get buried.

As Lufkin sat in the helicopter's cabin during liftoff into the darkness, all the various hoisting scenarios were going through his mind. He would need to combine quickness and strength in many of the procedures, such as dropping the swimmer into the sea, bringing the hook up, attaching the basket, and getting survivors into the helo as quickly as possible. Fortunately, Lufkin was a natural athlete and had the coordination required. Still, he had never flown into any weather remotely like Hurricane Sandy, and with possibly multiple survivors in the water, it would take every bit of concentration and endurance he could muster. Prior to launching, when he first heard that *Bounty* was taking on water, Michael went online and investigated the ship's website. On it was the path of the ship with the hurricane not far away, and for a brief moment he wondered what in the world the vessel was doing out there. But he pushed the thought out of his mind and tried to learn as much as he could about the ship and its crew. He knew for certain he didn't want his swimmer or the basket anywhere near the ship's masts. Should the cable become entangled in the rigging, it could pull the giant helo right out of the sky.

The pilots flew at an altitude of three thousand feet, using a strong tailwind to propel them at 170 knots. Off Cape Hatteras they slowly descended and reduced speed. Steve ordered his crew to "goggle up," meaning to don the NVGs, so they could see the water, which came into focus at about three hundred feet in altitude. Squalls of rain and wind gusts began rocking the Jayhawk, and a couple powerful gusts made the helo rise and fall unexpectedly by as much as fifty feet. Through their headsets the on-scene C-130 pilot, Peyton Russell, was updating them, and they knew conditions would deteriorate with each passing mile. Michael Lufkin paid particular attention to the talk about the many strobe lights blinking in the water. He knew they would be searching, and fuel could become an issue, making quick hoists imperative. Lufkin reckoned that not only would a second helo be needed immediately, but most likely a third, considering that up to sixteen survivors could be scattered around the capsized *Bounty*.

Jane Peña, who sat in the left cockpit seat, had already started making fuel calculations to establish their bingo time: the moment they absolutely had to leave the accident scene to make it back to land with the fuel left. She used a computer to enter the route of their flight, the wind, and other factors to help calculate the fuel being used. Most important, the return flight would likely be directly into strong headwinds. She wanted to be certain that the calculations were accurate, so she also kept a pad of paper nearby to manually record fuel burn rates to make sure the computer calculations were in line with her own. She had the responsibility to continually update Steve on their fuel status as they approached bingo.

The thirty-one-year-old copilot with short brown hair had been a bit on edge when they were flying at three thousand feet in the pitch dark, but now that she could see the ocean through her NVGs, she felt fine. Water was her element, and just seeing it had a calming effect. As with Michael Lufkin, this was her first major SAR case, and she knew she would be learning from Steve Cerveny, a top pilot, and felt glad for the opportunity. She had done a medical evacuation off a ship and rescued stranded kayakers from a sandbar, but flying into hurricane conditions to hunt down individual strobe lights and hopefully extract survivors was a bit more challenging. *This is what all those hours of training and studying were for,* she thought, remembering her long and difficult quest to become a pilot.

Jane had grown up in Washington State and was the quintessential tomboy—climbing trees, camping, hiking, playing soccer and baseball. She had always wanted to fly but was unsure how to go about it and instead majored in history at the University of Washington in Seattle. Her longtime boyfriend, who later became her husband, joined the coast guard, and Jane began to see the opportunities. She applied to Officer Candidate School, was accepted, and graduated in 2007. In her first position, she did offshore security boardings of foreign vessels, a job she loved, but she hadn't given up on flying and kept applying for flight school until she was finally selected. Graduating, or "winged," in March 2010, Jane's first air station was Elizabeth City. Now, she was about to see why the ocean off Cape Hatteras is called the Graveyard of the Atlantic.

It took about an hour to reach *Bounty*. Peyton Russell in the C-130 told Jane that he had passed over one strobe and survival suit that did not float like the others. "We've marked the location, and we think there might be a person in that suit." Jane and Steve understood this was the target they needed to go to first. Unlike the large rafts, this single strobe light, far from the *Bounty*, could be easy to lose sight of in the waves. And should the strobe light's batteries die, they might never find that potential survivor.

Steve guided the helo to the coordinates Jane relayed to him, a full three-quarters of a mile from the ship and the rafts. As they descended toward the lone strobe light, Jane got her first close-up view of the ocean—it looked crazed. "Normally," recalled Jane, "waves would be advancing from a single direction and there would be a set amount of space between each one. These waves, however, had nothing normal about them." They were coming from various directions, with no pattern, and oftentimes they slammed into one another, shooting spray into the dark sky. The pilots had a good view of the chaos below: besides the windows directly in front of the cockpit, small windows were at their feet and on the sides. In the cabin, Haba and Lufkin peered out small windows on either side of the aircraft, and they, too, were in awe of the unusual waves, varying in size from twenty-five to thirty feet.

Winds made hovering in place nearly impossible, and Steve did his best to hold the bird in position over the single strobe light. The crew could see the outline of the immersion suit, but there was no sign of life. To get lower, Steve let the wind blow the helo back a bit, then he angled the nose down, descending to sixty feet. Jane watched the radar altimeter, which shows exactly the distance between the aircraft and the ocean. It fluctuated between twenty-five and sixty feet, meaning that when a large wave passed beneath the helicopter, it was only twenty-five feet from them. Jane wanted to make sure they never got any closer than twenty-five feet, so she focused on scanning the seas to make sure no extreme or "rogue" waves were coming their way. Even if the wave itself didn't hit the helicopter, its spray could be ingested by the engine and cause flameout. If that happened, the Jayhawk would stall and drop like a stone. When it hit the water, it would turn turtle as the heavy rotors, extending fifty-four feet in diameter, pulled the helicopter upside down. The crew trained for this dire scenario, but successfully exiting the aircraft at night in thirty-foot seas would be a long shot. With that in mind, Jane kept her eyes peeled for an extreme wave that could kill them all.

Michael Lufkin removed his goggles in preparation for a possible hoist. Suddenly, over his headset, he heard Steve say, "I just saw the arm of the survival suit lift out of the water! We've got a person down there." A shot of adrenaline coursed through Lufkin, and he looked at Haba. They were officially out of search mode and into a rescue.

CHAPTER TWENTY-SIX

A SWIRLING VORTEX

Randy Haba had taken off his helmet with the radio set and exchanged it for a neon-green rescue helmet. Now he was donning his harness, flippers, mask, and snorkel, a determined look on his face. The rescue swimmer wore a dry suit that he knew would make him sweat profusely in the warmer waters of the Gulf Stream, but he was not complaining. Should disaster happen and he couldn't get back into the helicopter, the extra layer of protection against hypothermia might save his life.

He slid toward the open doorway. With the illumination from the helicopter's searchlight, he could see the person's head and arm sticking out of the ocean. Earlier Randy had used the aircraft's infared camera, which could help in the search for survivors by showing a person's body heat as white against a green background on the monitor. The lens of the camera was mounted in the nose of the helicopter, and Randy used a toggle to move it, while zooming in and out, to adjust the focus. He had seen a bit of white coming from the survival suit, figured someone alive was in it, and prepared for deployment. Wanting to do the hoist as quickly as possible, he told Lufkin he thought a direct deployment—in which the swimmer stays on the hook and brings the survivor up with him in a sling—would be the way to go.

Randy felt excited and tense, the same kind of feeling that builds in an athlete before the start of a big game. He always thought that if the day ever came when he didn't get that amped-up feeling before a rescue, he should resign as a rescue swimmer. Complacency made for mistakes.

Haba, at thirty-three, was a powerful, muscular man, standing at six feet one inch and weighing close to two hundred pounds. Like all rescue swimmers he was paid to stay in top shape. His background would not, however, suggest his career path. The first few years of his life were spent on the family farm in Nebraska, then later he lived in the farming town of Stratton, Colorado. He loved sports, especially football, and his high school team won numerous state titles. But he was not on the swim team, nor was he an especially strong swimmer.

Besides football, Randy's other passion was the outdoors—fishing, hiking, skiing, hunting, and anything else that took him into the mountains. A high school science teacher introduced him to the possibility of a career in the outdoors, particularly search and rescue. In college, Randy tried to get into a mountain search-and-rescue program at Western State College in Gunnison, Colorado. During his freshman year, however, his classes were the general required courses, and he grew disinterested and a bit financially strapped because he was paying for college himself without the aid of a scholarship. When he learned that one of the missions of the coast guard was search and rescue, he talked to a recruiter at the end of his freshman year. The recruiter showed him a helicopter rescue-swimmer video, and Randy was hooked—despite having never seen an ocean.

During coast guard boot camp Randy became up close and personal with the ocean when his company commander marched his squad into it. After he survived boot camp, his first assignment, like that of most who join the coast guard, was on a cutter, in Randy's case the 378-foot *Midgett*. One of his more memorable deployments was to the Persian Gulf as part of the US Navy *Constellation* battle group. His next base was in New Orleans, where, in 1999, he began training to become an aviation survival technician (AST) (rescue swimmer) and "doggy-paddled" his first five-hundred-yard swim. Despite not being as quick a swimmer as some of the other candidates, he was determined and completed the four-month program. Then it was on to Air Station Elizabeth City for the more grueling AST "A" School, where he quickly became a stronger swimmer. About half the trainees washed out of the program, but the football player in Randy wouldn't consider quitting, and he pushed himself both physically and mentally in ways he never had before. Instructors pressed the recruits to their limits and beyond, knowing that it was safer for a recruit to crack under stress in a pool than alone in the open ocean. Randy rose to the challenge.

After graduating he was transferred back to New Orleans and flew on over 150 SAR missions during the next four years and even received the Air Medal during a tropical storm when he was left on a shrimp boat for fifteen hours. A stint in Puerto Rico followed, then it was back to Elizabeth City, where he became a rescue swimmer instructor. Now it was Randy who was sizing up candidates, and he knew the best swimmers were not necessarily the fastest ones, but those who were the most committed and showed it through endurance and dedication.

After instructing for a couple of years, Randy was picked for a program that allowed him to go to college full-time to earn a bachelor of aeronautical science degree, and he also got married. In the beginning of 2010 he was sent back to Elizabeth City and shortly thereafter became a father. The coast guard life had been good to Haba, and now he was going to earn his pay by putting his life on the line for total strangers.

Crouched by the open cabin doorway of the Jayhawk, Randy squinted through the windblown rain and looked down to where the helicopter's spotlight illuminated the survivor being shoved around by the waves. The rescue swimmer attempted to get a feel for the way the waves were washing under the survivor and realized these were some of the most confused seas he'd ever seen. He suspected there was a strong current from the Gulf Stream, and he mentally prepared himself to fight both that and the towering seas.

The roar from the wind mixing with that of the rotors made it nearly impossible for Haba to talk with hoist operator Michael Lufkin, but they had previously discussed how to conduct the rescue. Randy clipped the cable and the sling, or "strop," to his harness. If the rescue went as planned, Randy would be lowered to the survivor, get him in the strop, and come up with him. Randy would wrap his legs around the survivor to ensure he or she didn't slip out of the sling.

Lufkin, kneeling by the cabin door, wore a gunner's belt around his waist that extended to a secure point on the opposite cabin wall to keep him from falling out the door should he slip. One leather-gloved hand gripped the cable, while the other hand held a pendant attached to a long wire cord that controlled the hoist. The cable, suspended from a steel arm extending from the airframe above the door, was composed of woven steel strands and was only about three-eighths of an inch in diameter, yet was strong enough to hoist eleven thousand pounds. The dozens of individual strands gave the cable its durability and strength, but they also presented a weakness. Individual strands had been known to break by rubbing against the aircraft or another object, and although this did not usually mean the cable would break, it could lead to fouling, or "bird-caging," in the spool. Should the cable become stuck while the rescue swimmer was in the water, the stranded swimmer would be in as much danger as the survivors and perhaps even at greater risk if he was unable to reach the life raft.

Steve positioned the aircraft in a hover just a bit aft of the survivor. The rotor wash kicked up foam and thick bands of spray, making it look as if the survivor were in the middle of a tornado.

Although the helicopter was equipped with an automatic hold feature that would keep the aircraft at a fixed distance above the sea, Steve couldn't use it because it would send the helo rising each time a wave approached, and dropping when it passed. It would be impossible for Lufkin to do the hoist with the aircraft fluctuating any more than it already did from the wind gusts. So Steve held his altitude by looking at the horizon and continually checking his vertical speed indicator, trying to keep that as close to zero as possible.

While the commander was working the levers that controlled the helicopter's movements, Jane continually scanned the ocean, particularly on the left side of the aircraft because no one else would be looking that way. So far no rogue waves had materialized, but every now and then she'd give an alert, such as "Larger one coming from the left," and Steve would increase altitude slightly to keep that cushion of twenty-five feet above the tallest of waves.

In the cabin Lufkin said through the radio in his headset, "Swimmer is ready and at the door."

Steve acknowledged and gave the okay for deployment.

Lufkin tried to stay as calm as possible, knowing he would now be doing two things at once: lowering the swimmer while telling the pilots exactly where he wanted them to move the aircraft during the deployment. His words had to be precise as the pilots would be scanning their instruments and the seas around them and would be unable to see the rescue swimmer much of the time.

Michael tapped Randy on the chest, the signal that he was ready, and the swimmer responded with a thumbs-up.

"Deploying the swimmer," said Michael.

Randy pushed off, and Michael started lowering him, saying, "Swimmer is outside the cabin, swimmer is being lowered."

Michael now knew just how strong the winds were. Haba went sailing aft of the aircraft, and Lufkin had to crane his neck just to keep him in sight.

Down went Randy, making contact with the water about forty feet behind the survivor. He immediately started swimming, but a wave dropped out from under him, and the cable violently jerked him back twenty feet, almost ripping his mask off. The next wave blindsided him, crashing into his back while he was in an awkward position. So much adrenaline was surging through Haba that he didn't feel any pain despite that later X-rays revealed a compressed vertebra with a hairline fracture. In the water, he was more mad than anything else, and he cursed to himself, realizing they had lost valuable time.

Michael also cursed as he worked the cable, lifting Randy out of the water before another wave could slam into him. Over his headset he explained to the pilots what had happened and said he was repositioning the swimmer, telling them to ease the aircraft "forward, ten feet."

Hanging at the end of the cable, Randy knew how hard it must be for Lufkin to time the descent in such conditions. The wind was so strong it felt as if the swimmer were sticking his head out of a speeding car.

"I could not wear my NVGs and do the hoist at the same time, so I had to rely on the fixed spotlight shining directly downward, which only gave me a small viewing area. Waves would appear out of the dark from different directions, and I had to make a split-second decision when to lower the swimmer again. When I saw what looked like a lull after a wave had passed, I pressed the pendant and Randy was back in the water," recalled Michael.

This time Randy was within a few feet of the survivor when a breaking wave and a wind gust pushed the helicopter upward, causing the swimmer to be jerked beyond reach of the drifting mariner. Randy gave Lufkin a thumbs-down to indicate the need for more slack in the cable to combat the unexpected gusts.

On the third attempt the rescue swimmer finally reached the survivor. Randy could see that it was a man, still conscious but quite pale and exhausted-looking.

Randy removed his snorkel and shouted, "Are you hurt?"

"I'm okay," croaked the man.

"Is there anyone else in the water nearby?"

"Don't think so."

Haba was relieved to see that the man was not only coherent but calm. Far too often swimmers have to subdue panicked survivors who, instead of following the rescuer's direction, claw or fight them.

"Okay, here's what we're going to do!" shouted Randy, holding on to the survivor's arm. Before he could explain, a breaking sea avalanched on the two men like a pile driver, pushing them downward, into a swirling vortex.

CHAPTER TWENTY-SEVEN

LIKE WE'VE FLOWN BACK IN TIME

Lufkin held his breath, searching for the men in the foam. It was next to impossible to hover in the same place with the varying wind gusts. Over his headset he spoke to the pilots: "Left, ten. Okay, now forward fifteen."

The neon rescue helmet appeared directly below Lufkin. It was one of the best sights he'd ever seen.

Below, Randy took a gulp of air and started to put the strop around the survivor, worried that in the dark another wave would separate him from the man. Randy cinched the strop up tight and hollered, "We're going up together! Keep your arms down on the sling. I don't want you falling out!"

Randy looked up toward the helo thundering overhead and signaled that they were ready to be retrieved. Lufkin started retracting cable, and soon the two men left the waves and were greeted by the howling wind, blowing them aft of the helo and spinning them.

Using his gloved hand, Michael, lying on his belly, held the cable as steady as he could. His big fear was that the cable could swing so far aft it would become jammed behind the open door. He kept retracting cable, and soon the men were at the door. Leaning out of the aircraft, Michael grabbed the harness on Randy and used all his strength to pull the two men safely inside.

In the back of his mind Lufkin wondered why the two men felt like the weight of three. Looking at the survivor's immersion suit, he had his answer. Water had collected in the feet and legs of the suit. *That thing must have a hundred pounds of water in it,* Lufkin thought. Then he moved to the door, continued updating the pilots as he had been all along, and with a sigh of relief finally said, "Swimmer and survivor safely in the cabin. Door is now closed."

The survivor was John Svendsen.

The C-130 flown by Mike Myers and Wes McIntosh was almost back to Raleigh when over the radio Sector informed them that the first survivor had successfully been hoisted. Roars of applause and cheering erupted on the plane. "It was utter elation," recalled Myers. "Our hearts had remained with the crew of the *Bounty*, and it was beyond nerve-racking to not know if they went down with the ship. But when we heard that helicopter crew had just arrived and already plucked one out of the sea, that gave us hope for the rest of them."

Once Wes and Mike had safely landed and refueled the plane, they entered the airport's flight-planning room. Someone asked, "Were you the guys out there with the *Bounty*?" Mike and Wes were taken aback; they were used to flying in anonymity, with no one outside the coast guard knowing what they did. Mike answered, "Yes, that was us. But how did you know?" The person pointed up at a television set. On it was a photo of *Bounty*, and a reporter was saying how the ship had sunk in the hurricane. Both C-130 pilots knew this case was turning out to be unlike any other, and they stayed glued to the television set, waiting to see if there was more news of survivors, prepared to fly again if needed.

The faint light of dawn filtered through the rain and clouds, and Steve Cerveny guided the helicopter into a wide turn, heading toward *Bounty*. On the way they saw another couple of lone strobe lights and hovered over them with the searchlight, determining the survival suits were empty. When they arrived at the ship, Jane thought, *This is surreal, it's like we've flown back in time.* Randy Haba had a similar reaction; he had seen many foundering vessels, but never a tall ship with three enormous masts. He hoped he would not have to be lowered to the ship, noting the tangled rigging fanning out from the vessel.

A blinking strobe light in one of the masts caught the attention of the aircrew, and Steve lowered the helo to forty feet for a better look. Within seconds it was clear that the strobe was on an empty survival suit, and the aircrew continued scanning the ship and the surrounding wreckage for survivors. As they fanned out into ever-wider circles, they saw another empty survival suit but no people.

Five minutes later Jane radioed the C-130, "We've searched the ship and the surrounding debris and there are no survivors."

The pilots on the C-130 acknowledged, then guided the helicopter to the nearest life raft, which was about a mile away. The raft's orange canopy was not inflated, and no one was on top of it or under it. Jane started getting worried. *Where are they? Surely there has to be more than one person alive.* They hovered over the raft, hoping a head or an arm would pop out from beneath the canopy.

"No survivors in raft we are over," said Jane to the C-130. "It is one of ours."

"Roger. The other three rafts are lined up in almost a straight line to the east. They are about a mile apart."

"Okay," said Jane, "we are proceeding to the next one."

This raft was also a coast guard raft. Again they hovered over the raft, and again no signs of life. *This is bad,* thought Jane. *There were sixteen or seventeen people on this ship. They can't all be gone.*

The Jayhawk moved on to the next raft. This one had a red canopy, fully inflated. Steve put the helo in a hover, slowly descending to thirty feet above the seas. He was worried his hundred-mile-per-hour rotor wash would flip the raft, but quickly realized that with such strong winds most of the swirl created by the rotors was being blown aft. The raft looked stable, and he took that to be a good sign: maybe there were people inside weighing it down. But there was no sign of life below, and he thought, *Please, not another empty life raft, somebody else has to be alive.* A second later a head popped out of the doorway and a survivor started waving. All four aircrew members breathed a sigh of relief.

Randy had decided against staying on the hook for the next rescue and would instead do a harness deployment, in which he would detach from the cable and swim to the raft. Michael Lufkin relayed this to the pilots, got the okay from Steve, then began putting Randy in the water.

When the swimmer hit the water, about forty feet from the raft, he unhooked and started knifing toward the little vessel as fast as he could. Without the cable on him he became aware of a strange sensation. The waves were going one way but the current was going the other. The current was so strong that if a wave didn't break directly on Randy, the moving water would propel the swimmer right over the wave top.

Randy arrived at the vessel in just a few seconds. Using handles by the doorway, Randy pulled the top half of his body into the raft. Panting and out of breath, he focused on the faces inside. A bunch of wide-eyed people looked back at him.

"How's everyone doing?" asked the swimmer.

Silence.

"Are there any injuries?"

The survivors just stared at him.

Randy tried a new approach. "Does anyone have trouble swimming?"

A man who was hunched over in the center of the raft struggled to sit up and looked at Randy. It was Doug Faunt.

Randy looked back at him, asking, "Are you ready to go?"

"Yes, I'm ready."

"Okay, relax and I'll take care of the rest."

Randy backed out of the cavelike shelter of the raft and into the howling wind and crashing seas. He waited at the doorway as Faunt, weighed down by his water-filled survival suit, inched to the door. When Doug got his first leg out of the raft, the water drained into the foot area, swelling it to three times its normal size. He flopped into the water and floated on his back. Randy wrapped his right arm around Doug's chest and started paddling with his other arm, using his flippers to thrust himself away from the raft. The swimmer kept glancing from the aircraft to the surrounding seas and back again, trying hard not to get blindsided by any big combers. One big wave came thundering in on the men, and Randy decided to swim through it rather than risk its breaking directly on the survivor.

Up in the helicopter Michael Lufkin began lowering the basket, watching in alarm as the wind sent it shooting fifty feet behind the aircraft. He brought the basket back inside, added weight to it, then told the pilots to move forward, deciding it best to let the basket hit the water in a spot where the waves would carry it to the swimmer.

"Okay, basket is in the water," Michael said over the headset. Then he did a double take while looking at the basket. Instead of being pushed by the waves, the basket drifted into and over the waves, away from Randy. To make matters worse, the weights he'd just added made the basket sink rather than ride on the surface.

"Current took the basket and the weights aren't working," said Michael. "I'm going to bring it back up and remove the weights."

Once that was done, he directed the pilots to a new hovering spot and let the basket hit the water just a few feet from Randy.

Despite the proximity of the basket, the swimmer had to drag the survivor through two large waves to avoid their cascading white water. Faunt swallowed considerable seawater before Randy stuffed him into the basket.

When Faunt was hauled into the aircraft and flopped out of the basket, he broke out into a wide grin. "I saw John Svendsen," recalled Faunt, "and I shouted his name, telling him I sure was glad to see him. I had been worrying about John and Dan, knowing how dedicated they were to the ship, the crew, and their responsibilities. I was afraid they would get caught up in their duties and not get away from the capsized *Bounty* fast enough."

Randy had watched Faunt be hoisted, and he figured he would try to save time by swimming back to the raft, which had now drifted almost two hundred yards away. He was swimming directly into most waves and helped by the current, but sometimes a large comber would slam him from the ten o'clock position and other times from the two o'clock side, driving him underwater. His progress seemed to take forever, and he realized he'd have nothing left in his tank if he continued this battle. Randy looked up at the helo and signaled to be picked up.

Once back inside the helicopter he cupped his hands by Lufkin's ear and shouted that six people were still on the raft but that no one appeared badly injured. "After we get the next survivor in the aircraft, just air-taxi me back to the raft! The current is unbelievable!"

"I know," said Michael, "it carried the basket the opposite way of the waves!"

The idea for an air taxi—where Randy would be carried just above the tops of the waves rather than lifted into the helicopter—would save precious seconds. Jane had been updating Michael and Steve, telling them they only had twenty minutes to bingo time, and Michael had been thinking air taxi just as Randy had.

Once the pilots had repositioned the helicopter, Randy lowered into the water, unhooked, swam to the raft, and stuck his head inside.

"Who's next?"

The survivors stayed quiet.

Randy looked at one of the female survivors closest to him. "Are you ready?"

Jessica Black answered yes, and off they went. This time the basket hoist went smoothly.

Randy used the next couple minutes to catch his breath, and soon the bare hook came down. He clipped the hook to his harness, and as he was about to give the thumbs-up to be lifted, he heard a roar, and out of the corner of his eye he saw a monstrous sea bearing down on him. All he could do was hold his breath before being engulfed in a torrent of white water. The force of the wave was so strong it ripped the mask and snorkel right off Randy's head.

Michael retracted cable as fast as he could and lifted Randy out of the swirling foam before the next wave buried him.

Well, that was some wake-up call, thought Randy. *Just got to do the rescue with no mask.*

The ocean wasn't quite done with him yet. Once he was back at the raft and telling the next survivor, Anna Sprague, to come out the doorway, a wave broke directly on the raft's canopy. Randy was hurled backward, landing ten feet from the raft. He coughed up a bellyful of water and kicked back to the raft, thinking, *This is not good. We gotta hurry, or we'll never get all these people out before bingo.*

In the cockpit, Steve was thinking the same thing. He knew another helo was on its way, and he had made up his mind he wasn't going to put the survivors or his crew in danger by extending the bingo time. He also surmised that the survivors were in pretty good shape because each time a new person came into the aircraft, the other survivors let out a cheer. *Just stay focused,* Steve told himself, *we're not done yet.*

He was so focused on his swimmer in the water and holding the aircraft in as steady a hover as possible, he never saw the second helicopter speed by. But Jane did, and over the headset she confirmed to both her crew and the C-130 that she had a visual on the other helicopter.

After Anna Sprague was safely in the helicopter, Randy extracted Mark Warner, and he, too, was quickly hoisted into the helicopter without incident. *Now we're going good*, thought Randy as he treaded water and waited to be air-taxied back to the life raft and the final three survivors.

At that same moment Jane said, "Okay, we are at bingo."

"Roger," said Steve. "Michael, we're at bingo. After we get the swimmer up, we're going home."

Randy didn't know this, and when he clipped onto the hook, he was expecting to be brought back to the raft. Instead, he found himself being lifted directly up, and he guessed that they were up against their fuel limit.

Once Randy was inside the helicopter, Michael hollered, "RTB" (return to base).

"We still got three people down there!" said Randy.

"It's okay, there is another helo on scene and a third one coming. We hit bingo." Michael grabbed the door handle and slid the door shut.

The five survivors who had been hugging and crying tears of joy all stopped and stared at Michael, not understanding why they were leaving their friends below.

Randy, who also served as the aircraft's EMT, started going from survivor to survivor, telling them another aircraft would get their friends and also asking each survivor how he or she was feeling. Only Svendsen was seriously injured, and he was still vomiting from spending so much time being pounded by waves.

"Door is shut, and everyone is seated and ready to fly," said Michael over the headset.

"Roger," said Steve, then he turned to Jane. "Take us home. You three did a heck of a job."

Josh Scornavacchi, Matt Sanders, and John Jones spread out as best they could to keep the raft from flipping. The loud roar from the rotors of the helicopter above them grew faint, and then the only sound was from the surging seas. *They're probably just repositioning,* thought Josh.

The three men sat patiently, expecting to hear the welcoming *thwack, thwack, thwack* of the helicopter's return at any moment. Josh peeked out the doorway, craning his neck so he could look up toward the sky. Rain and foam whipped at his exposed face, and he was forced to retreat back inside the raft. Then he thought, *What if something happened to them?* He quickly changed his thinking. *Well, they know the three of us are in here. We just got to keep this raft afloat a little longer.*

CHAPTER TWENTY-EIGHT

CATAPULTED

The second helicopter that reached the emergency scene faced what seemed like an insurmountable job. Eight potential survivors were in either a second *Bounty* life raft or drifting in the storm-tossed ocean. Further complicating the situation, the first helicopter crew said they were bumping up against their bingo time and might have to leave before they could extract everyone from the raft they were working on. A third helicopter had not yet launched, and no one knew what Sandy was going to do next.

Luckily, three of the four aircrew members in the second helo were quite experienced. In fact, aircraft commander Steve Bonn, age forty-four, was the pilot who had helped rescue Steve Cerveny when his helicopter crashed in the Rocky Mountains. Bonn had flown Black Hawks in the army for nine years, then joined the coast guard in 2000, where he flew Jayhawk helicopters, including a four-year stint at Air Station Kodiak, Alaska, performing rescues in dangerous weather. In 2008 he flew to the Mayday call from the *Alaska Ranger* in the Bering Sea, which developed into one of the largest and most difficult rescues ever conducted by the coast guard. The *Alaska Ranger*, a fishing-factory ship, had forty-seven crew members on board when it sank, and all but five were eventually rescued. Steve Bonn was in the air for eight and a half hours that night, in high winds and fighting snow squalls. That experience, along with a couple hundred other lesser SAR cases, would go a long way in the rescue of the *Bounty*.

Flying with Steve to the *Bounty* was flight mechanic Gregory

"Neil" Moulder, rescue swimmer Dan Todd, and copilot Jenny Fields. Neil had over fourteen years' experience hoisting rescue swimmers and survivors, and Dan had been a rescue swimmer for five years. Jenny, a graduate of the Coast Guard Academy, was the newest of the crew, having been qualified to fly Jayhawks in 2011.

All four had been called at home by Todd Farrell at the Operations Desk and told to report to the air station for a first-light flight to a tall ship taking on water. Dan recalled getting the phone and asking, "What's a tall ship?"

"It looks like a pirate ship," responded Todd.

"This better not be a bad joke."

"No joke. It's real all right, and you gotta come in right away."

Jenny Fields got the same call about launching at first light, but then "I got a second phone call," recalled Jenny, "just as I was leaving my driveway. It was Todd Farrell at the Operations Desk, and he told me that he needed me at the station immediately, that the sailors were abandoning ship that very moment. That's when my heart rate and adrenaline began pumping."

On the flight out, pushed by a strong tailwind to 170 knots, Steve Bonn said, "So who here has been to AHRS?" (Advanced Helicopter Rescue School, where crews practice over and in the towering surf at the Columbia Bar in Oregon). Dan and Neil had gone through the training, but not Jenny, so Steve gave her a quick overview of the additional duties of a copilot during extreme conditions.

"Watch the waves," said Steve, who was sitting in the right seat, "and learn their timings, and give advisories as best you can. Be a vigilant safety pilot on the controls and instruments, but more specifically be watching outside. I'm going to be mostly looking down and to the right during the hoists, so I need you to be looking everywhere else and paint us a picture of what's out there."

Then the four-person crew discussed what they would do when they located survivors, and all agreed that the swimmer would be put down in a sling deployment, followed by basket recoveries. Dan got the usual butterflies in his stomach thinking through the steps he would take when he got in the water. The shot of adrenaline was still kicking as he remembered that Randy Haba had once told him: "Big cases don't come along very often, and for some of us it's a once-in-a-lifetime experience. Everything you ever learned and practiced in training is going to be called upon."

When the crew arrived on the emergency scene, they were well prepared for what awaited them from listening to the conversations between the first helicopter and the orbiting C-130. They had enough light to see without using their NVGs, but depth perception was difficult. The only colors were shades of gray and white: gray water with whitecaps and variations of gray clouds all blurred by driving, horizontal rain. Wind tore the tops off the waves, sending bits of white foam and spray, like giant snowflakes, up in the air.

Peyton Russell, on the orbiting C-130, directed the helicopter toward the second *Bounty* life raft.

Steve Bonn, who had the controls, edged the helicopter ever closer to the top of the waves. Suddenly they could see the orange canopy of the life raft bouncing up and down in the seas like a cork in a raging river. Then a big wave rolled toward it and the raft disappeared behind the wall of water. The commander felt a building tension as he slowed the helicopter and got ready for the hoists—if there were hoists. No one knew for sure if the second *Bounty* life raft had survivors in it. Steve, however, was certain of one thing: if the sailors were not in the life raft, he would have to spend precious time and fuel investigating promising strobe lights, and the chances of hoisting all the potential survivors before bingo would be next to impossible. Jenny had calculated bingo at twenty-two hundred pounds of fuel to return to Elizabeth City, and she had also calculated lesser amounts if they went to Marine Station Cherry Point or had to set down on the nearest point of land, which was the beach at Cape Hatteras.

Looking down through the chin bubble of the aircraft, Jenny could clearly see the raft in the crashing chaos of foam and water. *Come on, come on, someone show yourself. There's got to be people in there,* she thought. She focused on two access door flaps, but no heads stuck out. The helicopter was now just fifty feet above the raft and was buffeted by strong crosswinds. *Where are they?* Suddenly she saw the canopy door open and three faces in red Gumby suits looked directly up at her. *Yes!* Then the survivors started waving their arms back and forth, and Jenny could almost feel their relief at knowing they were not alone.

Steve positioned the aircraft in a hover, nose into the wind, about twenty-five feet above the tallest wave tops, with the raft off to the two o'clock position. Jenny set the radar altimeter at twenty feet: if a wave came closer than twenty feet to the aircraft, an audible advisory would warn them that they were dangerously close to the crest. Between the radar altimeter and Jenny's scanning the seas, Steve could focus on flying while also keeping an eye on the rescue swimmer.

After the team went through the final checklist, Dan positioned himself at the door and then Neil lowered him toward the water. As soon as the swimmer's flippers touched the ocean, he straightened his arms and plunged out of the sling. It was a fifty-yard sprint to the raft, and Dan felt he had never swum so fast in his life. All that adrenaline could finally be used. At the raft, he pulled himself completely inside the doorway, sat down and faced the survivors, then yanked out his snorkel and raised his mask. He composed himself, took a couple breaths, and said, "Hey, I'm Dan. I hear you guys need a ride."

Unlike those on the first raft, this group of survivors were animated, with a couple yelling, "Way to go! You guys are awesome!"

Dan was hoping his casual greeting would give the survivors a feeling of confidence, as if swimming through thirty-foot breaking seas in a hurricane were an everyday occurrence for him.

"How many people in here?" asked Dan.

"Six."

"Nobody has fallen out?"

"No."

Dan pulled a small, waterproof radio transmitter from his vest, turned it on, and contacted Jenny. "There are six people in the raft." Then he put the radio away and turned back to the survivors, asking, "Does anyone have any injuries?"

The survivors pointed to Adam.

"Okay, he will go first. This is how I need you all to do this for me. When I get you to the basket, you're to sit inside and keep your hands and feet inside. The quicker you do that, the quicker you will go into the helicopter."

Just then a giant wave slammed into the raft, first hitting the spot where Dan was perched, catapulting him into the air. He flew toward the other side of the raft, accidently clotheslining two people on the way, and landed in a heap on a survivor. Water roared in after him, as if someone with a fire hose were aiming it through the doorway.

"Is anyone hurt?" shouted Dan, crawling back toward the door.

"We're okay!"

Dan wasted no time exiting the raft—he couldn't risk having another wave hit and becoming injured. If that happened, the survivors would be at the mercy of the seas until the next helicopter arrived. Dan wanted to get Adam out of the raft and into the basket immediately. He was trained to always take the injured survivors first, when the rescue swimmer had maximum energy. Should the survivor be torn from his grip by a wave, Dan would want to get that person fast because the survivor might not be able to stay afloat in the pounding seas for more than a minute or two.

Dan looked at Adam and shouted, "Can you get out of the raft?"

"I'll do whatever it takes," said Adam. "I got in the raft somehow and I can get out."

Dan motioned for him to come out of the raft. Adam clawed his way to the door, first sticking his head out and then struggling to lift one leg higher than the tubing that encircled the raft and eventually getting that leg into the ocean. Then with a push he dropped into the water and rolled onto his back. Dan wrapped his right arm around Adam's chest and began putting distance between them and the raft. With such high winds the swimmer wanted to get the survivor at least forty feet from the raft so that the helicopter could stay downwind of the raft. If the aircraft was over the raft, its rotor wash might flip it.

Steve Bonn, with a bird's-eye view of the raft at the two o'clock position, got a good reminder of what the other helicopter crew had warned him about—that the wind and the current would make the hoists more difficult than anything they'd ever before experienced. The commander watched Dan and the survivor be taken by the current and pushed upwind from the raft, meaning that Steve would have to move in that direction, passing directly over the raft. Without any other choice he moved the aircraft forward so he could keep the swimmer in view, and he held his breath. The raft stayed upright, and Steve awaited communication from Neil. It was impossible to hold the aircraft in one position with wind gusts sending it lurching forward, backward, or side to side. There would be no gently sliding the helicopter a couple feet at a time, for the wind had the upper hand and despite Steve's best efforts, any movement on the control levers, no matter how subtle, would send the aircraft rocketing ten feet or more.

"Big wave coming from the left," said Jenny in as calm a voice as possible.

Steve increased altitude another ten feet, letting the wave slide beneath them. Then he descended again, knowing the closer he was to the water the easier the hoist would be for Neil.

Neil had the basket ready at the doorway and shoved it out. With the pendant in his right hand and the cable in his gloved left hand, he started letting out cable. The wind shot the basket aft of the aircraft, and Neil told Steve to move forward twenty feet. Then, when the basket was halfway down, a crosswind caught it, shooting it forward and to the right. Neil was on his stomach now, trying to steady the cable, telling the pilots what was happening. He glanced ahead to where Dan held the survivor and couldn't believe how quickly the current was moving them.

Just as Neil was about to tell Steve to move to a new position, the wind changed and blew the basket backward and left. Neil let out cable as fast as he could and saw the basket hit the water.

"Hold right there! Hold!" barked Neil over the headset. The basket was only a few feet from the swimmer and the survivor, and Neil could see they would reach it without too much trouble. On the headset Neil could hear the automated voice from the radar altimeter saying, "Altitude, altitude." He knew a particularly large wave had come within their comfort zone, but he tried to ignore the warning—that was the pilot's worry. Neil had to keep his eye on the basket and the survivor.

Neil watched as the survivor was put in the basket, and as soon as Dan gave the thumbs-up, Neil started retracting cable as fast as he could. The basket, heavy with the survivor's weight, swung like a pendulum, and Neil, now on his knees, struggled to stabilize it. "Basket is coming up," said Neil. Then five seconds later, out of breath, he gasped, “Basket at the door.” Then grunting: “Bringing basket inside the cabin.”

While Neil used all his strength to lift the survivor—including the fifty pounds of water in the survival suit—out of the basket, Jenny said, watching the waves, “Couple really big ones coming.”

Steve dared to take his eyes off the swimmer drifting up and over the waves and saw two mountains of water approaching, their crests a snarling mess of white water.

CHAPTER TWENTY-NINE

FLIPPED LIKE A PANCAKE

While Steve powered the helicopter up and out of reach of the big waves, Dan, down in the ocean, wasn't so lucky. He saw the first comber out of the corner of his eye and took a big breath and dove downward into it, the same as a person might do at the seashore when he fears a breaking wave is going to knock him over. Holding his breath, Dan could feel himself get tumbled, but he knew he was much safer under the water than in the maw of the wave on the surface. He let the moving mountain slide past, then fought to the surface. Blowing water out of his snorkel, he was preparing to take in a deep lungful of air when the second wave caught him, driving him deep. Dan's entire body screamed for oxygen, and he kicked and stroked toward the light, toward the surface. When his head popped out of the foam, he coughed up green water, trying to clear his lungs.

Fortunately a small swell was next, and he let the current push him up and over it. He was far from the raft and didn't even think about swimming to it, knowing Neil would lower the hook as soon as he got the survivor out of the basket.

In the cabin, Adam struggled to get out of the basket, first pivoting so he could be on his knees, then lifting his chest out while placing his hands on the helicopter floor. Some water sloshed out of the neck of the survival suit, but most slid downward inside the neoprene, first forming a giant belly, then moving to his feet, making it look as if he had on enormous clown shoes. Neil grabbed him under the arms and helped get his legs out of the basket, then motioned for Adam to crawl toward the front of the aircraft to allow more room for removing the basket. Neil worked as fast as he could, but a nagging voice inside his head was saying to speed things up. He tried to balance haste with precision—one mistake could put the whole rescue in jeopardy. For a moment he considered asking how much time to bingo, but pushed the notion aside. *Just focus on what you can control,* he told himself.

Steve Bonn kept watch on Dan and updated Neil. "I've got eyes on the swimmer. He is being pulled far from the raft so we're going to have to pick him up. No way he will be able to swim back."

"Roger," said Neil. "Stand by. I'm disconnecting the basket now."

A minute later Neil lowered the hook to Dan, who clipped it to his harness. By prearrangement, Dan was hoisted just above the wave tops and air-taxied toward the raft.

Neil later recalled a frightening moment when he was looking down at Dan: "He was swinging like a wrecking ball because his fins were acting like sails. I grabbed hold of the swaying cable to steady it, and that's when I felt my shoulder pop."

Neil had dislocated his shoulder, but he could do nothing about it at that moment because the raft had just come into view. "Okay, ah . . . forward and right fifteen feet," he panted.

Dan was carried to within twenty feet of the raft, and Neil put him in the water, watched him unclip, and started retracting cable. The pain in his shoulder was radiating outward into his arm and down his back, and he thought, *We can't abort this mission because of me.* He decided he'd fix the problem himself. Positioning himself sideways to his jump seat, he took a deep breath and then launched himself—injured shoulder first—into the seat. A searing, burning sensation shot through his arm, but he felt the bone go back in the socket.

Adam Prokosh—in pain himself from several injuries—watched Neil with wide eyes, not sure why the hoist operator threw himself into the seat. Adam wanted to ask what had happened, but the rotors were too loud, and the hoist operator was already racing to reattach the basket.

Rescue swimmer Dan Todd had a more difficult challenge reaching the raft than he did the first time. He was in the midst of a series of waves that seemed ever more confused. "One minute," he later explained, "a big wave approached from the back and I'd be bodysurfing, but then the surge of the wave would carry my legs right over the top of my head and I'd have to ball up a little to avoid getting my back broken."

The waves were going toward the raft, but the current was moving the opposite way, and although he repeatedly bodysurfed, balled up, then swam, he still couldn't get to the raft. "Just when I'd get the hang of these waves coming up from behind me, another wave would materialize off to my side and slap me in the face, rolling me sideways. They were absolutely crazy. But it was the current that really made everything so difficult."

Trying to cover a mere twenty feet in such a strong current became a frustrating journey. He'd bodysurf a wave tantalizingly close to the raft, but as the wave passed Dan, it would collide with the raft, pushing the vessel beyond reach.

Dan's arm hit something in the foam and he grabbed it with his hand. A fifty-foot line trailed from the raft to a parachute-shaped sea anchor made of fabric, intended to slow and stabilize the raft. The rescue swimmer held on tight, let a wave push him forward, then pulled in a couple feet of slack until the wave hit the raft and straightened out the line, pulling Dan along, about three feet below the surface. The next wave propelled the swimmer forward, and again he hauled in a couple more feet of slack before being towed behind the raft. "I couldn't help but notice that while being dragged," Dan remembered, "how peaceful it seemed just a few feet below the surface. It was actually quite beautiful, and if I looked downward, the visibility was excellent. Then when I'd come to the surface, it was complete chaos, like being inside a washing machine. The difference was so unexpected it was striking."

After three or four of these rides, Dan reached the raft and motioned for the next survivor to come out. This hoist went like clockwork. The basket was just a few feet away, partly because Neil was learning to gauge the waves and the current, but also because Steve Bonn had maneuvered the aircraft to a mere ten feet above the wave tops. Normally the helo would be a good thirty feet above the biggest waves, but Steve knew the lower he positioned the aircraft, the less time the basket would be in the air and blown around. Steve relied on Jenny to warn him when a big wave was coming, and he ignored the continuous cautionary voice from the radar altimeter, squawking, "Altitude, altitude."

Jenny was juggling her duties of monitoring the instruments, managing communications with the orbiting C-130, recalculating the fuel burn, and operating the in-flight camera. She was looking through the camera to find Dan in the white water below when she reminded herself to scan the seas again. Just as her head was turning to look out the side window, something caught her eye in the chin bubble down by her feet. A snarling peak at the top of a giant wave was rushing up toward the belly of the helicopter.

Steve felt the pressure on his collective (the control lever for altitude) as Jenny announced in a hurried voice, "Up! Up! Up!" Together the two pilots sent the helo climbing, barely escaping the extreme wave.

Dan, treading water, watched the helo shoot upward, relieved to see it had dodged the three-story wave and gotten the survivor safely in the aircraft. Just as he pivoted to see if the raft was close enough to try to swim to, he witnessed the nightmare of every rescue swimmer. A big wave caught the raft just right and lifted it almost completely out of the water, flipping it like a pancake, so that its black bottom was now on the surface. The orange canopy was completely submerged. Panic shot through Dan. *Where are the people?* He started swimming with every ounce of strength he had.

Jenny saw the whole thing happen in slow motion. "I'd been scanning in all directions for extreme waves, and thinking that even though the magnitude of the seas was bigger than anything I'd seen, what really got my attention was the speed they were going. A mass of water moving that fast possesses an extraordinary amount of raw energy, and I marveled that Dan was in the midst of them. Then I looked toward the raft just in time to see it flip. Both Steve and I gasped, then watched Dan sprinting toward it."

The raft likely flipped because with two fewer survivors in it, the vessel was both lighter and unbalanced. Strong rotor wash from the aircraft might also have assisted the wave in launching the raft into the air.

The fear that people were either drowning or fighting to get out of the upside-down raft gave Dan an extra boost of strength, and he swam and bodysurfed quickly toward the raft, prepared to either dive down and through the doorway or perhaps cut through the fabric floor if he had to. Just as he arrived, heads started popping up, and he counted all four remaining people hanging on to the outer lifeline encircling the raft.

"Are you okay?" shouted Dan to the group.

Someone yelled back, "We're good."

Dan made a split-second decision not to try to right the capsized raft. *The raft is enormous,* he thought. *It may take forever to get it right side up. They have something to hold on to, and they all have survival suits and flotation vests. Let's get them out of here.*

"Okay," Dan hollered, looking at the person closest to him, "you're next. Just relax and follow my directions."

The decision not to right the raft was correct, and helped the remaining rescues go more quickly. Already outside the vessel, the survivors were ready to go. Over the next twenty minutes all four sailors were successfully hoisted up.

Neil was exhausted from nonstop hoisting and wrestling the loaded basket into the cabin over and over, but when he was finished with the sailors and was looking down at Dan, he had a chance to smile. He saw Dan pull out his knife and stab the raft, knowing procedure called for sinking empty life rafts so no other aircraft or vessels would get in a dangerous position for a rescue that wasn't needed. But what made Neil grin was that the raft had several compartments, and Dan had to repeatedly stab the raft to get it to start sinking. "At first," recalled Neil, "I wondered what he was doing. . . . It looked like he was trying to kill some creature from a horror movie, and the creature was winning."

Jenny glanced behind her in the cabin where the survivors were packed like sardines. Most were quiet, still in a daze or in outright shock from their ordeal. Jenny radioed the C-130 that they now had all six survivors safely in the cabin, and that they were about to pick up their swimmer. Peyton Russell suggested that when they got the rescue swimmer safely on board, they should investigate a possible PIW (person in water) before they moved on to the other *Bounty* life raft with the remaining three survivors.

When Dan was lifted into the helicopter, he slumped against a survivor, panting and trying to get his breath, after thirty-five minutes of nonstop exertion. He thought how in rescue swimmer school he went through the "six-man multi," where trainees had to rescue six "drowning" instructors in half an hour. He remembered that the rescue-swimmer manual required swimmers to have the strength to perform in heavy seas for thirty minutes. A wave of nausea rolled over him, partly because he had swallowed so much seawater, and partly because he was coming down off the adrenaline buzz and his body was crashing. He wondered how long it would take to get back to base.

Then Neil leaned in close to Dan and said, "The other helicopter had to leave because of fuel, and there are still three people in the raft. Mr. Bonn wants to know if you feel strong enough to get back in the water."

CHAPTER THIRTY

RUNNING OUT OF TIME

If the helo has enough gas to keep going, I'm going to keep going, too, thought Dan. He shouted to Neil, "Tell Mr. Bonn yes."

Jenny recalls how they first took a few moments to investigate the possible PIW. "We came across some debris, mostly survival gear out of the overturned life rafts, along with a couple empty Gumby suits. After a quick search we had to get to the raft with the three remaining people in it because we were getting low on fuel."

Steve put the Jayhawk in a hover near the raft, and down went Dan, now swimming markedly slower than earlier. To save time he did not enter the raft, knowing that rescue swimmer Randy Haba had probably already briefed the sailors earlier when he extracted four of the seven. Dan also remembered how when he was inside the first raft, he was thrown from one side to the other, and he wanted to avoid that possibility. So instead he stuck his head inside the vessel and hollered, "It's only three of you, right?"

The survivors acknowledged yes, and Dan then asked about injuries and they said they had none. "Okay!" shouted Dan. "We gotta move fast." Then he pointed to the person closest to him and hollered, "You first!"

He put the survivor in the basket without incident, but when he looked back at the raft, he saw that it had flipped. *Not again!* Just as before, Dan put his head down and began sprinting to the overturned raft. Only this time his depleted energy was no match for the waves and the current. *I'll never make it.* Both his arms and legs felt as heavy as tree trunks, and instead of stroking and kicking smartly through the water, the sensation was as if trying to push through mud. Rolling over on his back, he looked up at the aircraft and saw Neil crouched by the open cabin door. Dan gave a thumbs-up, meaning he needed to be picked up. He prayed that the last two people in the raft had escaped and were holding on to the lifeline.

Dan was hoisted above the wave tops and air-taxied toward the raft. He looked down and was startled to see the raft's orange canopy. Somehow the survivors had righted the raft, or perhaps a wave had flipped it back over. Dan could only hope the survivors were inside.

Once in the water, Dan felt a surge of relief: two heads poked out of the raft's doorway. The rescue swimmer fought his way closer, and without any coaxing one of the survivors slid into the water and Dan started towing him away from the raft to await the lowering of the basket. The two men were slammed by a wave, and Dan ingested considerable seawater during their tumble. When he popped to the surface, he still had the survivor in his grip, but now Dan was vomiting, willing himself to hang on to the survivor as the seas tried to tug him away.

Jenny watched Dan put this survivor in the basket, and when he entered the helicopter, she thought, *Why are they so slow? Don't they know we're running out of time?*

The copilot didn't know it, but this survivor had one of his arms outside the basket as it approached the doorway, and Neil had to lean out and smack the person's arm back inside. (An arm or even a hand outside the basket can be broken in multiple places if it gets trapped between the aircraft and the steel basket.) The survivor may have been gun-shy about leaving the basket once in the aircraft after the slap. Neil didn't waste time and yanked him out, unclipped the basket, and put the hook down for Dan, who had drifted far from the raft.

Dan clipped the cable to his harness, and as he was being lifted from a trough, he swung forward ten feet, directly into the face of a big wave coming from a different angle from the others. He slammed into the liquid wall, and spray from the impact shot high in the sky before the swimmer emerged on the other side of the wave.

Steve, worried about both fuel and the swimmer, said, "I hope I'm not swinging him too much. Just hold him below the aircraft and we will reposition him by the raft."

"Roger," answered Neil. "I'm going to bring him halfway up."

Dan careened wildly below the aircraft, and Neil, hanging on to the cable with his left arm, almost got yanked out the door.

Once the helicopter was near the raft, Neil set Dan down into the water and watched him unclip and begin methodically stroking. The flight mechanic wondered just how much strength Dan had left: *You can do it. Just one more left.*

Steve was thinking the same thing, and as if to will his swimmer more power, he blurted out, "Come on, Dan, reach that raft!"

An agonizingly slow minute went by, where it looked as if the current was getting the best of their swimmer. Then Steve spoke again, this time with relief: "Dan has the towline!"

The swimmer pulled himself to the raft and helped the last survivor out. As Dan was getting the final sailor inside the basket, the two were pushed by a wave from the right to the left side of the helicopter.

Neil's heart skipped a beat, and he craned his neck out the door to search underneath the helo for the two men. As soon as he saw that the survivor was in the basket, he retracted cable as fast as he could.

"This one is swinging really bad," said Neil.

Steve didn't respond, but instead kept his focus on holding the helicopter as still as possible. He felt the seconds tick by. *We've got to get this guy in, and then get the swimmer in, within five minutes or we're going to be up against our bingo.*

Jenny felt the same tension, and when the survivor was at the door, she looked over her shoulder and saw Neil yank him in. "When the last survivor was pulled inside," she later recalled, "I got really mad. Instead of getting out of the basket immediately, he put his hands up and cheered. I remember wanting to hit him upside the head and shout, *'Get out of the damn basket!'* I know they had just been in the worst situation of their lives and I should have been more forgiving, but getting Dan back in the helo and getting home safely depended on our fuel, and time is fuel."

With the last *Bounty* sailor out of the raft, the exhausted rescue swimmer slashed the raft with his knife and was lifted back to the helicopter. After he got his breath back, Dan, along with Neil, grilled the survivors about the exact number of people on the ship. Earlier reports had said sixteen or seventeen, and the survivors confirmed the correct number was sixteen. The first helicopter had extracted five, and this helo had nine jammed in the cabin, so two were still missing.

The three survivors who were picked up last were able to tell the others about the four shipmates taken from their raft by the first helicopter. So the group now knew that everyone was accounted for except Claudene Christian, Captain Walbridge, and Chief Mate Svendsen. But they also knew that the first helicopter had plucked out of the sea one sailor drifting alone—they just didn't know that person was John Svendsen. The bottom line was that two of their shipmates were still in the ocean.

Commander Bonn and Jenny knew they were almost at bingo, but because they always planned for a small cushion of fuel, they decided to do one last loop around the search area, hoping to spot a survivor. All they found was more debris. Steve made sure the crew went through its final checklist to ensure everything not needed was turned off, then he punched in the coordinates for Elizabeth City and turned over the controls to Jenny.

While Jenny was flying the aircraft, Steve used the aircraft's computer to predict fuel burn rate and fuel on deck when they landed at Elizabeth City. He updated the systems with the current headwinds, and the system flashed BINGO FUEL, meaning they would not be landing with as much of a cushion as they thought. In fact, should the headwinds increase, they might be in an emergency situation of their own.

Jenny's heart sank and her stomach felt as if there were a boulder in it. *What have I done?* she thought. *I failed everyone. This is my fault if the headwinds are worse than expected and we have to ditch.*

Steve read her mind and reassured her they would still be fine. To be on the safe side, though, he did another calculation using their current speed, and the cushion improved a bit. Both pilots knew they'd be cutting it close and would have to fly in an exact straight line; they could not let the winds push them even a few feet off course.

As the pilots discussed fuel and contingency landing plans, the survivors settled in for what was anticipated to be a two-hour, turbulent flight back to land. One by one the sailors began to fall asleep.

One survivor couldn't get the images of Claudene, Robin, and John Svendsen out of his thoughts. Two of those three people were at the mercy of the seas. He crawled closer to Neil and asked, "Are there any ships going for the last two people? We can't just leave them out there. I don't even want to think about the possibility that they didn't make it."

Neil tried to console the man. "We are very good at what we do. We will find your friends. A third helicopter is coming out."

Speaking into his headset, Neil said to Commander Bonn, "If you see the other helicopter approaching, let me know right away. One of the survivors is really upset, and I want to point the other aircraft out to him."

"Roger," said Steve, "I understand. And let him know the C-130 is still out there searching."

A short time later, Steve told Neil that the third helicopter would be coming by on the right side of the aircraft.

Neil tapped the survivor on the shoulder and positioned him at the window. A minute later the other helicopter went by. The survivor watched it go, heading into the teeth of Sandy.

On that third helicopter, flown by pilots Brian Bailey and Nick Hazlett, flight mechanic Tim Kuklewski was awestruck by the sight of *Bounty*. "When we arrived at the *Bounty*," he recalled, "I was surprised how big it was. Each time a wave crashed on it, various items would come loose, ranging from wooden planks to life jackets. It was an incredible scene, and it looked like the ship would be swallowed by the waves at any moment. I took my iPhone out, aimed it out the doorway, and snapped off three quick shots."

Tim and his crew saw how the debris field stretched for miles. With the C-130 guiding them, they hovered as low as possible over promising survival suits. Some suits were quickly identified as empty because they were folded over or were clearly flat, but others were filled with a combination of air and water, making it look as if a person were inside. Pilots Bailey and Hazlett kept approaching these suits from all different angles.

"Rescue swimmer Tim Bolen and I kept getting our hopes up," said Tim. "We were hoping to see a face or maybe a hand rise out of the water. We would not fly off until we were one hundred percent sure they were empty." But time and time again, the suits were unmanned, and after more than an hour of searching, they, too, hit their bingo and headed back to Elizabeth City, where they rested and refueled, preparing to head back out later that day.

A fourth helicopter was launched at noon and resumed the search. Rather than go to the *Bounty*, which had been examined several times, this crew followed the debris field a full two miles out from the ship. The crew, consisting of pilots Matt Herring and Kristen Jaekel, flight mechanic Ryan Parker, and swimmer Casey Hanchette, scanned the storm-tossed seas below them, hoping for some sign of life. After completing the first search pattern and coming up empty, they began their second search. Ryan noticed how one Gumby suit floated differently from the others. "It was more spread out than the others suits we investigated, so we came back around and got in a low hover. Then the hood of the suit flopped open and we could see blond hair."

Rescue swimmer Casey Hanchette was immediately lowered, and once in the water he unhooked and swam toward the unconscious sailor, who was floating facedown. The sailor was Claudene Christian. Casey immediately got her in the sling and clipped his harness back on the hook, and they were lifted up to the helicopter together. He and Ryan administered CPR the entire hour-and-a-half ride back to the air station. But their nonstop efforts were for naught. Claudene was dead.

Claudene had a laceration on her nose, but showed no other signs of trauma. We will never know if she survived for a time in the water or if she was pulled down by the rigging and died quickly.

After an incredible rescue of fourteen people by the coast guard, one *Bounty* crew member had been taken by the hurricane and Captain Walbridge was still missing, and the odds of his being found alive were shrinking with each passing hour.

CHAPTER THIRTY-ONE

HELD BY THE SEA

When the survivors touched down at Elizabeth City, they were swarmed by people trying to help: police, paramedics, other coast guard staff, and the Red Cross. Those sailors still in survival suits needed help exiting the helicopters because of all the water inside their suits. They could barely take a step, and the rescue swimmers and flight mechanics asked the survivors to sit on the edge of the helicopter doorway while slits were cut in the feet of the Gumby suits to let the water drain out.

Once off the aircraft and inside the station, everyone was interviewed by coast guard officials. Claudene and Captain Walbridge had not yet been found, and the search-and-rescue teams were desperate to find out anything that would help in their efforts.

Adam Prokosh was treated at a hospital for his separated shoulder and the fractured vertebra in his back, then he was reunited with the rest of the survivors at a hotel, where he shared a room with Josh. A couple hours later they learned that Claudene had been found but was unresponsive. Some thought that meant that she was alive, but a short time later word came back that Claudene had died. "Right after we found out," said Josh, "the Red Cross came to the hotel and we boarded cabs to go to Walmart to get some clothes. Everyone was crying because we had just learned Claudene didn't make it."

Claudene's parents, Dina and Rex, had been worried about their daughter since *Bounty* first set sail from New London, and their anxiety only increased when Claudene called them at the beginning of the voyage to tell them how much she loved them. Their concern mounted when they later received the text message from Claudene that said, "If I go down with the ship and the worst happens, just know that I AM TRULY, GENUINELY HAPPY. And I'm doing what I love! I love you."

Days of sickening worry passed, and then came the dreaded phone call from the coast guard when Claudene was first located and lifted into the helicopter. The Christians were told Claudene was unresponsive and being given CPR. Dina and Rex immediately began flying on a series of connecting flights to get to Elizabeth City as fast as possible. While waiting for one of the connecting flights in Atlanta, Dina's cell phone suddenly rang. It was a doctor at the hospital where Claudene's body had been taken, and he broke the news that Claudene had died. The Christians were heartbroken but also angry. *How could this have happened, how could an experienced captain set sail when the whole world knew a hurricane was heading in their direction?*

As images of the sinking *Bounty* glowed from television sets and computer screens across the United States, the entire country was asking the same question. Part of that answer is held by the sea. After searching twelve thousand overlapping square nautical miles, the coast guard suspended the search for Captain Robin Walbridge. His body was never found.

COAST GUARD INVESTIGATION

Three days after *Bounty*'s crew abandoned ship in 77-degree water, the coast guard suspended its search for Robin Walbridge. That same day, coast guard rear admiral Steven Ratti ordered a formal investigation to determine the cause of the sinking.

By then, Thursday, November 1, *Bounty*—a ship that Walbridge once told his crew couldn't sink because of the buoyancy of its wooden construction—had indeed sunk, leaving only a few bits of debris—unused immersion suits among them—floating on the surface.

In the weeks immediately following, coast guard commander Kevin M. Carroll began his investigation, talking informally not only with survivors but with experts who knew *Bounty* well. His goal and that of his agency was to take "appropriate measures for promoting safety of life and property." Although the investigation was "not intended to fix civil or criminal responsibility," Carroll nevertheless was charged with determining "whether there is evidence that any act of misconduct, inattention to duty, negligence, or willful violation of the law on the part of any licensed or certificated person contributed to the casualty."

Thus when Carroll opened public hearings on February 12, 2013, into the loss of *Bounty*, the ship's owner, Robert Hansen, exerted his constitutional protection against self-incrimination and refused to testify. The four surviving *Bounty* officers and eight of ten surviving crew members did appear as witnesses during the eight days of hearings. Their sworn testimony and that of others provided much of the basis for this book.

First to testify was John Svendsen, chief mate and the person whom Robin Walbridge anticipated would be *Bounty*'s next captain. Svendsen was considered a party of interest in the case, because he was the senior surviving officer and could be held responsible for his actions aboard.

Carroll's questions led Svendsen through the tale of *Bounty*'s fatal voyage, a story that would be repeated in many details by the eleven crew members who followed him at the witness table in a hotel ballroom in Portsmouth, Virginia. The chief mate's testimony was unique, however, in his claim, under oath, that he had confronted Walbridge in New London, challenging his decision to sail toward Sandy. The confrontation was private, he testified. No one but he and the lost captain knew what words were exchanged. The testimony could, given Svendsen's precarious legal position as the ranking survivor, be seen as an attempt at self-protection, except that crew member testimony that followed seemed to buttress Svendsen's version.

The next two to testify—Third Mate Dan Cleveland and Bosun Laura Groves—both told Carroll of their meeting with Svendsen prior to departure, where concerns about the voyage were discussed.

By the time Cleveland and Groves testified, Carroll and his panel had questioned Todd Kosakowski, the shipyard manager, who revealed his discovery of rot aboard *Bounty* and detailed his discussions with Walbridge. It was Kosakowski who testified that Walbridge had urged Hansen to sell the ship as soon as he could.

Kosakowski was followed at the witness table by Joseph Jakimovicz, who had been manager of the shipyard prior to Kosakowski and who said he was less concerned with the rot found in *Bounty*'s timbers. "I've seen a lot worse," he testified. "I'm basing my judgment on forty years experience. He [Kosakowski] is basing his on five or six years' experience. That's probably the difference."

Carroll asked all of the crew members about the work done on *Bounty* in the Boothbay Harbor Shipyard and the condition of the ship. Second Mate Matt Sanders, Engineer Chris Barksdale, longtime volunteer crew member Douglas Faunt, and crew members Joshua Scornavacchi, Jessica Hewitt, Anna Sprague, and Jessica Black appeared in person. Adam Prokosh and Drew Salapatek were interviewed by telephone, their voices amplified for the audience in the ballroom.

For the benefit of the coast guard, each crew member relived their experiences on board *Bounty* during Hurricane Sandy and, after they jumped or were thrown from *Bounty,* in the ocean until they were rescued.

Among those who attended every day of the testimony were Robert Hansen and the parents of Claudene Christian, Harry Rex, and Dina Christian. The Christians were represented by a lawyer who, along with Hansen's lawyer and Svendsen himself—all parties in interest—were allowed to question each witness.

A representative of the National Transportation Safety Board, which was conducting its own investigation of the incident, was included in the panel that assisted Carroll.

Three months after the hearing adjourned, Ralph J. Mellusi, on behalf of Claudene Christian's estate, filed suit in the US District Court in New York, seeking $20 million in damages from HMS Bounty Organization LLC and Robert Hansen for, among other claims, "negligence, gross negligence, willful, callous and reckless conduct and conditions" and another $50 million in punitive damages.

On June 26, 2013, Commander Carroll's completed report was forwarded by the Fifth Coast Guard District to Coast Guard Headquarters in Washington, DC.

In a statement in late September 2013, the coast guard explained that "The report will be reviewed to ensure that all relevant matters of fact have been explored and adequately documented; all findings of fact in matters of controversy are justified; all conclusions are logically consistent with the findings of fact and their analyses; causes have been adequately analyzed; human error has been documented and analyzed; all evidence of violation of law or regulation has been referred for appropriate enforcement action; and all recommendations are in reference to conclusions, address conditions observed and are supported in the case file.

"The investigation contained several safety recommendations, and Coast Guard Headquarters must take the time to review, coordinate with responsible oversight offices, and then draft for the final action response for the Commandant's signature. Given the complexity of, and comprehensive nature of the review at the Coast Guard Headquarters level, the final date of completion of all Coast Guard activities pertaining to the investigation remains undetermined."

Not all of the survivors wanted to talk about *Bounty*. Already they had endured a period of constant high-level stress, near drowning, the loss of friends, and a barrage of media requests. They then had to relive what happened during their testimony at the coast guard inquiry. It was not, nor has it been, an easy time for some of the crew.

Yet they knew they would never forget Claudene and Robin and attended memorial services for their lost shipmates. Throwing wreaths into the sea, they wondered what happened to Claudene and Robin in their last hours. At one memorial service they huddled in the snow, knowing this would probably be the last time the surviving crew of *Bounty*'s final voyage would all be together.

In the months that followed the loss of *Bounty,* some surviving crew members took positions on other tall ships and some of the surviving officers were being courted by other tall ship captains.

AFTERWORD

Michael Tougias

When *Bounty* was first encountering heavy seas, I was, coincidentally, on TV talking about storms. One of the hosts of *Fox & Friends* asked me if I thought any ships might be in harm's way with Hurricane Sandy coming up the eastern seaboard. I paused and then explained that the storm had been so well forecast that all ships would be in port. Imagine my surprise when two days later news reports of the dramatic rescue of *Bounty* splashed across my TV set. That launched my quest to learn more, and later I contacted Doug Campbell to team up and write the definitive account of what happened and why.

What struck me during my research was how much worse this accident could have been. The sailors' donning of survival suits and gathering on deck occurred just minutes before the ship rolled to its side. Had they been belowdecks during the capsizing, I doubt anyone would have gotten out alive, especially because there was just a single passageway to the top. Equally important was the coast guard's decision to launch Wes McIntosh's C-130 into the heart of the storm. If that plane had not been on scene when *Bounty* heeled over, the loss of life would have been higher because the aircraft was the only communication link between the ship and the outside world. Without the C-130 crew to relay news of the disaster back to Elizabeth City, the helicopter commanded by Steve Cerveny would not have launched until at least two hours later. The immediate launch of that helo likely saved the life of John Svendsen, who was floating alone in the raging sea, far from both *Bounty* and the life rafts.

The airlift rescue of the first five sailors is remarkable not only because it occurred in hurricane-force winds and thirty-foot seas, but also in the dark. The second helicopter had just as dangerous a task: to extract nine sailors from two different rafts under tight time constraints due to fuel limitations. President Obama had it right when he lauded the coast guard. Speaking in New Jersey just after the storm struck, he said, "One of my favorite stories is down in North Carolina where the coast guard was going out to save a sinking ship. They sent the rescue swimmer out and the rescue swimmer said, 'Hi, I'm Dan, I understand you guys need a ride.' That kind of spirit of resilience and strength—but most importantly looking out for one another—that's why we always bounce back from these kinds of disasters."

We often think of the coast guard men and women as "just doing their jobs" because most are humble and downplay their role. We assume that when one mission is complete, they move right on to the next. They do, but every now and then a rescue or rescue attempt comes along that moves the rescuers deeply and has an impact that will last well beyond their careers. I recall how Mike Myers, the copilot on the C-130 with Wes McIntosh, wrote to me saying, "It was so painful to experience the *Bounty* crew's emotional highs and lows. There was a bond and connection between our crew and theirs. Then to have them go in the water, at night, exhausted, and hastily forced overboard, it became our worst case scenario. We made repeated radio calls, we flashed our lights when in over-flight, we dropped rafts, survival gear, homing devices . . . everything we could to keep their hopes of survival alive. But we had lost our connection with our fellow mariners—we would not hear any other radio calls, see any flares, nor observe any people in the water. It was heart-breaking thinking that the worst had happened."

The survivors knew it was a combination of their own gritty determination to live, coupled with the coast guard's resolve to find and rescue them, that had allowed them to have more tomorrows. But for some, the ordeal wasn't over after the rescue, and they were plagued with nightmares, post-traumatic stress, and being second-guessed by others.

• • •

Most people will remember Robin Walbridge for his disastrous decision to leave port. But we have all made mistakes, and it seems unfair that over a lifetime of difficult choices a person gets labeled for his last one. Coast guard captain Eric Jones explained it this way: "One bad decision does not undo all the positive influence Robin Walbridge had on sailors." I think he's right, and almost every crew member who survived Sandy agrees—they almost all spoke highly of Robin's leadership and training skills.

We also need to remember that Hurricane Sandy was unlike other hurricanes. It was epic—nine hundred miles wide, the largest storm ever recorded in the North Atlantic. Captain Walbridge and all those who followed him as he steered *Bounty* out of New London, Connecticut, believed they could skirt the storm. Had it been a "typical" hurricane, they might have done just that. But Sandy's reach was so massive that by the time they realized its magnitude, there was no safe direction to sail.

Still, the captain should have thought of his crew first, and not that "a ship is safer at sea than at port" during a storm.

A critical decision occurs in the opening pages of this book when Captain Walbridge calls the crew together to announce his plans to sail despite the oncoming storm. He told them anyone could leave and he wouldn't think any less of them or hold it against them. Why, I wondered, did every single crew member agree to remain on the ship? Most said they had confidence in the captain, the ship, and their own training. But I think another, more subtle factor was at work—the group itself. Perhaps no one wanted to be the first to walk off *Bounty*, appear to be afraid, or be perceived as letting their crewmates down. Remember, most of the crew were under thirty years old, and they felt a loyalty to each other and to the captain without the benefit of decades of sailing. Also, the manner in which Captain Walbridge made this announcement likely influenced the outcome. The crew was forced to make a quick decision, without having the time to check various forecasts themselves. Nor did they have the luxury to sleep on their decision, discuss it with family, or have a private conversation with the captain. Instead, when none spoke up and said they were leaving, the captain ordered them to prepare the ship to get under way.

When I think of *Bounty*, a cascade of thoughts flows through me. I recall how I went on the ship briefly twenty years ago with my father and my son in Fall River, Massachusetts. I thought she was beautiful. When I was just fifteen years old, I consumed the trilogy of books related to the *Bounty* written by Charles Nordhoff and James Hall in the 1930s (*Mutiny on the Bounty*, *Men Against the Sea*, and *Pitcairn's Island*.) They were wonderful stories and likely fueled my future writing career and love of the sea. While I generally think that Hollywood remakes of books fail miserably, I loved the two *Mutiny on the Bounty* movies. The first was released in 1935 and starred Charles Laughton as Captain William Bligh and Clark Gable as Fletcher Christian. The second movie was a 1962 version starring Marlon Brando and Trevor Howard. Many viewers like myself fell in love with the South Pacific and the graceful ship that saw so much turmoil.

Now when I reflect on *Bounty*, I feel mostly sadness. My thoughts are of the majestic old ship in its death throes and how Sandy took the lives of two crew members. But what bothers me most is that it didn't have to happen.

Douglas A. Campbell

Jan Miles, co-captain of the tall ship *Pride of Baltimore II*, wrote a scalding "open letter" to Captain Robin Walbridge and posted it on the Internet a month after *Bounty* sank. In that letter, Miles echoed the sentiments of many in the maritime community when he asked:

"Why did you throw all caution away by navigating for a close pass of Hurricane Sandy? I was so surprised to discover that BOUNTY was at sea near Cape Hatteras and close to Hurricane Sandy Sunday night October 28th! That decision of yours was reckless in the extreme!"

Few among the dozens of individuals—other than *Bounty* crew members—interviewed by Mike Tougias and me disagreed with Miles. One who did was Cliff Bredeson, an occasional volunteer *Bounty* crew member who had made numerous ocean crossings with Walbridge.

Bredeson said that in his opinion Walbridge's decision to leave New London was appropriate. Had the pumps not failed, *Bounty* would have been fine, Bredeson told me.

I am a sailor of small boats and have logged numerous miles offshore—far, far fewer than Robin Walbridge. In that limited experience, I have made my share of decisions to sail that I've later regretted. I've been lucky. While some of those decisions have led to discomfort, none has led to disaster.

When I heard *Bounty*'s story in October 2012, I—like most other sailors—wondered why a captain would think his crew would be safer at sea in a hurricane than onshore. To be absolutely clear, the safest way to deal with boats is to stay off them. There are always risks in going to sea, some of which cannot be anticipated. But the ocean floor is littered with the wreckage of ships—particularly old, wooden sailing ships—and the bones of crews that left port and didn't make it back. There was no question in my mind in October that Walbridge should have anticipated problems with Sandy and that *Bounty* should have remained at some dock, someplace, and should not have ventured out toward an approaching hurricane.

I was grateful, then, when Mike offered me the opportunity to investigate *Bounty*'s saga and ask what to me was the critical question: Why did Robin Walbridge take his ship to sea?

I found a handful of individuals who knew Robin Walbridge well and could tell stories that transported him from a caricature that a news story makes of anyone to a real person with unique qualities, passions, and abilities. Those tales showed me why this man could be adored by so many, respected by almost all he met. They also gave shape to an intelligent, driven man who was, in the end, trapped by his own success, almost universally unquestioned, and, perhaps as a result, unaccustomed to being challenged.

I owe a debt of gratitude to these people and hope that in repayment of that debt our work will provide readers with an honest portrait of a man whose enthusiasm for his life touched many, often young, people and no doubt changed their lives in positive ways.

ACKNOWLEDGMENTS

The authors wish to thank the following people we either interviewed or corresponded with. There were not one or two people who were crucial to this story. Instead, there were dozens, and each was an important piece of the mosaic of this dramatic saga. You were gracious with your time and opened up your hearts.

Kristin Andersen
Marco Angelini
Captain Richard Bailey
Michael Beck
Steve Bonn
Cliff Bredeson
Marc Castells
Steve Cerveny
Dina Christian
Jennifer Clark
Captain Bernard Coffey
Connie DeMarus
Todd Farrell
Doug Faunt
Jenny Fields
Captain Christopher Flansburg
Randy Haba
Darren Hicks
Herb Hilgenberg

Lucille Walbridge Jansen
Peter Jansen
Gary Kannegiesser
Tim Kuklewski
Shirley R. Lawyer
Ned Lightner
Michael Lufkin
Barbara Maggio
Wes McIntosh
Jim McNealy
Captain Jan Miles
Bill Miller
James Mitchell
Neil Moulder
Hal Mueller
Tom Murray
Mike Myers
Barbara J. Neff
Chris Parker
Ryan Parker
Jane Peña
Adam Prokosh
Captain Beth Robinson
Peyton Russell
Jonathan Sageser
Jim Salapatek
Joshua Scornavacchi
Andrew Seguin
Rochelle Smith
Larry Sprague
Ed Sychra
Dan Todd
Captain Eric Van Dormolen
Michelle Wilton
Gerald Zwicker

—Michael J. Tougias and Douglas A. Campbell

ABOUT THE AUTHORS

Michael J. Tougias is a versatile author and coauthor of twenty-one books. Two of his previous books, *A Storm Too Soon* and *Overboard!* (both written in the present tense), received critical praise because of their fast-paced style and "heart-pounding" narratives. His bestselling book *Fatal Forecast: An Incredible True Tale of Disaster and Survival at Sea* was praised by the *Los Angeles Times* as "a breathtaking book . . . [Tougias] spins a marvelous and terrifying yarn." His earlier book *Ten Hours Until Dawn: The True Story of Heroism and Tragedy Aboard the* Can Do was praised by *Booklist* "as the best story of peril at sea since *The Perfect Storm*." This book, about a sea rescue during the Blizzard of 1978, was selected by the American Library Association as an Editor's Choice: "One of the Top Books of the Year."

Tougias and coauthor Casey Sherman teamed up and wrote a combination history/ocean-rescue story titled *The Finest Hours: The True Story of the U.S. Coast Guard's Most Daring Sea Rescue.* This drama occurred in 1952 off the coast of Cape Cod when two oil tankers, in the grip of a nor'easter, were split in half and eighty-four lives were in jeopardy. The Disney Corporation is currently making a movie based on this book.

On a lighter note, Tougias's award-winning humor book *There's a Porcupine in My Outhouse: Misadventures of a Mountain Man Wannabe* was selected by the Independent Book Publishers Association as "The Best Nature Book of the Year." The author has also written for over two hundred different and diverse publications including the *New York Times*, *Field & Stream*, *Fine Gardening*, and the *Boston Globe*. He has just coauthored two new books: *The Cringe Chronicles* and *Derek's Gift: A True Story of Love, Courage, and Lessons Learned.*

Tougias has prepared slide lectures for all his books, including *Rescue of the* Bounty, and his lecture schedule is posted on his website at www.michaeltougias.com. (Interested organizations can contact him at michaeltougias@yahoo.com.) The author also has an archive of maritime rescue articles and personal stories on his blog michaeltougias.wordpress.com, and he has an author page on Facebook at "Michael J. Tougias."

Through research into dozens of survival stories, Tougias has also prepared an inspirational lecture for businesses and organizations titled "Survival Lessons: Peak Performance & Decision-Making Under Pressure." Tougias describes this presentation as "an uplifting way to learn some practical strategies and mind-sets for achieving difficult goals from those who have survived against all odds." He has given the presentation across the country for all types of organizations, including General Dynamics, International Administrative Association, Massachusetts School Library Association, NYU Surgeon's Roundtable, North Platte Town Lecture Series, Lincoln Financial Services, Raytheon, United States Coast Guard, and many more. Interested organizations can contact him at michaeltougias@yahoo.com. For more details see www.michaeltougias.com.

Douglas A. Campbell, the author of two nonfiction books, *The Sea's Bitter Harvest* and *Eight Survived*, has spent his career in journalism. For twenty-five years, he was a staff writer at the *Philadelphia Inquirer*, where two of his stories were nominated for the Pulitzer Prize. After retiring from the *Inquirer* in 2001, he resumed his career as senior writer at *Soundings* magazine, covering all aspects of recreational boating. His stories for *Soundings* have won numerous awards from Boating Writers International Inc.

Doug began sailing on the Delaware River in 1979 and still keeps a small boat moored there. He and his wife, Monica, also sail a thirty-two-foot blue-water boat, *Robin*, with which they've competed in the biannual Bermuda 1-2 Race. Doug has placed third out of thirty-nine boats on corrected-time sailing the single-handed leg of the race from Newport, Rhode Island, to Bermuda.

SUMMARIES OF MICHAEL J. TOUGIAS'S LATEST BOOKS, AVAILABLE FROM SCRIBNER AS TRADE PAPERBACKS OR AS E-BOOKS

A Storm Too Soon: The True Story of Disaster, Survival, and an Incredible Rescue

Seventy-foot waves batter a tattered life raft 250 miles out to sea in one of the world's most dangerous places, the Gulf Stream. Hanging on to the raft are three men, a Canadian, a Brit, and their captain, JP DeLutz, a dual citizen of America and France. The waves repeatedly toss the men out of their tiny vessel, and JP, with nine broken ribs, is hypothermic and on the verge of death. The captain, however, is a tough-minded character, having survived a sadistic, physically abusive father during his boyhood, and now he's got to rely on those same inner resources to outlast the storm.

Trying to reach these survivors before it's too late are four coastguardsmen battling hurricane-force winds in their Jayhawk helicopter. They know the waves in the Gulf Stream will be extreme, but when they arrive they are astounded to find crashing seas of seventy feet, with some waves topping eighty feet. To lower the helicopter and then drop a rescue swimmer into such chaos is a high-risk proposition. The pilots wonder if they have a realistic chance of saving the sailors clinging to the broken life raft, and if they will be able to retrieve their own rescue swimmer from the towering seas. Once they commit to the rescue, they find themselves in almost as much trouble as the survivors, facing several life-and-death decisions.

Also caught in the storm are three other boats, all in Mayday situations. Of the ten people on those boats, only six will ever see land again.

"By depicting the event from the perspective of both the rescued and the rescuers and focusing only on key moments and details, Tougias creates a suspenseful, tautly rendered story that leaves readers breathless but well-satisfied. Heart-pounding action for the avid armchair adventurer."

—*Kirkus Reviews*

"The riveting, meticulously researched *A Storm Too Soon* tells the true-life tale of an incredible rescue."

—*New York Post*

"Tougias deftly switches from heart-pounding details of the rescue to the personal stories of the boat's crew and those of the rescue team. The result is a well-researched and suspenseful read."

—*Publishers Weekly*

"Few American authors—if any—can better evoke the realities that underlie a term such as 'desperate rescue attempt.'"

—*Fall River Herald*

"Already a maven of maritime books with *Overboard!* and *Fatal Forecast*, Tougias cinches that title here. Working in the present tense Tougias lets the story tell itself, and what a story! Anyone reading [*A Storm Too Soon*] will laud Tougias' success."

—*Providence Journal*

Overboard!:
A True Blue-Water Odyssey of Disaster and Survival

A nerve-racking maritime disaster tale from the masterful author of *Fatal Forecast* and *The Finest Hours*. Michael Tougias has left countless readers breathless with his suspense-packed, nail-biting disaster-at-sea narratives. And now one of the survivors of a perilous tale has sought Tougias out to tell his terrifying story, for the first time described in *Overboard!*

In early May of 2005 Captain Tom Tighe and First Mate Loch Reidy of the sailboat *Almeisan* welcomed three new crew members for a five-day voyage from Connecticut to Bermuda. While Tighe and Reidy had made the journey countless times, the rest of the crew wanted to learn about offshore sailing—and were looking for adventure. Four days into their voyage, they got one—but nothing that they had expected. A massive storm struck, sweeping Tighe and Reidy from the boat. The remaining crew members somehow managed to stay aboard the vessel as it was torn apart by wind and water. *Overboard!* follows the simultaneous desperate struggles of the boat passengers and the captain and the first mate fighting for their lives in the sea. (An interview with the author and the survivors, along with actual footage from the storm, can be found on YouTube, "Michael Tougias—Overboard Parts I, II, III.")

"A heart-pounding account of the storm that tore apart a forty-five-foot sailboat. Author Michael Tougias is the master of the weather-related disaster book."

—*Boston Globe*

"*Overboard!* is a beautiful story deserving of a good cry."

—GateHouse News Service

"Tougias has a knack for weaving thoroughly absorbing stories—adventure fans need this one!"

—*Booklist*

The Finest Hours: The True Story of the U.S. Coast Guard's Most Daring Sea Rescue

(coauthored with Casey Sherman)

On February 18, 1952, an astonishing maritime event began when a ferocious nor'easter split in half a five-hundred-foot-long oil tanker, the *Pendleton*, approximately one mile off the coast of Cape Cod, Massachusetts. Incredibly, just twenty miles away, a second oil tanker, the *Fort Mercer*, also split in half. On both fractured tankers, men were trapped on the severed bows and sterns, and all four sections were sinking in sixty-foot seas. Thus began a life-and-death drama of survival, heroism, and tragedy. Of the eighty-four seamen aboard the tankers, seventy would be rescued and fourteen would lose their lives.

Going to the rescue of the *Pendleton*'s stern section were four young coastguardsmen in a thirty-six-foot lifeboat—a potential suicide mission in such a small vessel. Standing between the men and their mission were towering waves that reached seventy feet, blinding snow, and one of the most dangerous shoals in the world, the dreaded Chatham Bar. The waters along the outer arm of Cape Cod are called the Graveyard of the Atlantic for good reason, yet this rescue defied all odds when thirty-two survivors were crammed into the tiny lifeboat and brought to safety. (Coast guard officials later said that "the rescue is unparalleled in the entire annals of maritime history.")

Several cutters and small boats raced to the sinking sections of the *Fort Mercer*, and valiant rescue attempts were undertaken—some successful, some not. (An interview with Michael Tougias and photos of the disaster unfolding can be found on YouTube, "Finest Hours—Adam Knee (producer).")

"A blockbuster account of tragedy at sea . . . gives you a you-are-there feel."

—*Providence Journal*

"A gripping read!"

—James Bradley, author of *Flags of Our Fathers*

Fatal Forecast: An Incredible True Tale of Disaster and Survival at Sea

On a cold November day in 1980, two fishing vessels, the *Fair Wind* and the *Sea Fever*, set out from Cape Cod to catch offshore lobsters at Georges Bank. The National Weather Service had forecast typical fall weather in the area for the next three days—even though the service knew that its only weather buoy at Georges Bank was malfunctioning. Soon after the boats reached the fishing ground, they were hit with hurricane-force winds and massive, sixty-foot waves that battered the boats for hours. The captains and crews struggled heroically to keep their vessels afloat in the unrelenting storm. One monstrous wave of ninety to one hundred feet soon capsized the *Fair Wind*, trapping the crew inside. Meanwhile, on the *Sea Fever*, Captain Peter Brown (whose father owned the *Andrea Gail* of *The Perfect Storm* fame) did his best to ride out the storm, but a giant wave blew out one side of the pilothouse, sending a crew member into the churning ocean.

Meticulously researched and vividly told, *Fatal Forecast* is first and foremost a tale of miraculous survival. Most amazing is the story of Ernie Hazard, who crawled inside a tiny inflatable life raft—only to be repeatedly thrown into the ocean as he fought to endure more than fifty hours adrift in the storm-tossed seas. By turns tragic, thrilling, and inspiring, Ernie's story deserves a place among the greatest survival tales ever told.

As gripping and harrowing as *The Perfect Storm*—but with a miracle ending—*Fatal Forecast* is an unforgettable true story about the collision of two spectacular forces: the brutality of nature and the human will to survive.

"Tougias skillfully submerges us in this storm and spins a marvelous and terrifying yarn. He makes us fight alongside Ernie Hazard and cheer as he is saved . . . a breathtaking book."

—*Los Angeles Times*

"Ernie Hazard's experiences, as related by Tougias, deserve a place as a classic of sea survival history."

—*Boston Globe*

"Tougias spins a dramatic saga. . . . [He] has written eighteen books and this is among his most gripping."

—*National Geographic Adventure* magazine